# MR PAPARAZZI

# DARRYN LYONS
# MR PAPARAZZI

JOHN BLAKE

Published by John Blake Publishing Ltd,
3 Bramber Court, 2 Bramber Road,
London W14 9PB, UK
www.blake.co.uk

First published in hardback in the UK by John Blake Publishing Ltd, 2008
First published by Penguin Group (Australia), 2008

ISBN: 978-1-84454-600-8

British Library Cataloguing-in-Publication Data:
A catalogue record for this book is available from the British Library.

Design by Debra Billson © Penguin Group (Australia)
Additional design by www.envydesign.co.uk

Printed in the UK by CPI William Clowes Beccles NR34 7TL

1 3 5 7 9 10 8 6 4 2

Papers used by John Blake Publishing are natural, recyclable products made from wood grown
in sustainable forests. The manufacturing processes conform to the environmental regulations
of the country of origin.

Every reasonable effort has been made to contact relevant copyright holders. Any omission is
inadvertent; we would be grateful if the appropriate people could contact us.

For Mum and Dad
*(Sorry about the rude parts and the swearing!)*

# Contents

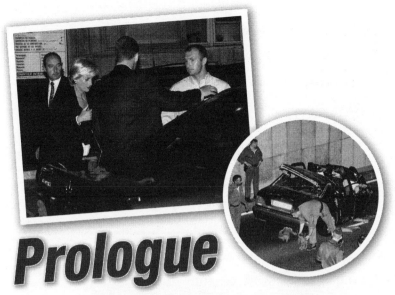

# Prologue

**'Something had gone terribly wrong' – see inside for full story**

**IT WAS JUST PAST MIDNIGHT** on Sunday 31 August and I was at home watching television when the phone rang. It was my agent in Paris and he had shocking news. He told me that Princess Diana had been in a major car accident, he had men at the scene and the pictures would be with me soon.

My agent's photographers had lost the trail of Diana's car when its driver, Henri Paul, jumped a red light immediately after leaving the Ritz hotel in Paris. While most of the other paparazzi kept trying to find the car, our men decided to head for home and happened upon the wreck of the car as it lay in the Alma tunnel. They ran down and began helping administer first aid to Diana as they waited for emergency services to arrive. Once it became clear they could do nothing more to assist, Fabrice clicked into work mode and took some pictures of the biggest new story he would ever be a part of.

I rang a few newspaper editors and offered them the tip of the year for a healthy fee. They reacted to the news with incredulity, but started chasing it up while I raced into the office. The pictures from the accident started dropping onto our computer system and I realised it was serious. I whispered a prayer. I didn't know what to do. I knew this was big, but the little boy from Geelong didn't know how big.

Initial reports said that Diana was concussed and had a broken arm and the images I was looking at seemed to confirm that. I spoke to the editor of the *News of the World*, who offered me a quarter of a million pounds for one-time use of the images. We did the deal, and a low-res shot was sent to News International – the only one that left my office.

And then I got a call telling me that Diana was dead. I immediately withdrew all of the images from the market. It was a big call, but once the tragic news came, my mind was set. I just had to answer a simple ethical question. I felt a wave of shock. Truly this, too, was like losing a member of the family. I was gripped by a deep feeling of sickness and felt like my soul had been pierced. Something had gone terribly wrong. Fairytale princesses weren't supposed to die.

INSIDE THE DOG-EAT-DOG WORLD OF THE FREELANCE SNAPPER

# THE BIG BREAK

**THE *NEWS OF THE WORLD*** and the cut and thrust of London's media were in every aspect a long way removed from my upbringing in provincial Victoria. But that upbringing made me the way I am and sharpened my natural instincts to make bold moves and to achieve.

I had an idyllic childhood in Geelong, a middle-class, country town an hour out of Melbourne. Everyone knows everyone else's business and if they don't, they make it up. It's still a funny mix of being a very friendly, safe place to bring up a family and the Wild West. The P-plate burnouts still happen down Moorabool Street on a Saturday night. The radio station is still playing the same music it did twenty years ago – 'April Sun in Cuba' by Dragon. But that's what Geelong people like and that's what I love about Geelong. As they say, if it ain't broke don't fix it. Everyone in town seems to go off to work at Ford, Alcoa or Shell or becomes a plumber or electrician. I broke the mould. Not only did I break the mould at school but also at home. My family were quite strict Baptists – it's odd because there's nothing strict about me.

School was the start of my entrepreneurial activities. At around the age of nine, I wrote to the great Australian cricketer Dennis Lillee and asked him for five autographs, telling him to write in one of them: 'Good luck in your cricket, Darryn'. I intended to sell the others for 20 cents a time. Lillee was my idol. I was successful in my request, and was delighted when he even spelt my name right. I copied his signature and to this day mine is very similar to his.

Competition and ambition were a big part of my character. In my bedroom was a picture of a Lamborghini Countach. I dreamed of that car, just because it was different – the doors opened upwards. My friends remember me telling them that I would have that car one day, and in fact the Lamborghini that I ended up buying from Rod Stewart was the same colour as the one on my bedroom wall. My main mates from school were Mario Gregorio (Mars), Shayne Van Dreumel (Vanny or Drumes), and David Lewis (Lewy). During our high school years we stuck together like glue.

Undoubtedly the biggest influence on me outside the

family unit was Mal Donnelly, my art and photography teacher at East Tech Secondary. I come from a family of architects, builders and painters, but when I discovered photography I was gripped by a massive passion for it. The school had been given the most incredible facilities by the state government – when I got my first job at the *Geelong Advertiser* the paper didn't have the facilities that the school did!

I owe Mal my career because he encouraged my love of photography. He was a huge influence – compassionate, caring and with an intuitive understanding of how a kid's brain operates. He saw I had the right attitude, and the fortitude to be a good photographer, and he saw the amount of work I was willing to do. Mal also taught adults in the evening on a paying course, which ensured that he had good equipment for the kids to use. He was also able to duplicate his adult lesson plans for the brightest kids in the day class.

I wouldn't call my discovery of photography luck; I really think it was fate. I was never going to do anything else – didn't even have to think about doing anything else. I loved the creative side and always felt that photography was art. My interest started with a pinhole camera. We built them at school, took them home and took one picture, and then came back to school and developed it. It was fascinating. I found I had a knack for composition, and I went to extraordinary lengths to do something different. I would go to my grandma's place and put hessian or Vaseline over the lens to get different effects while taking hundreds of shots of her dog, Midge. When I discovered Cokin lens filters, I was in my element. My poor sister Vikki spent several hours posing for me in the style of the Mona Lisa.

Mal says that I picked up the basics very quickly. He says that kids like me are a real challenge and that we raise the bar. I was inquisitive, inquiring and challenging – basically a pain in the arse! While he was teaching, he would look for that flicker of disinterest in my eyes and know he would have to expand his projects and ideas.

We covered a lot of theory, but the practice was very important too. There was a darkroom attached to the class-room, so we covered developing and printing. I was very interested in the chemistry aspect of photography, and that certainly helped with the course. Mal reflects that if you can get a kid interested in the darkroom process, it's amazing what they can achieve. East Tech had an old Pentax K1000 that pupils could borrow at weekends, though you had to go through a major process to get it. It was the first proper camera I ever used. I was thirteen.

Mal also operated field trips for the students, generally just around town during daylight hours. We worked on cityscapes, portraiture, the full range. We were limited in terms of film stock and studio time, but this probably helped me become a better photographer. I knew how to make a shot work, and I also knew that I couldn't waste frames.

By Year 10 I was integrating photography with other subjects. For one science project I went up to Kodak's facility in Melbourne and learned about the history of photography, how film was made with silver oxide, the whole thing. I put everything into that project. (Until he retired in 2005, Mal used my work on that project as a teaching aid.)

The school built a new music and art wing and I volunteered to be the photographer for the opening ceremony. Mal was also responsible for the school magazine and was always looking for content, so was happy to give the job to me. My involvement in the magazine also meant that he could allocate more studio time for me.

The *Geelong News*, one of our local papers, came down to shoot some images of the opening ceremony, too, and the following week in class we went through the spread that had run in the paper. Mal talked through the photographer's approach and where it might have been better, and remembers me immediately challenging him and defending the photographer.

Initially my parents thought that my photography was just a hobby. They got nervous when it became obvious that it was my chosen vocation. I took a job at Coles New World supermarket, working alongside my best friend Mario, and soon bought my first car and more importantly my first camera – which in turn made me my first million.

My first bit of kit was a Ricoh XR2S from Fletchers in Melbourne. It had all the amazing features I wanted. I remember walking in there with Dad, who said, 'There are a lot of cameras here. Are you sure this is the one you want?' He couldn't believe I knew what I wanted. I used to walk around the house and the garden taking pictures of everything – especially Sasha, the family dog.

During years 10 and 11 at East Tech I got my first taste of life on a newspaper when I was sent on a work experience secondment to the *Geelong Advertiser*. My first printed picture, of three boys at a local fete, was used big and I was as pleased as punch. The *Addy* placement was over all too quickly, but I was soon back there working for free during my school holidays.

When I wasn't partying I was practising my photography, but it was all in my spare time – I wasn't even studying it at the Gordon Institute of Technology (where I went to do my final year of school). At sixteen, I started doing voluntary work experience. My mother almost had a fit when I came home from my first unpaid photographic job with pics of a decapitation on a railway line. A purple Jaguar had got stuck on the tracks and been decimated by the 3.15. This was real news. I thought my photos were unbelievable and threw the prints down on the table for her to look at while she was cooking dinner. She was speechless for a moment. Eventually she said, 'Wouldn't you like to be an architect, son?' I'll never forget the look on her face. You don't really register the bad stuff when you're in a high-octane news situation. You get tunnel vision and just focus on doing the job.

As my photographic career took off, my formal education started to fall away. I had decided that I couldn't do both well, but it was an easy choice. During one of the infrequent lessons I actually attended, I looked at the algebra on the board and thought, 'I am never going to use this in my life.' And that was that. Predictably, I flunked at the Gordon.

Despite the fact that I had completed work placements at *The Addy*, I knew there was no space there and no chance of a job, so I targeted the other major paper in town, the *Geelong News*. I had been wagging school a lot and covering shifts for Brian 'Harry' Hamilton at *The News*, as well as doing whatever scraps they threw me.

I stuck with it, kept grafting and, over time, did more and more for *The News*, mostly unofficially. *The News* was biweekly and *The Addy* was daily. That in itself taught me to be more creative and take a different approach. If I was somewhere at the same time as an *Addy* photographer, I couldn't shoot identical pictures as his would usually be published before mine and I didn't want to be seen to be regurgitating the same material as my rivals. We loved getting exclusives at *The News*, turning *The Addy* over. A biweekly should never really be able to do it, but we managed to all the time. We'd all socialise in the Press Bar in the Criterion Hotel after work, but I always wanted to win.

I ended up getting banned from *The News* because, as an unpaid member of staff, I wasn't covered by the workers' compensation insurance scheme. I was very upset about that.

The editor, Dale Jennings, was a real by-the-book man and we weren't close, so the situation seemed impossible. I was much more friendly with his deputy, Gary O'Regan, and the sports editor, Ondrej Foltin. When Jennings moved to *The Addy* and O'Regan became editor my career began to flourish.

Harry Hamilton was on his way out, and I focused on making sure I was there, front and square, to step into his boots. O'Regan soon found out that I had been moonlighting and, according to Ondrej, far from holding it against me, when Harry left to set up a new company, I got my first break. O'Regan took me on rather than hiring an experienced hand.

I was ecstatic: at eighteen I was an official First Year Cadet with a weekly pay packet of $23. I signed up for as much as I could, regularly covering twenty or more jobs a day. If there was nothing in the job diary I would go out and set up my own stuff. It was never about the money – it was all about the idea. I was a real experimenter. My goal was to get the front and back pages every day. I achieved it many times over.

When Glen 'Quarters' Quartermain joined *The News* he became my right-hand journalistic buddy. He's a great writer and one of the funniest characters I've ever met – a classic. Glen says that I am the most competitive little bastard he's ever met and that I annoy him at times. This has been a constant in our friendship; we often fall out for a couple of weeks before carrying on as before, but I count him among my closest friends.

We were quite a team and some of the stories we covered

together were unbelievable. One of our first jobs was to cover a horse race and instead of remaining behind the barriers, I clambered onto the track about five metres behind the finishing line. The officials were screaming at Glen to get me out of the way, but he knew that I wouldn't listen to him any more than I was listening to them. They thought I was going to be killed, and I nearly was. As the horses finished they actually bowled me over, but I got a great shot of the winner on a 24 mm lens.

I was also there to help Glen cover his first fatal car accident, which is always a gruelling experience for any reporter. Glen kept his distance, but I was shooting through the car window, even though the macabre shots were obviously never going to be used in a family newspaper. I turned to see Quarters throwing up over a farm fence, entertaining the local cow population.

At the time we made good use of radio scanners, which were illegal but very useful. One day we picked up details of an armed siege on the emergency services frequencies. The police were there, marksmen, the lot. I came up with the great idea of circling behind the property to get into the garden. Once installed, Glen would try and get an interview with the guy holed up in the house and I'd get a shot of the guy. Glen's response was simple, 'Darryn, he's got a fucking gun!' But then he realised I was serious, wished me luck and started interviewing whoever he could. I headed round the back, climbed over the fence and knocked on the door. The guy barricaded inside actually opened the door and it became obvious that he was holding a water pistol. We chatted together for about ten minutes, he even posed for some set shots with the pistol. Then I nipped out the front and told the cops that I'd just been having a chat with the guy and he'd be out in a couple of minutes. Which he did. Of course, when the story ran it was as a Glen Quartermain World Exclusive! I told Glen that his was the greatest act of cowardice I'd ever witnessed. He retorted that mine was the greatest act of idiocy he'd ever seen.

There were only six or seven of us at *The News*, all news-hounds. The atmosphere was electric and the team was probably the best I've worked with in terms of competitiveness and hunger for success. We worked till midnight and wanted to be the best. I learned about the equipment, the pressure, the darkroom and how a newspaper worked – which in those days involved a lot of time in the pub. That was where you got your stories.

**'The atmosphere was electric and the team was probably the best I've worked with'**

Though I continued at *The News* for several more productive months, my career began to get a little bumpy. Ted Brown took over as editor and he hated me. We just didn't gel. He would scream at me and I would just tell him to fuck off. He fired me a couple of times, but couldn't really get rid of me. Tony Aitken, the senior photographer and my immediate boss, hated me too. Everyone else around the office loved me because I was such a character.

In 1987 I won third prize in the cadet division of the Australian Press Awards with an image captioned 'Polly Wants a Snapper' – a shot of a cockatoo and a fish. Success of this kind was unheard of for a photographer at a biweekly regional paper. Clearly it was time to move on, and finally a vacancy came up at the *Geelong Advertiser*. I was twenty years old. The editor at the time, Graham Vincent, had had his eye on my work, and remembers bringing me on board. I was a little rough around the edges when I arrived, but Graham saw my total commitment.

I trod on a few toes, certainly, but I think Graham admired my flair. He knows that I took some criticism in the early days about my attitude and that it hurt me, but that I dealt with it. He loved my outrageous behaviour. He also realised that underneath all that bravado and bullshit was a fairly complex character. He always knew that I thought about things a lot more than some people gave me credit for. He loved that he could sit at a news conference at five o'clock in the afternoon, see that he had nothing for the next day's front page and call me. I would ask what he wanted, he would reply that he didn't know and, invariably, I would come back with a front-page image. I always produced the goods and wasn't worried about what I had to do to get the splash.

My first major scoop was a shot of the Queen, a brilliant image that Graham Vincent ran across the whole front page of *The Addy* – something that had never been done before. Leaving the scrum of the official photocall behind, I managed to hide myself in the middle of a flock of sheep at a shearing demonstration during the Bicentennial celebrations and popped up and nailed a fantastic picture of Queen Elizabeth. She was throwing her head back and laughing at a dog wearing a watch. Pretty fucking surreal all round! The boy from the one-horse town had scooped the whole royal rat pack. Although I was covered in sheep shit I was delighted, and so was the paper. The shot is known as 'My Queen of Hearts'. It relied on my patience and tenacity, and my desire to be the only person in the right place. Graham thought it was a sensational photograph and says that like all good photographers, I see things differently. I wasn't afraid of anything – be it royal protocol or a perilous environment.

Though I had many close friends on the paper, my attitude would have annoyed some of the staff. Ondrej says that my arrogance really started to show at *The Addy*. He remembers me often striding into the office, flinging down some prints and announcing, 'That's it – I've got the front page!' Those on the team who knew and understood me liked me; the ones who didn't thought I was a real smartarse, which was no biggy; I knew I was a smartarse!

*The Addy* was fantastic and slowly I moved up the grades. I was known as 'Scoop'. I was also big into the nightclub scene in Geelong at that time. One day I went to the Golf View Hotel (the first hotel in the area to have a revolving dance floor!) to do an advertorial and happened to meet the owner, George Ramia. We hit it off instantly, both being Leos. Then I started DJing for him with George Toppa. I also helped George with the night club renovation and began living at the hotel. This was at the risk of offending my parents who were anti drink and anti nightclub. Whenever my father was given booze for Christmas, he poured it down the sink. He had such disdain for alcohol. My mother's parents had battled alcoholism, so she couldn't bear the stuff either.

It was girls, beach, tinny, DJ, picture, and giddy up! In many ways I was at the top of the social ladder in Geelong. My connections with the newspapers, radio and nightclub gave me some serious cachet, and I was having fun. I could have had a wonderful life and a very good career there, but I had bigger ambitions. I talked to two buddies, George Ramia and Don 'Mad Dog' Dwyer from the local radio station. They said, 'What more have you got to do here? Everyone knows you.' Though he was a very well-known figure in Geelong, Mad Dog had cut his teeth in radio with the BBC in London and when my situation started to change he was a real driving force in encouraging me to break out of my comfort zone and follow my dream. Graham Vincent encouraged me, too.

I had several reasons for wanting to leave. The main one was that I had always been desperate to make it on Fleet Street. That was where the world's biggest-selling newspapers were and it's where I wanted to work. I'd also lost my driver's licence for drink driving after one night at *The Addy*'s Christmas party. Working in Geelong was going to be hard without a car. Fleet Street had always been a magical kingdom in my mind; the ultimate dream and test was to make it there. It wasn't just the big league – it was the World Cup final.

While I wasn't flush, it didn't take me long to get the money together. None of my jobs paid big money, but I had plenty of them. The night I left *The Addy*, I took a big cheque with me – my final payout was around $1400. One hour later I was on the end of a serious beating at a card game and was left with about $500 – my total budget for a new life. However, I was armed with a determination to take on and beat the world's best: 'If you can dream it, you can do it.'

I left in September. The good weather was coming to Geelong and I was moving to England for the winter. I was going to have to get used to a rather different climate! It was 1988 and I was twenty-two.

I couldn't help looking back as the plane thundered on and I don't mind admitting that I cried as I flew out over the northern coast of Australia. There's an emotional bond that holds you to your country, and I was testing it.

The plane seemed to crawl its way to Los Angeles. Immediately upon arrival, I collected my gear and went from LAX to a horrible hotel in Orange County. I was on a package deal and had no choice; we were bussed in like prisoners. I was only in LA for three days and had to make sure I used my time wisely. I was on a mission.

I had come to LA to go to the legendary Samy's Camera,

the cheapest camera shop in the world, where I knew I could pick up some really good second-hand equipment. I was there browsing for a whole day, like a kid in a candy store, wishing I was rich but knowing I would have to choose well as my budget wasn't going to stretch far. Despite my financial restrictions, I was able to get some great stuff – a photographer's jacket, lenses and a beaten-up Nikon FM2 body, and a Quantum Turbo battery-flash. All this would get me through my first month in the UK. Once I had bought as much camera equipment as I could, I decided to visit Disneyland. I hated it – thought it was crap. London was calling and I was more than ready to leave La-la Land behind.

My plane flew into Gatwick and I cleared customs at around 6 a.m. and caught the next train to Victoria Station. My first destination was the business centre on the concourse, where I bought a phone card, borrowed the telephone directory and tried to get an appointment at every national newspaper picture desk for later that day. It was a tough process. I was an unknown foreign national begging for time from some of the busiest people in London. But my enthusiasm had its reward – I was able to secure an appointment with the *News of the World*, one of the major players in the tabloid field. I wanted to work there, or at one of the other big papers – the *Daily Mail*, *The Mirror*, *The Sun* or *The Express*. These were the Fleet Street leaders. At one time *The Express* had ninety staff photographers working for it around the world!

I was very low on cash by this point and, though I

shudder to recall it, opted to walk from Victoria to Wapping carrying all my luggage on an unseasonably hot day. It's a bloody long way, and took me around four hours.

Seeing the Tower was surreal, and in fact the whole city looked like a film set to me. London seemed so olde-worlde, so quaint. Everywhere I looked I saw clichéd images like the famous red double-decker buses. I wasn't impressed with Big Ben – it had looked much bigger on television. Initially, London struck me as a doom and gloom, 'Get out of my way' kind of place. No one seemed too keen to help a lonely Australian with directions. Lack of assistance notwithstanding, I made my way to the News International HQ and went to find Mr Frank Hart, who was the picture editor at the *News of the World*.

**'My jaw dropped as I realised that I was now sharing the lift with Rupert Murdoch'**

Inside the lift I jabbed the button and the doors closed, then suddenly reopened to admit a group of men. My jaw dropped as I realised that I was now sharing the lift with Rupert Murdoch and some of his immaculately turned-out henchmen.

I hadn't come this far to miss an opportunity, so I introduced myself. 'G'day, Mr Murdoch!' I said cheerfully, and told him I used to work at his Geelong paper, *The Advertiser*. Not only that, but I had in fact been part of the *Addy* dragon-boat team that bore his name – Rupert's Raiders. In between floors, I even managed to produce a team T-shirt featuring his caricature.

Whether or not he thought I was insane I don't know, but he seemed interested – or perhaps just amused. He asked me what I was doing in London. Without hesitation, I told him who I was going to see and that I was planning to make it on Fleet Street. He smiled and was gracious enough to wish me luck. Probably to the relief of his associates, the doors then opened at my floor and I got out and headed for Frank Hart's office.

After my meeting with the Boss I was feeling pretty confident, but it immediately became obvious that Frank didn't have a lot of time and was only going to give my portfolio a cursory look – not least because it was a Friday and they were fairly manic, being the world's largest-selling newspaper.

Just as Frank was telling me that I would probably be better off trying to cut my teeth in the UK at a suburban daily, and that he had a mate at the *Croydon Advertiser*, there was a frantic knocking on the window. I didn't know what was going on at this point – the only Croydon I knew was in Melbourne and I had just flown from there. Frank went out to take a call and I figured I had reached the end of my appointment. I could see him chatting animatedly when suddenly he sat bolt upright and started nodding furiously.

I still don't know who was on the other end of the line (so give me a call, Rupert, I'd love to know), but Frank came straight back in and said that my portfolio was great. 'You start tomorrow, son,' he told me, and that was that. I was to pull my first shift as a freelance the following day.

My mouth fell open, but I managed to recover enough to make sure I didn't fumble this opportunity. Now it was my turn to start nodding furiously.

Five minutes later I was back on the street, Frank's words ringing in my ears. I was off to Bournemouth with the paper's chief reporter to find out if Windsor Davies was gay. My final question had been simple. 'Great,' I had said. 'Who the fuck's Windsor Davies?'

After the chance meeting with Murdoch and the incredible offer of some immediate work, I was on a real high. That night I took a bus to Muswell Hill to beg a favour from an old colleague at *The News*, Tracey Linguey, and her husband, Tony, who were living in London. I desperately needed somewhere to crash as my money was gone. Tracey had landed a plum gig at the *Daily Mail* but Tony, I was secretly amused to learn as we had never got on, was delivering TVs for Rumbelows. Tracey and I had agreed to rendezvous in her local pub, the Maid of Muswell. I was early and it wasn't long before the travel, the excitement of the day and a couple of pints of British beer caught up with me. When Tracey arrived, she found me sound asleep under a table.

The following day, I was still tired and jetlagged. The chief reporter picked me up from Muswell Hill and we set off for Poole in Dorset. He told me that this was going to be an easy gig and that I was going to sample the best seafood I'd ever had in my life. It wasn't the best of course. (I'm Australian, for fuck's sake! I know good seafood.) However, the trip did teach me about the expenses fiddle. It was regarded as a kind of unofficial overtime for a newspaperman in the UK, and I had to learn quickly, otherwise everyone else was going to get caught out. I hated having to fill in all those forms. It was a pain in the arse, but you had to do it. Everyone had a regular expenses fiction and my own favourite creation was 'Use of galibea, £20'. I was never once asked what the hell a galibea was, but I've since discovered it's the name for the flowing robe worn by Muslim men!

After that first job, I got work almost every day. Freelancers were always advised not to rely on one source of jobs, so I also covered the odd job for *The Sun* and *The Standard*. I was truly a free agent, covering sports, trailing outside restaurants or celebrities' houses for a possible shot – otherwise known as doorstepping – anything for any paper I could get work from. At one point I did go for an interview at the *Croydon Advertiser* because the regularity of the pay attracted me. I went down to *The News* in Portsmouth, too. Thank God something made me turn them down.

Tracey remembers all too well my stay with her in what she describes as her 'broom cupboard' in Muswell Hill. I was out on the road every day with my portfolio, tapping up new contacts, certainly not afraid of rejection. I only stayed with them for three weeks, sleeping on the floor, pretty much living on Wimpey burgers and bad Indian food. After I moved out they still saw me – I was always keen on a backyard barbecue.

Not that the weather was any good, but when a barbie is on offer I am there by hook or by crook.

My expertise was growing with every new day and my horizons were certainly expanding. My first experience with the royals was right after I arrived in London: I covered Prince William's first day at school. There were about 150 photographers there in the morning and everyone shot the proceedings, but I hung around at the back door for the rest of the day and got a shot of the young prince leaving for home. I was the only photographer to get something that was informal and natural and it was my first exclusive. I sold the picture to *The Express*, who paid me £75 for it – at that point I had no idea how to negotiate. They used it big and then I took it to an agency, Rex Features, who syndicated it for me. Mike Selby, the head of Rex at the time, looked at me slightly askance. It was as if he was thinking that I was the kind of guy who might one day come back to haunt him. BIG is now bigger than Rex.

People don't know the work that goes into this career. When I started out it was far from glamorous. After moving out of Tracey and Tony's place, I shared a bedsit over the road from them in Muswell Road, Muswell Hill, with an English couple. We had a room each and not much else for £50 a week. It worked out fine for quite a while. I was hardly ever there; it was very much shift, shift, job, job. The room was big enough for a bed, a desk and a sofa. I had all manner of ridiculous things covering the walls – pictures of me dressed as Rambo, silly, tacky things that made me laugh.

When I first arrived in London I was incredibly naive about life in general. One day I was sent to get some shots at a trial and I just walked into the High Court and started taking photographs of the guy in the witness box. Of course, I was jumped instantly by the security guys. I had no idea I wasn't allowed to take photos in there. I'd been used to just waltzing around Geelong doing whatever I liked.

I was always a big networker, a pusher. The desire to go out and achieve burns bright in me. London is a special place – all people do there is work, and I love it. To make my space in the business I had to make it happen by building relationships. I worked hard at getting to know people, even though I am not by nature a schmoozer. Usually this meant going out drinking with people. One thing that threw me was the early pub closing time. It reminded me of the 'six o'clock swill' in Australia in the 1960s – the bell would ring and everyone would rack up fourteen beers to down. (Not that I was a big drinker in the 1960s, of course, being four years old and not even at primary school!) In Australia I was used to getting a drink whenever I wanted, and the system in the UK seemed archaic.

My working day would see me up at six and out by seven, and taking on a night shift meant that I finished at 3 a.m. twice a week. Most of my jobs were for the *Daily Mail*. I wasn't on a shift rate and could pull in £65 a job, which was a lot of money then, especially when you do the maths in Aussie dollars (in those days you multiplied by three) – the most I did was twenty-nine jobs in one day! There was no hanging around; if I hadn't been briefed the night before, I always rang in early to see if there were any loose jobs available. I knew that most photographers were quite lazy, so if I could get the first call in as the picture editor arrived, I would be away. Something usually always came up, though if I didn't get a job for some reason, I would be out on the road looking for pictures. I craved that elusive exclusive.

Often when everyone else was in the pub, I'd be out looking for pictures. My average workday was eighteen hours. I enjoy getting up early, but it's not so easy in England in the winter. I really missed the sun. Pushing the limits meant that I would always come home knackered. I didn't have a large circle of friends in the early days and much of my socialising was work related. Despite that, I was never really lonely. People have always been drawn to me, and my home was always open to strangers.

Having arrived in the country with nothing, very quickly I had a lot. I was one of the first people to have a mobile phone – one of the enormous versions with a gigantic battery pack; I still remember the number. That was one of my brightest moves because it meant I was always ahead of the pack when the jobs got handed out. My first pay cheque was around £6000 and most of that was reinvested

◄◄ At 41 Fraser Street, Herne Hill, with my billycart and the bear that never left my side. The picture below shows me preparing to 'go to work' with Dad during the school holidays – I've always been ahead of the curve on fashion.

A Manifold Heights Primary School mug shot, with me aged about 10.

*My first-ever published picture appeared in the Geelong Advertiser while I was there on work experience.*

Belmont Primary School was full of surprises yesterday when it held its annual parade on the theme of "Mythical Creatures, fantasy Characters and Child book heroes", with this week being Children's Book Week, with pupils and staff dressed as their favourite characters for the parade.

One of the most exciting of the costumes was that of the Geoffrey Rose hiding this fantastic creation. Mrs. Dowsett, a Who, joined in the mas and a genie. Twelve entrants tokens for their e

*Darryn Lyons' photograph that won third prize in the cadet division.*

# Advertiser photographer wins praise from judges

*Geelong Advertiser* photographer Darryn Lyons has won third prize in the cadet division of the Rothman's Australian Press Awards.

Lyons, 21, took third prize for a photograph taken for his former employer, the *Geelong News*.

The picture of a cockatoo kissing a snapper appeared in the *Geelong News* last September.

The panel of six judges praised Lyons' "innovative approach to what could have been an ordinary subject".

*Brisbane Sun* cadet Martin Johnston took first prize and Genevieve Edwards of the Melbourne *Herald* finished second.

Former New South Wales Premier Neville Wran presented Lyons with a trophy and $250 for his efforts.

Lyons said the award came at a time when it was difficult for papers outside the metropolitan area to pick up awards.

*Darryn Lyons*

*I was 19 when I got my first business card.*

-195 Ryrie Street,
elong, Vic. 3220.
lephone: 22-3622

**geelong news**

## Darryn Lyons
### Photographer

◄◄ A year after I got my business card, I won my first photography award with my 'Polly Wants a Snapper' shot – a first for someone at a free suburban paper.

My first Geelong Advertiser business card. I was 21. →

**GEELONG ADVERTISER**
197 RYRIE ST.,
ONG 3220
Telephone:
052-222322

**DARRYN LYONS**
PHOTOGRAPHER

◄◄ Dealing with the sharp end of a rhino at Werribee Zoo was all in a day's work back then!

One of my talents has always been photographing animals. Another is creating a great picture from virtually nothing. I called this shot 'Birdy' and it made the front page.

• GOLFERS beware of Duncan the duck in a hole at Queens Park. The web-footed Watson was checking out the fourth in search of his elusive feathered friends — birdies, eagles and albatrosses — when photographed by DARRYN LYONS yesterday.

⬧ With John Lucas (centre) and long-time partner in journalistic crime Glen Quartermain (right) at a *Geelong News* party. We were reunited at my 40th birthday party in Geelong — as you can see I have aged better!

# THE BIG TRIPLE HEADER !!!!!!

**geelong news**
Centrepoint, Geelong. Ph: 22-3622

◄◄ The Big Triple Header was a hedonistic party thrown by me, George Toppa (centre) and George Ramia (left) at the Golf View Hotel to celebrate our birthdays. The Golf View was a great party venue, as was the Venus Dance Club, where I was a DJ in the early '80s.

The tremendous trio, Darryn Lyons, George Ramia and George Toppa, cordially invite you to celebrate their birthdays in festive fashion on Sunday, August 17 at the Golf View Hotel.

The grand occasion promises to be talked about for decades so don't miss out on the fun and frivolity.

The evening tees off at 8pm in the hotel's Fairway Convention Room and beer, wine and soft drink will be supplied.

It is also rumored a punch packed with more potency than a distillery will be available.

Dress formal - let your hair down when you get there!

YOUR COMMUNITY NEWSPAPER

The Venus Dance Club

Gary Ablett (or 'God' as he was known then) captured in full flight at the MCG. My pictures made the front page of the Advertiser and were picked up by many other publications too.

The Australian Bicentenary 1788-1988
DARRYN LYONS
PHOTOGRAPHER
THE GEELONG ADVERTISER
Valid for: 27-29 APRIL 1988
PASS NO.: 16V

**MEDIA 88**

Too early | Try again | Gotcha | Delight

A famous picture of the Queen taken during the Australian Bicentenary tour. The shot was used globally and I scooped the royal rat pack of photographers – though I did have to get covered in sheep shit to get it.

◀◀ My first year on Fleet Street was also my last! The *Daily Mail* was the last paper to move out of the most famous street in the world, and this was our final day there. The shot below shows me and *Sun* photographer Terry Richards freezing on the day of the Downing Street mortar attack in 1991.

Crash Bang Wallop! On my way to a glorious double hundred for the *Daily Mail* team on Hatfield Heath, Hertfordshire.

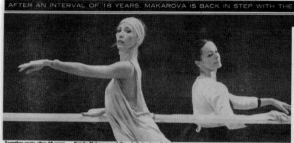

AFTER AN INTERVAL OF 18 YEARS, MAKAROVA IS BACK IN STEP WITH THE KIROV

Together again after 18 years ... Natalia Makarova and Kirov ballerina Irina Kolpakova

## Ballerinas meet again . . . across the b

BALLERINA Natalia Makarova danced again with the Kirov Ballet yesterday ... 18 years after she defected from the Russian company.

After a tearful reunion with the dancers — in Britain for the first time since her shock departure — she joined their rehearsal session.

And with her at the exercise barre was an old friend, Irina Kolpakova, the last member of the Kirov to dance with Miss Makarova in 1970.

It was only after months of careful negotiations that the Russian authorities agreed to the meeting.

In the Soviet Union, Natalia Makarova is a legend and this year, for the first time since her defection, she has been included in an encyclopaedia of Russian ballet.

'In Russia I have come back to life,' she said yesterday. 'I didn't exist for 18 years.'

The 47-year-old dancer, now a British citizen and an international star, thanked the spirit of glasnost for the historic reunion. 'It is very symbolic,' she said. 'The circle is complete. I am not a defector any more. I felt confident on stage. It is so exciting and very emotional.'

She has danced with the world's major companies and starred in the hit Broadway show On Your Toes.

Last night she was hoping to fulfil another dream — to dance with the Kirov again, in Swan Lake at the Business Design Centre, in Islington, North London, ...

'I just hope to be able to return to Mother Russia one day and introduce my ten-year-old son to his grandmother. That's all I want now.'

← My first big hit for The Mail: page 1 and a double-page spread inside. I stayed long after the photocall, and my patience paid off!

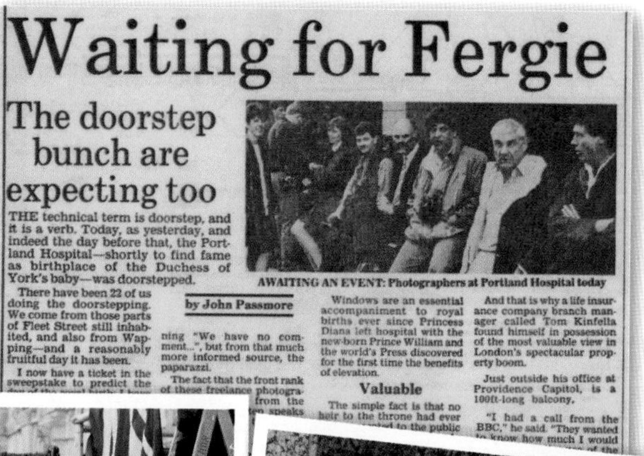

# Waiting for Fergie

## The doorstep bunch are expecting too

THE technical term is doorstep, and it is a verb. Today, as yesterday, and indeed the day before that, the Portland Hospital—shortly to find fame as birthplace of the Duchess of York's baby—was doorstepped.

AWAITING AN EVENT: Photographers at Portland Hospital today

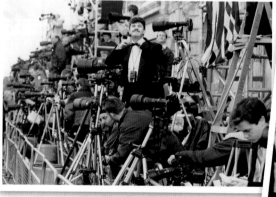

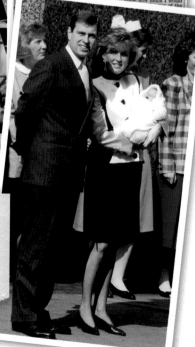

by John Passmore

There have been 22 of us doing the doorstepping. We come from those parts of Fleet Street still inhabited, and also from Wapping—and a reasonably fruitful day it has been.

I now have a ticket in the sweepstake to predict the ...

... ning "We have no comment...", but from that much more informed source, the paparazzi.

The fact that the front rank of these freelance photogra... from the ...

Windows are an essential accompaniment to royal births ever since Princess Diana left hospital with the new-born Prince William and the world's Press discovered for the first time the benefits of elevation.

### Valuable

The simple fact is that no heir to the throne had ever ... to the public ...

And that is why a life insurance company branch manager called Tom Kinfella found himself in possession of the most valuable view in London's spectacular property boom.

Just outside his office at Providence Capitol, is a 100ft-long balcony.

"I had a call from the BBC," he said. "They wanted to know how much I would ...

➽ My introduction to doorstopping: the rat pack outside the Portland hospital waiting for news of Fergie's baby. On the day of the birth, I turned up in black tie to pay my respects – I do like to stand out from the crowd.

My shot of the new arrival, Princess Beatrice. By then I felt like I had been waiting nine months too!

➤ In my early days at *The Mail* I'd use my own time to find pics. I took the shot of the kissing toddlers at Hyde Park, and the one of the little fella dwarfed by his dad's cricket pads in Kensington Gardens.

into gear. Whenever I got a new piece of kit, I was like a kid at Christmas.

Working like a dog during the week wore me out, so I would try and catch up on sleep at weekends. Fine in theory, but I was often offered extra shifts. Sometimes they were news shoots but frequently it was football. I'd never seen soccer before and was amazed by how fast it was. Though I was happy to take the money, the English winter was not for me and as soon as I could afford to give up the freezing Saturday arvos at the pitches, I did. On at least a couple of occasions I fell asleep on the bus on the way home and woke up in the depot feeling like Reg Varney of TV's *On the Buses*: 'Where are the clippies?'

Though I have always been a keen cook, I hardly went near the kitchen at Muswell Hill. My life was work and my work was life. I was very fit, but I was living off Kentucky Fried Chicken and burgers from the cafe round the corner – bloody great burgers, though. I didn't want to let a minute go past without trying to make money. To this day, I won't go near washing and ironing. It's such a bad use of time. Thanks, Mum – but I would rather buy new than waste time.

My hectic schedule meant that I was getting plenty of exercise and my youth kept me going – adrenaline is an amazing thing. The excitement of chasing jobs and the thrill of competition meant that I felt strong.

Tracey and Tony – he grudgingly and only by extension – were really good to me and took me under their wing. A few weeks after my arrival, Tracey inveigled me an appointment with Andy Kyle, the picture editor of the *Daily Mail*. At stake was a 'regular' freelance position, still not a coveted staff position but one up the ladder from my truly hand-to-mouth role at *News of the World*. There was a real class system on Fleet Street. It ran on a sliding scale from staff photographer down to regular freelance to freelance to scum.

Tracey had got me the introduction; now I needed to seal the deal. I had to prove myself. Thankfully, my tenacity, enthusiasm and – let's not forget – an excellent portfolio carried me through. I had done it. I was numb. This was a huge, momentous event in my life. I'd got my first job on Fleet Street! I called Mum from around the corner from *The Mail*'s Tudor Street offices, crying tears of happiness. At *The Mail* I would be working with photographers of incomparable quality.

When I first started at *The Mail* I was on around £60 per job. I was doing multiple jobs, treble shifts. I didn't sleep – fuck that. My sales reports very quickly totalled at least £8000 a month. I was cleaning up. It wasn't long until the accountants got wise and forced me onto a day rate – but not before a memo had been circulated asking why I was earning more than the editor. The memo appeared after I had received a monthly statement from accounts that came to more than £10 000. This was a lot of money, but I did have a huge backlog of expenses that had finally come through in one chunk – and those galibeas weren't cheap!

I was certainly making the figures, but I needed wheels. The first car I purchased in London came through one of the drivers at the *Daily Mail*, Dave Bully. He was a real character, very charismatic. It was a Renault 5, a total rust bucket that cost me £150. My first experience driving in England was terrible. A very troubled guy threw a rock through my window as I proceeded up the Archway Road. I knew he was off his nut because he threw an ice-cream first.

**'This gig was like being put into a tumble-dryer on full speed'**

Scary as that was, I knew I was going to have to be tough to make it in this city. The requirements of the job were that I had to be physically and mentally very strong. This gig was like being put into a tumble-dryer on full speed. I could handle it, but I came out a different man. Working regular freelance was all about speed and efficiency. You had to be the best to compete with the best.

Getting jobs through the paper's diary wasn't enough for me. I also used to go out and look for pictures on my own and submit them. I had a couple of great page-three shows in the early days – I was only doing what I'd been doing at *The Addy*, but it impressed the picture editors. Most of my peers were very lazy and just sat in the photographers' room waiting for the phone to ring and for them to be spoon-fed something. When it did ring, they'd be too scared to pick it up as they hated working, but I'd be diving for it. Sometimes the other staff photographers told me to say I was the only available person, so I would get the job. Good.

To get a great picture, you needed thought and a bit of luck. Ray Collins of *The Sun* and I rode our luck when we were chasing shots of a youngster who had committed a very serious crime and got sent down at Slough Magistrates' Court. The police smuggled the kid out of the court and into a van; we jumped into Ray's car and gave chase. We hit the M40 and charged along after the van like the proverbial bats out of hell. I opened the sunroof and stood up through it, camera at the ready. Ray pulled the car in behind the police van and then, at my signal, yanked the wheel around and moved up next to the window. The guy turned around in surprise and I melted him. Unbeknown to us, though, we weren't allowed to take shots of juvenile convicts, and I got hauled over the coals when I got back for endangering public life and bringing the profession into disrepute. Of course, I told the desk that the whole thing had been Ray's idea.

My bull-in-a-china-shop approach may not have been subtle, but it got results. Chief reporter Dave Williams and I were sent abroad to cover a story involving a British admiral who been taken to the cleaners by his mistress. After the whole drama blew up he had been hospitalised in Spain. While Dave was back at the hotel trying to go through official channels, I waited till siesta time and just walked into the hospital, took the admiral's picture and asked him a few questions. When I got back, Dave told me I was out of order and there were protocols to be observed. He was happy to take a copy of my notes, though. As we were operating abroad, we got away with it.

Despite the staff's differing work ethics, we all loved a good drink-up together at the old Fleet Street bars – the Punch, Ye Olde Cheshire Cheese, Scribes or the Mucky Duck, which was over the road from *The Mail*. The odd opening times used to confuse me at first, but I soon picked them up.

Though the general life was dog-eat-dog, there was a degree of camaraderie. To survive I had to be part of the gang. The most important clubs were the Golden Scissors Club and the GANS (Give Us A Neg Society). GANS involved sharing out negatives if any of the hard-core membership had missed the moment and would not otherwise have been able to file an image. We were a close-knit community and were judged on what we produced. If only one of us had the picture, then sometimes that person was forced, by convention, to share. Naturally, that kind of action was never in my mentality, but it was part of the game and I had to play it. The old guys whose car-chasing days were over loved it, of course. My competitive edge could be salved, however, just by the knowledge that I had got the shot, and I loved getting a pat on the back from some of the old stagers who had been there and done that.

A great example of this was in 1994, when I nailed a shot of convicted serial murderess Rose West through a police-car window at 5 a.m. the day after her accomplice husband,

Fred, had hanged himself. The other guys were all sleeping off their hangovers. Though I knew that my success would be shared by GANS members, I didn't expect to be the only photographer who wasn't given a byline by his paper. What a cruel irony. I had taken the shot that was on the front of every national paper, credited to Tom, Dick or Harry – all fortunate GANS members!

There were some real characters in the group I ran with. The notorious snapper 'Beastie' Burton was someone I spent a lot of time with. He looked like a rogue, but was a lovely guy. He was one of the younger breed but had an older mentality – he loved the style of the classic Fleet Street snappers, which basically meant that he loved a drink! In many ways he was born in the wrong era. I could imagine him wearing a fedora with a press card sticking out of the band, toting a classic Speed Graphic camera. He truly had the look of a movie press photographer, straight out of central casting. He was a great guy to be around, great company, and never slow to get a round in.

**'Send the Aussie in – he'll kick their arses'**

There is no doubt that my time at the *Daily Mail* was the making of me and shaped my future business. My company, BIG Pictures, is very much modelled on the way *The Mail* ran – lots of screaming, lots of conferences and an attitude of 'Let's beat everyone'. The editor of *The Mail*, Sir David English, was a gentleman of the old school and a born newspaper man. I idolised him. He was the boy from nowhere who had made it, and I wanted to be him. He oozed aura and presence and I loved the way he spoke. He even used to swear 'in posh'. He had really lived the life, and had been in papers long enough to have broken the story about the death of JFK. English became a real influence on my career. He used to take the piss, but he loved my attitude. 'Send the Aussie in – he'll kick their arses,' he would command. In my early days at *The Mail* I was known for putting myself in harm's way to get the shot. I ended up on quite a few car bonnets and several of my colleagues weren't sure if I was employed as a snapper or a stuntman.

As a *Daily Mail* photographer, you were part of the 'royal family' as far as other photographers were concerned. *The Mail* was the place to be at the time, but they worked us fucking hard. English had been there since it was turned into *The Mail* from *The Sketch* under Lord Rothermere, and he wanted results. That suited me, as that was my agenda too. Rothermere, who's now passed on, was a true gentleman and a ladies' man. He had a Japanese mistress in Paris, where he spent a lot of time. Bubbles Rothermere was his wife; she had been a Tiller Girl and liked to party. She was a constant source of amusement and there were all sorts of rumours about her.

The *Daily Mail* picture editor, Andy Kyle, and I had a good relationship. He was very diligent and a good politician – it's a bloody hard job keeping all those egos satisfied, believe me. By the time Andy came in, the role of the picture editor on Fleet Street had changed from being all-powerful to being more of a picture collector. They just had to get as many pictures in as possible and chuck them over to the back bench. The powerhouse of any newspaper became the subeditors who laid out the paper. It was up to them who got the front page.

I was making friends with all the right people. Obviously the top brass were important, but Johnny, the head of the darkroom team, was the boy. The darkroom guys were real East End types, but they knew how to make your pictures look good. There was an entrepreneurial atmosphere to that place, with a lot of backhanders going around for extra prints. I'd hate to be able to compare how much film came in against how much went out the back door.

In my first weeks at *The Mail* I spent much of my time loitering outside the Portland maternity hospital with Pete 'Rosie' Rosenbaum and Chris Grieve, who were freelancers at *The Mirror*, waiting for the Duchess of York's first child to be born. Pete, and Kleggy from *The Sun*, were laughing at me because I didn't know how to pull off a 'car shot'. This shot required technique, luck and whole lot of guts. Pete gave me the low-down and left me to practise. The premise was as follows: set your aperture at F8 to F11, full manual power on the Quantum flash unit, 250th of a second on the shutter speed, run at a car, and crash-bang-wallop with a wide-angle lens. Rosie and I used to run up to people driving home past the Portland and practise on them. Must have scared the living crap out of them. (Funnily enough, just recently I took a call from the police, who were making a complaint about a couple of my BIG guys. They were outside TV personality Ulrika

Jonsson's house and had been practising their car shots on a family and almost caused a major accident. While this was in truth no laughing matter, it did remind me of the old days.)

Fergie was a long, cold doorstep at the Portland. Mike Forster was the *Daily Mail*'s royal guy, and there were five of us making sure that everything was there for him. I pulled twenty-four-hour shifts for two weeks and made a killing – £280 a day. In those days I was a staunch royalist, and I was so excited when the Duchess was about to come out with the new Princess that I turned up in black tie. A sea of photographers from all over the world, two or three hundred, surrounded me. I'd been guarding the spot for three weeks, but when the moment came the favoured royal photography rat pack turned up, took the best positions and got their shots.

That was the way it was most of the time. Out on the street there was no time for pleasantries. It was a free-for-all. There'd be fighting, pulling people's Turbo leads out of their packs if they weren't looking, it was dog-eat-dog and anything went. But the adrenaline . . . !

We had some real breaks at the back door of the Portland. Rod Stewart emerged once with his new baby when none of us had known he was there, and one afternoon I melted the actor David Jason walking past. I felt a little sorry for him as he didn't enjoy the experience, but the pictures got used.

There was time to learn new tricks, but in general there was no fucking about. I had to watch and learn fast. I was flying with the best: Chris Barham, Bill Cross, Mike Forster, Mike

Hollist – the big boys. There were some great characters there. One of my favourites was Eric Faulkner, the night picture editor of the *Daily Mail*. His version of the truth always had a certain economy; apparently he'd 'made' the Rolling Stones when they came in unkempt to have pictures done and he clipped them round the ears and sent them away to get haircuts and some decent threads. According to Eric they came back as pop stars and the rest is history.

Another interesting *Mail* guy was Monty Fresco. He had once been David English's favourite photographer and was finishing his career as I was starting out. His eyes weren't what they'd been and he used to get me to cover jobs for him, because he rated me. Well, I thought he did. Maybe I was just gullible. Another Harry Hamilton! I didn't mind because I wanted the experience and I liked Monty. Rumour had it that he had an entire room at home devoted to his collection of hotel toiletries. Maybe light-fingeredness ran in the family – I'm fairly certain his son Michael once nicked a lens from me on a job at Croydon Crown Court.

As well as perfecting the car shot, I also discovered a very low-tech piece of kit – the ladder. It was as important as the camera on some jobs – if there were forty guys there, you had to get above them. I was always out with my ladder; I was like a window cleaner. I had ladders with two, three, four and five steps. They were all a pain in the arse. Much of the art of being a photographer is being prepared. It is as much about getting ready and getting in position as it is getting the shot. It's not always easy, and most of the pressure came from myself.

My first major success for the paper was when the Kirov Ballet came to town. I was given the theatre gig, which the others figured was a dead-end job, but I knew was important because David English himself was attending the theatre that night. I stayed on after the photocall even when every other photographer had left. This gave me unrestricted access to shoot the full dress rehearsal and the results were excellent. Andy Kyle looked at the long roll of negatives and was immediately impressed. He hurriedly made marks with a Chinagraph pencil on a couple of shots to be cropped slightly, and with a finger and thumb nicked each of the neg proofs that he wanted to see prints

**'It was a scene of devastation and mutilation, but I had to get on with the job'**

of immediately. The prints the process guys turned out were the old style, 16 by 20 inches – huge. The picture editors in those days used to influence the back bench or the editor by turning up with prints the size of posters. Luckily for me, David English loved the shots, too. 'This is marvellous stuff. Maaarvellous stuff!' he boomed. Through going the extra mile and waiting for the shot that was worth hitting, I ended up on the front cover with a double page inside. That pissed some people off, I can tell you!

Horror was part of the job too, and news photographers had to deal with it. I covered the Clapham train crash on 12

December 1988, which left thirty-five people dead and scores injured. It was a scene of devastation and mutilation, but I had to get on with the job. In situations like that I switch everything else off except my focus on the job. I become unemotional. Maybe only journalists understand that. I'm not saying that distancing yourself from your feelings is a good thing, but you can't get too emotional in the field and still capture what is happening in front of you.

As well as expanding my experience and portfolio, *The Mail* also helped to fill my extremely limited down time. Chief reporter Dave 'Willow' Williams was captain of the paper's cricket team, and always roped in any Australians who joined *The Mail*. The team would play in and around London and the home counties every Saturday, and once a year there was 'the tour' – a real highlight. We travelled all over the country, from Yorkshire to Somerset to Norfolk – although we were scared to go to Yorkshire because we always got slaughtered. It was the most dangerous county for us. I called it 'Lillian Thomson county', after Australian fast bowlers Dennis Lillee and Jeff Thomson.

Some of the greatest cricket arenas are in the UK, and I'm not talking about Lord's. One pitch had a 40-foot oak tree at second slip – I edged many a six there. Another had a road running literally 20 feet behind the stumps. The wicketkeeper had to watch his back to avoid passing cars shaving the hairs off his arse with their mirrors! I loved these grounds.

*Daily Mail* cricket tours were usually four-day affairs. We would depart on a Friday morning, hit a local pub for lunch and that evening turn out to play a twenty-overs-per-side game at 5 p.m. It was real 'hit and giggle' stuff, and we were usually slaughtered. We would then play a full match on both the Saturday and Sunday, and come crawling back on the Monday. A very, very long weekend, with a lot of drinking and a lot of cricket.

All the top-echelon *Daily Mail* reporters were on the team. After a game in August 1989 we were in a curry house somewhere in South London having a great night together when we all got called back to central London. I was briefed on the cell phone as I drove, but details were hard to come by. All we knew was that a party boat, the *Marchioness*, had gone down on the Thames with half of London's 'beautiful people' on board. It was a models' party on the boat, with the next generation of supermodels on board. The scale of the event kept being revised and it wasn't until we reached the riverside that the true horror became apparent.

It was a foul night and somehow evoked an atmosphere of Jack the Ripper's London. It was windy and there was a real chop on the water. The darkness was almost palpable, cut only by searchlights and the desperate screams of the dying. I swung my camera around, trying to follow the searchlights and blindly banging off frames. I could hear but not see people in the water all around me, screaming and then disappearing into the inky water to their deaths. Everyone who was present wanted to do something to help, but diving into the Thames to try and pull some unseen victim to safety would have been a suicide mission.

I had a long (300 mm) telephoto lens, but was unable to find anything. The atmosphere was terrifying – it had the same sense of panic and fear that I imagine the Blitz must have engendered. I couldn't hit anything in the water; the only images I got were of the heroic rescuers doing their best and of the upended vessel. No one got a shot of anyone in the water – not even Bill Cross, who actually lived right next to the river.

I didn't question our right to be there doing the job while these devastating scenes unfolded around us. I am not a qualified lifesaver, and I and my colleagues were there to record history. After the event, of course, I had an emotional response. Over the following weeks I had a recurring nightmare featuring a drowning girl slowly losing her grasp on the stays of one of the bridges and being dragged under the water. While that may have happened, it was certainly not something I witnessed.

The *Marchioness* disaster was a chilling event, and sobering in every sense of the word. Fifty-one people drowned. We were all commended for our efforts by *The Mail*'s deputy picture editor, Nick Skinner, but it was a terrible experience – an extreme event. The following day was almost even more harrowing. I was sent out as part of a team to round up 'collect pictures'. This involved knocking on the doors of people who were freshly bereaved and asking if they had a photo of their loved one that we could copy. It was true gutter press stuff – probably the worst job a photographer had to do, but if you could pull it off the more you were rated by the tabloids. It was hard, but I was amazed at the grace of the families I spoke to.

## LOCAL SNAPPER SCOOPS PRESS AWARDS

# FAR HORIZONS

**WORKING AT *THE MAIL*** made me into a complete photographer. Experiencing the terror and emotion of war brought me some of my most memorable days. My war experiences began in the company of a reporter called Geraint Jones, with whom I headed into Romania in 1989 to cover the revolution. Before leaving London we converted our white Kennings hire van into an 'ambulance' using rolls of red electrical tape to make it look like we were with the Red Cross. Sorry about that, Mr Red and Mrs Cross, but we needed to borrow your image. (It wasn't as bad as it sounds because we were actually carrying medical supplies for various hospitals.)

We drove that van right across Europe. The night before

entering Romania, we stayed in Szeged in Hungary. It was Christmas Eve, I was twenty-three and it was my first experience of war; Geraint's, too. We were in a hotel right on the border and I remember the sound of sniper fire and falling mortar shells as I lay under my bed talking on the phone to my mother. She and Dad were just about to open their presents, due to the time difference. I wished them a happy Christmas to the sound of sporadic gunfire.

**'As I was saying goodbye, all the windows in my room were blown out'**

As I was saying goodbye, all the windows in my room were blown out. I thought this was great – a boyhood dream come true. Now I was a real war photographer. I tried to pass the noise off as the TV and the boys partying and told Mum not to worry and to have a great Christmas – that's all, folks!

As we prepared to enter the country, there was a huge queue of aid and media vehicles at the border. Amazingly, we got in with them. I had been convinced that we would be turned away. There's a picture of me at the border with a Romanian soldier posing with his Kalashnikov. It was about minus 10 degrees. Fucking freezing! It was only later that I realised I had been standing there with a *Daily Mail* cap on; I couldn't have made our status more obvious, but I guess they didn't read English.

A German TV crew in front of us was travelling with a German charity. Taking the wheel of our van as we cleared the border, I heard a shot and saw a little puff of dust. One of the German guys had copped a bullet in the head. It could have been any of us – we would all have been in the sniper's sights. Thinking back, I know that I had my window up and that the German's was down – perhaps it was a clearer shot for the sniper.

Though that was a scary experience, I had no fear for the duration of the trip. I genuinely believed I wasn't going to get shot, that something would save me. Perhaps it was the confidence of youth; I don't know. I wanted to continue in the tradition of the great war photographers, people like Tim Page and Donald McCullin. Donald covered the Vietnam War and on one occasion his camera stopped a bullet. I figured the same would happen for me. My dream at the time was to work for the Magnum agency, a gritty war and real-history picture agency that employed the world's best photographers.

We headed towards Timisoara, which had been one of the strongholds of the Securitate (secret police). Snow had begun falling gently, and looking ahead on the road we saw a quite surreal scene. A guy with a huge, frozen handlebar moustache was driving towards us in an enormous horse-drawn wooden cart with stone wheels, complete with a wooden chuck on the axles. His whole family was on board; it was like something from *The Flintstones*. I felt like Michael J. Fox in *Back to the Future*, but instead of a DeLorean I had a Ford Transit. The family wasn't far from the border, but whether they got out of the country I don't know. I guess that's why I felt invincible. I couldn't get shot, because I was dreaming. For the boy from

Geelong, it was like walking onto a movie set; the problem was that it was, in fact, all too real.

I drove on for a couple of kilometres before being forced to brake abruptly as there was a child in the road. He was around nine or ten and was pointing a .303 at me. We were prepared for most eventualities and were equipped with the main in-demand items for bribery – namely alcohol, cigarettes and sweets. The kid came up to the window and started shouting, 'Bonbon!' (sweet). I translated this as 'Boom boom' and figured we were in big trouble. Luckily Geraint's grasp of foreign languages was better than mine and he reached for the sweets. We hurled bags of Mars Bars towards our would-be killer and he wandered off, sat by the dusty road and put his gun down. His mission complete, he started eating happily. Had we not handed over the goodies, he would certainly have shot us. I don't know where his mum and dad were; they were probably dead.

The whole country was extremely dangerous and I don't know how we managed to blag it. Before we left London we had learned a few stock phrases in Romanian and that certainly helped. There were checkpoints every five kilometres and the only way through was by bribing the guards with cartons of cigarettes or mini-bottles of Tullamore Dew whiskey.

After hours of driving, we made it to our destination. The Intercontinental Hotel became our base of operations, but it was very primitive. The top three floors had been the Securitate's headquarters. We had rooms there, but the hotel was basically a concrete shell and we lived rough. Occasionally the power came on, but it was sporadic at best. We travelled with a neg scanner and I had my darkroom kit with me. Those school photography lessons really came in handy. I developed my own film and transmitted black-and-white images via our wire machine. The maximum that could realistically be sent was around four or five images a day, and the chances were very high that the line would cut out.

If you weren't in the hotel you were fucked. There was a camaraderie among the media who were based there. Everyone was looking for three things: a reliable phone line to get copy and images out, the next big story, and a stiff drink. All the journalists sat together on the roof at night and got smashed on looted bottles of red wine or whatever we could find. We would place the empty bottles on the ledge and wait for them to get smashed by a flying piece of ordnance or a sniper's bullet. After nothing to eat for days, and too much drink, we went crazy. I danced around, playing chicken with the snipers – poking my head up to invite potshots. Everyone else had fucked off. There were no rules; it was like the Wild West. All around us was the most amazing pyrotechnics display as gunfire and tracers lit up the sky. It was like a press room crossed with a borstal, a beehive with a death buzz.

The Securitate had left in a hurry; the rooms were filled with files and high-frequency surveillance equipment. By that stage the whole town was full of snipers, but I was still fully gung-ho. As well as danger, there were great pictures everywhere. The hotel's basement held a torture chamber; one poor guy had been left to die there on a concrete butcher's block. A huge knife protruded from near his genitals, and piano wire was tightened around each of his fingers. Appallingly, the wire had been used to drag his body over the block so that the knife sliced through him. It was horrifying, but I took the picture. This was the first time I truly smelt death. Once you have experienced that, it never leaves you.

I coped in this environment better than I thought I might. There's a parallel of sorts between a sniper tracking down his target and a paparazzo chasing his. Though of course our object is not murder. I hate guns, let alone shooting people for real.

There was no real plan to our travels around Romania; we had to use our initiative. Our brief was just to do what we could do. We were there for about a month, though at times we thought we were never going home. I think the office forgot about us. The classic command from the desk to the team on the ground was, 'Stick with it!' The number of times we heard that . . . It was also true that, to an extent, we concealed from the office the real level of danger unfolding around us because we didn't want to be pulled out early. We wanted to get stuck in. I was John Wayne with a camera in a world of complete lawlessness, and for a boy who liked danger this was everything – the real deal.

One problem was that at the time no one at home really knew what was unfolding there. I don't think the desk knew what they were sending us into. They were more worried about who'd won Lotto than our safety. We were among the first journalists in, though, of course, we were Red Cross, not journalists! We did in fact have a fairly significant cargo of aid items that we distributed to hospitals and orphanages for *The Mail*'s charity.

Geraint was an excellent writer and had a cool head – though we were both pretty scared at times. I was able to deal with the overload by going into a kind of professional trance. By operating almost as a robot I lost touch with the passion and care within me. It sounds bastard-like, but it was the only way to cope and keep my sanity. I certainly didn't sleep. Adrenaline is the most incredible drug and when you're on it all the time you can do anything. It kept me alert to what was unfolding around me. It was exciting and exhausting.

The irony was that the only picture I got into the paper was a head shot of Geraint to accompany his daily foreign feature page. I was taking the greatest shots of my career, we were recording history, but I couldn't get a fucking picture in the paper to save my life. It became quite demoralising. The only real avenue for my work was through news features. I got a Romanian guy to pose with a ripped-up copy of *The Mail* to try and get something in, but even product placement failed me. Nothing got syndicated elsewhere; Solo, *The Mail*'s syndication arm, was so useless I'd be surprised if they ever sold a picture. In many ways it was easier for *The Mail* to get hold of Reuters stuff for the news as they were wiring all the time.

In the end we were pulled out. Geraint left first and then I was off. We dumped the van, which was wrecked by now, and headed off – I guess we lost our deposit at Kennings. My destination was not London but Berlin, where I arrived just in time to miss the Wall coming down but in time to catch the euphoria of it all. I was in and out in a couple of days.

I had the war bug now, and in 1989 when the Czech revolution happened I was on the first plane to cover it as a freelancer. Andy Kyle just told me to go for it and we'd work something out later. I flew Aeroflot and the plane was like a converted troop carrier. The flight was very scary; the crew were celebrating and as drunk as skunks. The flight attendants were enormous women who tottered down the aisles handing out jugs of beer to everyone as the plane lurched from side to side; at one point it was almost upside down.

I arrived in the Czech capital on the night of the regime change. History was unfolding and the atmosphere was unbelievable. The Iron Curtain had fallen and everyone was ecstatic. I was there for a week, and for some reason I got more pictures into *Time* magazine than into *The Mail*. I had some wonderful colour transparency stuff and syndicated it to loads of titles through Rex Features.

The *Daily Mail* cricket team featured some of the paper's big-hitters – in every sense – and was a real social affair. There were plenty of characters, and I got on with some better than others. Hal Austin was our dynamite West Indian fast bowler, and I also enjoyed spending time with Stewie Payne and Paul 'Cros' Crosbie. Despite not having a great deal of natural talent, Stewie and Cros loved the game and were the heartbeat of the team. Both took some unbelievable catches. They made a major contribution to the social side of the team – especially Stewie, who was a real party animal. Ian Walker was also part of the drinking hard core and we would always be up until God knows when. The landlords of the pubs would often just leave us to it and go to bed. We would calculate what we'd drunk and pay up the next day. Our bar bills were enormous.

Bill Greaves was a big part of the team, a real posh old-stager. He would turn up in his blazer and whites, smoking a Hamlet cigar. Being more laid-back, he didn't really approve of my bombastic approach to the sport, but I guess he appreciated my contribution to the scorecard. Generally I would bat at three and either make nothing or a lot. I admired Bill for getting out there and doing it at his age. He never missed a match and we had some good nights together, though Dave Williams was forever acting as mediator between us. I played to win and sledged like hell. I enjoyed fielding at silly mid-off, a great sledging position. Talk to anyone who plays polo with me now – nothing has changed. I'm sure that on occasion I pissed off the whole team, and I know that Dave sometimes struggled to arrange the fixture for the following year due to my outspokenness and constant sledging. Once we got to the pub, though, everything was forgotten. In fact, I regularly became the life and drunken soul of the party.

There was always something to amuse us on those trips. In one game, all of the opposing team had the same surname! I remember one legendary match in particular that took place in Somerset. The Friday was fairly typical. We had lunch in the local – a ploughman's lunch and a few pints – and then took to the field for the twenty-over match. I was on fire and bowled my heart out. The Saturday match, coming as it did after a heavy night of drinking, was truly exhausting. The pitch was on a plateau at the top of a massive hill. It looked like Robin Hood's hat with the top cut off and you felt like you were playing in the clouds. If anyone really got hold of a delivery, an unlucky fielder – usually me – was looking at an 80-metre run! I went up and down the hill a few times that day. It was more like mountain trekking than playing cricket.

On the Sunday we were in illustrious company. The celebrated British author of *Cider with Rosie*, Laurie Lee, owned the pitch at Sheepscomb on which we were playing, and he turned up to watch. Laurie had built a wonderful pavilion and pitch, all for the love of the game. I had no idea who he was at the time. It had been pissing with rain and was a really sticky wicket. When it was our turn to bat, I made a combative eighty while the others dropped like flies around me. As I left the field, Laurie kept hailing me as 'The champion!' and told me he was going to write a book about me. I loved that guy, he was fantastic, so eloquent – a real eccentric, loving life, with his cane and his young-looking girlfriend hanging off his arm. By the end of the evening people were claiming that his next novel would be called 'XXXX with Darryn'.

Being at *The Mail* gave me the chance to witness the greatest tournament of another, very different sport. I had covered plenty of football matches since arriving in the UK, but getting sent to the Italia 90 World Cup was a real coup – and a bit of a fluke. Jim Hutchison and Brian Bould were initially covering the event, but Brian had to come back to the UK as his father was ill. As ever, I was the first guy to pick up the phone in the photographers' room. I was told to get the next flight to Italy and couldn't believe my luck. Giddy up!

This was it – the pinnacle of achievement for a photographer, as far as I was concerned. It was a privilege to be trusted to cover such a massive event. I'd covered a lot of big sports events in Australia – VFL (now AFL) grand finals and the like – but this was huge. The passion aroused at the World Cup is amazing. I don't think even winning the Ashes compares to its power, and I'm a cricket nut. The first match I covered wasn't exactly the greatest in the World Cup's illustrious history – Argentina became the first team ever to fail to score in a final and were beaten by West Germany due to a late penalty converted by Andreas Brehme. But the buzz was unbelievable.

As well as covering the matches, we were there to cover

the England camp. Everywhere they went, we went. There was a press conference or story every five minutes around this team, which boasted some truly great players and characters – Lineker, Gascoigne and Shilton among them. It was very much a news trip, not a 'Let's stitch up the players' trip. Though England played well, the only thing they won was the Fair Play trophy, which was no big deal in my eyes. There was only one trophy that counted, after all. The team's final match was the third and fourth place playoff, and they went down 2–1 to the host nation.

I was the packhorse on that trip, the 'dev and wire' man (developing film and transmitting the images). My role was to make shuttle runs from the press room to Jim at pitchside and send stuff out to the paper as fast as I could. There was a lot of pressure. Everything had to be perfect, and we tested everything twice. I had an enormous amount of gear to carry with me. There were some consolations – the women were unbelievable. The World Cup hostesses were everywhere and they were stunning, breathtaking and, above all, willing!

Our brief gave us the opportunity to travel around Italy and to see its cities. Over there, going to a football match is like going to a royal ball. The stadiums were stunning, some even featured marble stairs, and the crowd were elegantly turned out and classy – not something you associated with British football fans. Some of the women were wearing ball gowns! In Bari, a couple got married in the centre circle before the match. The atmosphere in the stadiums was always electric;

I would get chills up and down my spine just from plugging into that excitement.

Of course, the ultimate experience was the final. Being in Rome for a World Cup final: what could be better? I felt like Caesar in the Colosseum watching that match. They used to feed Christians to the lions here, and now the Lyons was a photographer there! The roar of the crowd was unbelievable. After the final whistle heralded the West German victory, I just slumped back in my chair, worn out by the sheer emotion and intensity of it all.

At *The Mail* I had access to the top news events and celebrities, and my work began to be recognised. On one of the most memorable nights in my career I witnessed the lights going out for one of the world's greatest-ever performers. The paper had received a tip that Rudolph Nureyev, the legendary ballet dancer, didn't have long to go and I was sent to Paris in October 1992 with Rebecca Hardy, a

**'Under the coat I had a metre-long 600 mm lens with a doubler**

real go-getter, great foot-in-the-door merchant and brilliant writer. Another *Mail* photographer was with us, Brian Bould, who opted to be the processing man. The show that was Nureyev's true swan song, *La Bayadère*, was to take place at the Palais Garnier theatre.

Luckily it was a cold night when I strolled up to the theatre in my trench coat, because under the coat I had a metre-long 600 mm lens with a doubler. My excitement faded a little when I discovered that Europe's most feared paparazzo, Daniel Angeli, was already there on the job, but I kept going and got past security somehow. I walked up to the private boxes at the back, from where I could see the auditorium. Over to one side, Nureyev was slumped in the box nearest the stage, surrounded by close friends.

Needing a vantage point, I seized the nettle and, after knocking politely, barged into the box opposite Nureyev's. It turned out to be filled with a Japanese delegation from Toyota who spoke not a word of English between them. Courteously they all got out of my way, bowing madly and chattering excitedly as I set up my gear. It was like *National Lampoon Goes to the Ballet*. They must have thought I was very important. The way I pulled the lens out, though, it could have been a bazooka!

There was no light at all in the theatre, so I was using 1600 ASA film pushed to 18 000. Brian was going to need to be on top of his game to get anything from the shot I was attempting to pull off. I couldn't believe what I was seeing through the lens, and kept shooting. Just as I decided to leave, Nureyev left too. Expecting security to get me on the way out, I rushed off and palmed the film to Rebecca. She managed to get it out to Brian, who processed it in our hotel room. As I left the theatre I walked out past Angeli (who had missed the shot) and into the street. I realised that Nureyev's car was about to come past me and, with clinical precision, whipped my camera out and nailed him again with a perfect car shot. That was the last picture ever taken of him.

In photographic terms, getting any image at all that night was a miracle. Not only did the film have to be pushed to the end of extremes, but I was shooting on a 600 mm lens, hand-held, on a 15th to a 30th of a second shutter speed. Any photographers reading this will realise just how hard that is. I'll never forget that job. It was one of the pictures I hit against all the odds.

It was a shame to see the great Nureyev pass, but I won a hatful of awards for my images. The shot inside the theatre was voted into the top of *Time Life*'s Pictures of the Decade award and I won the 1992 News Photographer and Press Photographer of the Year for the photos, too. Brian did an amazing job on the processing – I owe him those awards. Incredibly, *The Mail*'s editor of the *Night and Day* magazine, Christina Appleyard, didn't use the pictures in the next edition. They have certainly been used a lot elsewhere, though.

Despite the fierce pressure, there were plenty of perks. Probably the cushiest job I ever handled for the *Daily Mail* involved a trip to the fantastic Eden Roc hotel in the south of France. At the time, it was the most opulent hotel I'd ever seen, and now it's my hangout when BIG Pictures works the Cannes Film Festival. I don't know whether the gig was ever intended as a story for *The Mail* or whether it was an attempt at getting a bargaining chip or even revenge. The renowned British QC George Carman was staying with a woman on Sir Donald Gosling's boat, *Leander*, which was moored at Antibes. Sir David English had sent me to cover this.

I spent a month tailing Carman, watching him on the yacht through binoculars from my sun-lounge. Tough gig! None of my material was ever used, and at the end of the month I had to pay a gigantic bill – in cash, which was the only method of payment accepted by the hotel. It was about twenty grand, sterling.

You never know when a great shot is going to appear. On one of my last nights at Eden Roc, I noticed that Sting and his wife, Trudi Styler, were at the table next to me at dinner. Always with my eye on the bottom line, I took half an hour off from Carman the following morning and got some sensational shots of Sting performing his yoga routine. Those pictures got picked up everywhere. It's important to focus on the job in hand, but I always look for the bonus, the icing on the cake, whatever you call it. I call it cash, or 'Ka-ching!'

*The Mail* liked to play a little dirty at times and I covered quite a few undercover jobs that were motivated by shady politics – both internal to the paper and national – as much as by the quest for a great page lead. I was involved with a team that checked out the infamous beauty Pamella Bordes, who was linked to many important people in Britain.

The celebrity side interested me and I wanted to know more, so I befriended the night pap guy on *The Mail*, Alan Davidson, or 'Bruiser' as he was affectionately known. He was the 'elbows man' and looked like he'd walked off the set of *The Godfather*. He was a nightmare, always getting in there, getting in the way and giving everyone the shits. The opposition hated him, but he always got the picture. I used to go around with him in the evenings and just watch, listen and learn. He used to bully and bribe the back bench to get his shots in the paper – in those days he was paid by usage – and would always be either berating them or bringing them gifts.

I became Bruiser's protégé; perhaps he thought he could take me under his wing and make something of me. Although I was interested in the celebrity side, it wasn't the kind of thing I ever thought I'd seriously work in. I was a news man, a features guy. The modern celebrity market didn't really exist at the time, apart for pics from night paps like Bruiser. Most of the images of famous people were wooden, posed-up shots taken at parties. The photography was not at all creative or intrusive and never upset the celebs – they had the upper hand then.

**Mel**

**I FIRST LAID EYES** on my wife-to-be, Melanie, at the Casanova Club in Mayfair. It was after the Press Photographer of the Year awards ceremony and I was with my mate, Bruiser.

As well as having the sharpest elbows in London, he was a mad casino buff. I was twenty-two and it was my first time in a casino. I walked in and there she was – a gorgeous brunette with eyes to die for. I'll always remember her long, flowing peach dress. She was the most beautiful thing there, and casinos are pretty glamorous. Her presence seemed to have taken over the whole place. She threw the chips to me at the roulette table, and I guess it was love at first sight. I won 1200 quid – the numbers were 4, 13, 15, 17, 27 and 36 – but I left the casino thinking only about Mel. We didn't exchange a single word, but I was smitten.

As soon as I had seen this vision, that was it for me. I was back there every night. I got hooked on the gambling, too, and did well. Mel was known as the Hoover; she was the one they brought in to clean out the high rollers when they started winning too much. I should have stayed away from her! I recruited a friendly waitress who helped me pass my phone number to Mel. I think I was a blast of fresh air compared to the ageing, wealthy foreign clientele. I think she found me amusing – the funny Australian bloke who stood out a mile in a Mayfair casino. Gradually I managed to get into the after-hours social circle – for the usual £25 black chip, of course – which was very much against the rules. I left flowers on her car in the middle of the night, romantic notes under the windscreen wipers. For the first time in my life there was a serious possibility that I was in love – whatever the hell that word means.

Though she had my number, Mel didn't phone immediately. When she did make the call, she turned up at a barbecue party at my place in Muswell Hill with a chaperone, Steve Ward, who wanted to hit me up for information about getting work as a pap. He was a real estate guy who had boomed in the good years and then gone spectacularly bust in the lean years, and now he wanted to get photography work.

I had to win Mel over. I guess it wasn't love at first sight for her, but she was intrigued. She was from one of the nicer council estates in Bishop's Stortford and I went up to see her in my XJS, a purple Jag with gold stripes down the side – a fantastic car, until I smashed it into a police car after hitting black ice on the way to a Cliff Richard gig. (Thanks, Sir Cliff. I didn't exactly love your music, but I did love that car.) I was on my best behaviour and her father and I got on very well. Over the following months we enjoyed several days out together, either golfing or watching the cricket. He would often come down to arbitrate if Mel and I had argued about anything major, but in truth he usually seemed to side with me.

Three weeks after the barbecue, Mel had a key to my flat in Muswell Hill so that she could come and go as she pleased. She introduced me to the world outside newspapers, which was something of a novelty. We had a great social life. There was always something going on. We moved in together pretty much straight away, and Mel would say that – perhaps contrary to people's expectations – I was easy to live with. I am a very laid-back character, good company and a good cook, which she said was a huge bonus. However, she did find me to be rather messy and used to joke that I would never be seen dead using a vacuum cleaner.

One evening, she finished her shift and headed back to Muswell Hill in her red Peugeot 205. I had been out on a late job in Trafalgar Square and we went straight to bed. That night we got burgled. I have a vivid recollection of it. Even though I was half asleep, I saw the whole thing – a guy with a knife by our bed lifting watches and camera gear. Thank God I didn't completely wake up.

The minute Mel and I got together I stopped gambling, as she was very hot on observing professional niceties. I was fine with that; I figured I had hit the jackpot anyway. She and I weren't allowed to converse much while she was working; the laws in the UK are very stringent. After we'd known each other about six months, Mel left the job, which made things easier. The casino had asked her to move onto blackjack, which wasn't really her thing. She has always been a grafter, just like me. Her next job was selling cellulite-reducing machines, which she lasted a day at before applying for a job at the Shiseido counter at Harrods, which she got.

Just as Mel and I became serious, so did my work commitments. I was eager to learn and so, as well as my normal shifts, I tagged along with people like Bruiser in order to pick up tips. It was he who, after much cajoling on my part, took me to the Belvedere restaurant in Holland Park for the launch of film director Michael Winner's biggest flop of all time. Starring Michael Caine, it was a horrible film called *Bullseye!* – though it became known as *Bullshit*. Bruiser snapped me with Caine, Winner and Roger Moore. I was always a huge James Bond fan and meeting Agent 007 was truly an ambition realised. I look back at that photo with some regret. Maybe I can get my tech guys to get rid of that pathetic little moustache I had . . .

As well as cutting my teeth on the night circuit, I was also shooting a lot of studio images for *The Mail*. I met some interesting people, but lining them up against a background was too boring for me. Innovation is my watchword. The pop group Right Said Fred came in for a shoot just as their huge hit 'Deeply Dippy' was charging up the charts, and I was struggling to produce something memorable. To the horror of the studio manager, after a lot of thought I ended up taking a knife to the background and slashing it into a huge star shape, open down the middle. I shot them emerging from the star, and it looked brilliant. This plumber and his mate who had suddenly become famous really looked like pop stars. I syndicated a couple of negs myself and made pretty much every teeny magazine. In fact, that picture was published all over the world.

Relating to the subject is important. If people relax and work with you, then the shot is always better. Many of the professional models really know how to work a camera, and shooting beautiful women has always been a passion of mine. I had the opportunity once to take pictures of Cindy Crawford on a freelance shoot. While we got some incredible images, I missed a huge scoop. Cindy kept disappearing into the back room of her suite and talking to someone.

**'If people relax and work with you, then the shot is always better'**

I could just see a grey-haired head and thought it was some old bloke. Later it became obvious that it had been Richard Gere. Shame we didn't nail that shot. The story of their liaison wasn't out at that point and it would have been worth a fortune.

Cindy is enormously tall and has quite a 'horsy' face, but she photographs amazingly well. There are lots of women like that: they just shag the camera. Look at Sophia Loren, Liz Hurley, Kate Moss and so on. They are real stars, but the problem with modelling is that if you have the looks, then other personality deficiencies are not important. That explains the success of models like Naomi Campbell. I've never taken a shot of her when there wasn't an incident. For every person like her, however, there will be someone wonderful. I got to shoot Cheryl Ladd for *The Mail*; by then she had taken over from Farrah Fawcett-Majors as my main fantasy. I could hardly keep the camera still.

Simple jobs with lovely people were by no means the staple. I got myself into serious trouble at the High Court during the Jason Donovan libel trial that had resulted from *The Face* magazine claiming he was gay which Donovan contested and won. Perched above the masses on my longest ladder I had a brilliant view, but I ended up getting arrested on assault charges. A police superintendent was jumping around in front of me demanding that I get down and out of the way. It was a simple situation – I was either going to get the picture or not, and failure never really appealed to me. The situation quickly descended into farce as he accused me of hitting him. I ended up in the slammer for hours. I got the shot off, though. The paper sent a bike to the nick to collect the film. I was shitting myself, but *The Mail* had excellent lawyers and I ended up with a suspended sentence – and the front page. I wanted to fight the sentence, but in the end we lay down just to bring the affair to a close.

*The Mail* always looked after me. I was grateful and I respected them. David English and managing editor Brian Vine offered to sponsor me when it looked like my visa was going to run out. They thought I was important to the operation of the paper and would have been there for me, but in the end I married Mel and no longer needed the visa.

# CALLED TO WAR

### Confronting images from a brutal conflict

**FROM PRAGUE** to the Bosnian conflict was not so far in kilometres, but in terms of emotion and experience there was no comparison. This campaign was dark and frightening. Andy Kyle made the call to me: 'Pack your bags – you're on.'

Once the enormity of the situation I was about to enter had sunk in, I burst into tears. I was scared. The fear was tangible, but underlying it was the excitement I had felt in Romania. I was terrified but also couldn't wait to get started. I didn't know how long I was going away for, or indeed if I was coming back. The price on a journalist's head at the time was 10 000 Deutschmarks. For the first time in my life, I was worth money!

The day I left, I grabbed Mel and broke down. It was nervous energy more than anything. Once I was on the road, though, I started to focus. This was a more serious conflict than Romania and my experiences there were scant preparation. I was weighed down by hundreds of pounds of gear; the satellite phone on its own was four times the weight of a normal suitcase, and twice the size. It was so heavy that one of us had to be upgraded on the way out of Britain as we needed the extra baggage allocation. Wire machine, transmitter, Mac computer, camera gear, flak jacket, helmet – you name it, I was carrying it and it weighed a ton.

Our arrival in Split was bizarre. The war hadn't really arrived there. I had expected tanks to be rolling up the beach, 'I love the smell of napalm in the morning', that kind of thing. Although there was a touch of *Apocalypse Now*, everything seemed pretty sanitised and it was much like arriving at any major airport. I was travelling with Dave Williams, my old mucker on the cricket team and the chief reporter at *The Mail*. He knew what he was doing. We went from the airport to the hotel to get our bearings and there were people sunbathing on the beach. Split was more like a soldiers' holiday camp than a front. We went out that evening for dinner. I had the risotto al nero, which was excellent. What war?

The following morning we picked up our maroon Russian-built Lada Niva 4x4. That little fucker was more like a tank than a car, but it got us out of some very tight spots. Dave used to say you could drive it up a wall if you needed to. We met up with some of the troops and some other journalists; Kate Adie was there, as was John Swain, the inspiration for the film *The Killing Fields* and a legendary war correspondent. We sank a few Tullamores with him. We even had dinner with John Schofield, the BBC correspondent who later died out there from a bullet to the neck. As it was the height of summer, we stretched out in the sun with our flak jackets on. I thought it was all pretty cool. There were choppers overhead, regiments marching in the streets and bikini babes on the beach – an incredible scene for a boy from Geelong. I could almost hear the soundtrack from *Apocalypse Now*.

Reality dawned very quickly. Our initial destination was a farmhouse in Vitez owned by a farmer, Lucas, and his wife, Katja. This would be our operational base. It had two types of running water: freezing and fucking freezing. But it was home. We had the run of the place, as they trusted us. Katja cooked for us and we would wash it all down with gallons of Tullamore Dew or the local brews, slivovitz and rakija. Toasts would be proposed, then 'Ziveli!' (cheers) and down the hatch. We had some really good nights around the fire there: Lucas, Katja, myself, Dave and our British army link, Major Peter Bullock.

**'There were choppers overhead, regiments marching in the streets and bikini babes on the beach'**

The booze was pretty horrible stuff. Lucas would have a shot of slivovitz every morning at six, and would expect me to join him. He saw me as a kindred spirit because I was up for trying anything and everything.

The dish for the satellite phone had to be installed on the roof of the farmhouse, which took Dave and me at least half a day. Our presence allowed Lucas and Katja a window onto the world. Through us, they could phone friends and family and let them know they were still alive. Bizarrely, their son was living in Melbourne at the time. The other side resented people like our hosts because they got all the money from the visiting armies and media, and not so much of the pain. This part of the country was not in an area directly riven by warfare, so the local people benefited from the available business and investment. Even now Vitez is a boom town because of it.

Lucas was involved in the struggle himself and would head out to fight every night. He and his colleagues were Croats fighting Muslims and Bosnian Serbs on the frontline at Turbe. It was a crazy war where you could be fighting against your own family. Every night in Vitez, the local postman, whose allegiance lay with the Bosnians, would launch mortars at his neighbours. He would deliver letters by day and shells by night. That homicidal idiot was always trying to put something through your door special delivery! I shot him every single day – but unfortunately only with my camera.

I had to be careful not to shoot too much, as I had to develop by hand and then transmit using the Hasselblad wire machine through the sat phone. I had a dark bag in the bedroom of the farmhouse and we heated the water and colour chemicals on the fire for processing. I also had an element component that I had ripped out of a kettle at home. If the electricity was on,

I could plug that in and use it to heat things. It was a serious pain in the arse.

The farmhouse was near the UK forces so we spent a lot of time with them. They held a daily morning briefing for the journalists. While we were not required to attend, it was useful to know what was going on and get up to speed on the movements of troops and aid. We would ask the army for certain resources and to be allowed to embed with certain units. Sometimes plum jobs would be drawn from a hat. The briefings were open to all media, but as we were British press we had priority to a degree. I spent quite a lot of time with other photographers, particularly *Today*'s Colin Davey and the *Daily Express*'s John Downing. Technically, as an *Express* man, Downing was the enemy, but I got on with him very well and he's a fucking good snapper. There was a bit of sharing. John Swain was a seasoned operator and a great journalist. When he attended the briefing, it was like a deity entering the room, and then he would do his own thing.

On one occasion Dave and I won the army briefing 'lottery' to join some British forces on a Chinook mission to drop aid. These aircraft are the most cumbersome, unstable, unwieldy elephants I've ever seen. Our destination was in the far north of the country and the tonnes of aid dangled below us in a huge net. The Chinook was bristling with soldiers and guns. On the way up, a surface-to-air missile locked onto us and the pilots took immediate gut-wrenching evasive action. They wobbled the aircraft and deployed decoy tinfoil from each engine to draw the missile. I saw it streak past the window. It was fucking frightening and there were no pictures to be had on that trip, other than some of the crack soldiers holding their heads in their hands in fear and dismay on board the shuddering helicopter. A few weeks later, many of the American top brass were shot down in a Chinook.

We used the farmhouse as a general base, but also stayed in bombed-out hotels or inns when we were on the road. We arrived in Srebrenica the day after the infamous massacre by the Serbs of 8000 Bosniaks. We wired images back to London from the Holiday Inn. The hotel faced a hill where the gunners were based, and one whole side of it was missing. We were on the 15th floor and there were only three walls. Obviously the lifts weren't working, and I couldn't be bothered to go down to reception and complain, so I just put up with it. The town's street market was already returning to some semblance of normality, though there seemed to be a funeral taking place every five minutes – and I mean that in all sincerity. The wailing of woman and children still echoes in my head and the stench of murder was everywhere – in your nose, your clothes, everywhere.

Understanding what had happened in Srebrenica was made a little easier by the 'fixer' that Dave engaged. Yanu was a live wire in every sense and our guide to what was going on. He took us to meet another contact who he said would give us information to help us gain safe transit to an enclave. We met him and his bodyguards for lunch in a secret location.

I wandered back to the car to get my Walter Wolf lung-busters. (Those cigarettes were horrible, not dissimilar to smoking rolled-up sawdust. They kept me sane, though, and got me through the day.) I couldn't find them anywhere so I looked under the seat. I saw an AK47, two pistols, five hand grenades, essentially a whole arsenal. If any of it had gone off I would have been blown back to Oz, not to mention kingdom come. I asked Yanu what the hell was going on. 'Protection,' he told me simply, but somehow I didn't feel so safe racing over the bumpy dirt tracks after that. I didn't know until the following day that he had a rocket-propelled grenade (RPG) in the boot! I said to him, 'Listen, buddy, what's your day job?' (As it happened, his day job involved the local mafia and in the end it was his downfall. Dave ran into him a few years later and found him hobbling around with his legs in callipers. While he claimed he had been in a car crash, his wife admitted to Dave that Yanu had run out of luck and been kneecapped by the local hoods.)

Dave had been to the region before and knew what to expect. He kept us as safe as we could be, given the circumstances. The frontlines were always moving and it was vital to have your wits about you at all times. Upon arrival at a checkpoint, knowing which language to speak and whether or not to offer a pack of cigarettes as a bribe could be critical. In fact, this knowledge could mean the difference between life and death.

Dave had great contacts, was able to secure fuel for us on the black market and knew who we needed to avoid. Unfortunately for us we were stopped twice by the mujahadeen. These guys dressed in black and carried huge swords across their backs. Only their eyes were visible through a slit in their masks; they looked like ninjas and were fucking dangerous. On both occasions when we met them I thought it was curtains.

The first time we met them we had already had a rear tyre shot out by a sniper. Not a good day. Never have two men changed a tyre faster – being stationary was not a good idea in that terrain. Further along the road, we were stopped by the men in black robes. Dave did the talking and I just focused on the goats and the winding creek I could see in the distance. I was a bit like Dave's cocker spaniel; Dave was certainly in charge. My heart was in my mouth and I didn't want to make eye contact. In the end they waved us through and we continued our journey.

I was quite taken with the black robes, but adopting that attire would not have been a good move. Our uniform was jeans, shirt, flak jacket and helmet, all day, every day. My jacket read 'A-positive' for my blood group and 'Digger' (my nickname from *The Daily Mail*) to identify me. Our pockets were filled with field first-aid kits and anything else we thought might be useful. *The Mail* supplied us with a lot of gear, but the British soldiers were fantastic. I felt safe in my jacket and used to get in the freezing bath still wearing it if we were in a dangerous area. We knew we were in someone's sights almost all of the time. It was a very weird feeling to know that you were being watched by someone who wanted to kill you. It was a bit like a pap chasing a celebrity, but at least if you get hit by a snapper it's not fatal. If the celebs feel bad about what we do to them, they should try war! There's a bit of a difference between firing off a frame and firing a bullet, of course. Someone told me that if you hear a bullet being fired, you're not going to die; if you don't hear it, the round has probably already killed you.

**'It was a very weird feeling to know that you were being watched by someone who wanted to kill you'**

We travelled all over the region, in and out of refugee camps on a daily basis. The scenery was beautiful – 'God-given', in Dave's words. The blue of the lakes was unbelievable. Amid these gorgeous surroundings lay millions of unexploded mines that are still there, and every home was riddled with bullets. It was like seeing a crack house in Disneyland. There was pain and suffering everywhere, but I was excited by the possibilities. Everywhere I looked I could see World Press Photographer of the Year shots. I hate to compare war photography to golf, but to me it makes sense – you might be an average player, but the chance that you can go out and hit that shot is what keeps bringing you back. We knew that unimaginable horrors had been visited on these people. Rape and murder were everyday experiences. Bloodied corpses in ditches and carbonised bodies that would snap like twigs were not uncommon sights.

The war was brutal and angry, and there was no logic to it

at all. The ethnic combatants seemed incredibly disorganised; half of the soldiers were pissed or on drugs. It was very hard to determine which side was which. Obviously this complicated matters enormously. The uniforms were marginally different but in truth most of the fighters didn't have uniforms – they wore tracksuits. I couldn't fathom why they were fighting in the first place. The conflict was totally unpredictable and oftentimes seemed medieval – we saw utes with 40 mm cannons fitted to the back. Added to this were the hordes of mercenaries who had come from all over the world to play little war games.

The stories that emerged were heartbreaking and the cruelty breathtaking. We spent a night with some snipers on the Serb side, watching as they trained their sights on women desperately making shuttle runs to collect water for their children. They were allowed to get down to the river, fill their buckets and start back before the snipers took them out – the buckets, not the women. It amused these guys to see the precious water trickle back into the river and not reach the children. On one grim afternoon we discovered three bodies: a woman and her two children. All three had been shot in the head; they were still holding hands as they lay in the mud. Horrors like these are the realities of war.

Dave and I reported from Tusla, where a massacre had taken place in the town square. It had been a public holiday and the square was crammed with scores of children when it was hit by four mortars. Much of the evidence of the carnage had been removed, but I managed to shoot images of women hiding in doorways to avoid sniper fire, desperate to get food for their children. People were trying to go about their business, but every so often one would just get picked off. Everywhere I looked there were orphaned, displaced kids; it was heartbreaking. Around seventy died that day and their bodies were apparently buried beneath the pine trees growing around the town.

So far my luck was holding, though at one checkpoint I was accused of being a Serbian spy and imprisoned for three hours. We were on the way back from Mount Igman, which overlooked Sarajevo, and someone decided they didn't like my face – I can understand that. It was a very scary experience and I was lucky to be released. The winding road down from Igman reminded me a little of the Great Ocean Road and the Grampians area in Australia, though at home the roads aren't littered with the shells of blown-up vehicles – just the odd wallaby who'd decided to take on a bullbar.

Igman was near the site where Torvill and Dean won Olympic ice-skating gold for Britain. The Olympic village was now completely blown to smithereens and the venue in which the duo had won their gold was a graveyard. British troops were heavily involved in the region and we spent days with them, even helping them dig in at one point.

We knew there was a price on each of our heads of 10 000 DM. The people in charge of the mayhem didn't want the story getting out. It was wholesale murder, after all. There were guns everywhere. Even at weddings they would fire hundreds of rounds up into the air, not seeming to realise that what goes up must come down. I heard about one guy who was celebrating his nuptials; as he raised his gun to fire, he hit the trigger early and cut his new wife in half.

On one occasion Dave and I covered an orphanage, which was hugely upsetting. I wouldn't have wished to raise pigs in that squalor, let alone kids. We were trying to help, working with Gordon Bacon, the head of Save the Children. He was a fucking gutsy bloke, there for the duration. There was a huge surge of troops in the area and it was even more unstable than usual. We spent the night in the orphanage to keep a low profile and moved on the following day.

We ended up at a Croatian checkpoint where the guards were uncharacteristically jumpy. You never looked anyone in the eye over there – a lesson I learned by experience. The previous week I had been tailgated for miles by a driver who eventually came alongside me and asked me to pull over; he did this by running me off the road. As he was leaning out of his window pointing a gun at my head, I decided it would be a good idea to do what he wanted. He got out of his vehicle and came towards me and I held his gaze. He pistol-whipped me as hard as he could. Apparently I had not indicated before changing lanes. I almost had to laugh. The apocalypse was going on around us and he was worried about the fucking highway code! Arsehole.

Back at the checkpoint, the soldiers were asking a lot more

questions than usual. Unwittingly we were trying to pass through an assembly point for a major push and they didn't want us there. I didn't dare get the camera out. I felt a silence descend over me. It was like a horror movie, with bats and evil spirits flying through my mind. I knew we were in a really bad situation. The soldier who was interrogating us walked away, commanding us to wait, and in a moment of madness (or serendipity) I floored the accelerator and we roared away. Dave was shouting in my ear that I had just killed us both, but I concentrated on hammering the pedal and waited for the bullets that never came.

Sometimes you have to make your own luck. I had experienced a strong feeling that we were about to die at that checkpoint and somebody upstairs had told me to go, so I did. I believe I saved both our lives that day. There were lots of foreign fighters in the area, and two Brits had already been killed. Robbery was as likely a motive for murder as anything else and we were carrying lots of expensive gear and had our own vehicle; certainly we were targets. Photo and television equipment was worth serious dough on the black market and was regularly stolen. As we made our way on the winding road an RPG exploded metres in front of us. It could have been someone taking a pot-shot at us or just bad luck; either way, we made the rest of the five-mile journey across some of the most scarred roads in Europe with our lights off.

Driving in the region was a fine art and one you picked up quickly if you wanted to stay alive. A stop-start technique, varying pace and to some degree varying direction was as much as you could hope to do to throw off target anyone who might be pointing a gun at you. On one of our excursions, we realised that one of the tyres had blown. Staying where we were and waiting for the RAC was not an option, so I got us back on three tyres and a rim – no mean feat in those conditions. We found out from the man who changed the tyre for us that it had been shot out.

My most vivid memory is of the day that myself, Colin Davey, and John Downing were operating around Mount Igman and decided to cover the United Nations Protection Forces (UNPROFOR) tanks heading off to Sarajevo. The city was surrounded by a sea of white crosses, a massive graveyard that was cinematic in scope and unbelievable in range. It was truly heart-rending. As the tanks rolled off, a white Suzuki jeep raced up behind us. I saw guys in bandanas looking like the rhinestone cowboys from hell, weighed down by chains of bullets, and I started feeling uneasy. We were in trouble, and we weren't more than 500 metres from the main British base in Vitez.

The jeep's occupants jumped out and ran over to us. One of them pulled a huge silver handgun with a beautiful bone handle out of his holster – I could see my face reflected in the barrel. He was wild-eyed and sporting a camouflage singlet and army dungarees. He shouted something at us, so I decided to produce my press card. Bad move – there was a bounty on journalists. The press card was immediately torn from around my neck, thrown to the ground, stamped on and spat on. The guy with the gun then punched me hard in the head. Reeling, I watched him take one bullet out of his belt, spin the gun's chamber with a theatrical flourish, insert the round and put the .44 to my head. I had a bitter, coppery taste in the back of my throat. Though I was transfixed by fear, a feeling of total calm washed over me. I was unaware of anything around me. I was floating through a silent-movie version of my life; the laughter, tears, good times and bad times slipped past me hazily.

Immersed in this dream-like state, I replayed my life and waited for the end. This phenomenon is well documented; I guess it is a defence mechanism and gives you something to think about other than how far your brain is likely to be blown out. I had a one-in-six chance of survival and I won the lottery that day. I heard a dry click that echoed in my brain as the pin fell on an empty chamber. I went numb. Our assailants were laughing, but I was too shocked to muster any kind of emotion. Falling to my knees, I dry-retched over the dusty road. I was glad to be alive, but the calm I had felt was replaced by numbness.

They demanded that we follow them and, as they were toting machine guns, we did. We drove about 10 miles and were locked up in a Croatian camp. Luckily for us an interpreter who was acting as a double agent was at the camp. I recognised him immediately as we had met the night before. Here he was with the bad guys – a stroke of luck. He was able to alert our side and the British army negotiated our release. I was back on the beat that evening – back in the game of survival.

Life in this war had no value. People could shoot you because there was a bounty on your head, or because they wanted your camera or whatever was in the van, or for no reason at all. No one would ever know what had happened to you. In time of war there's generally no such thing as money. It's a barter world. I've got a million-denomination banknote from Serbia somewhere; it wasn't of much use at the time. In Romania I also managed to acquire a flag with the Communist symbol burnt out of the middle. I always planned to get it framed, but some fucker nicked it from my office. That was one of my biggest disappointments – that and my first passport being stolen, full of the border stamps that had presaged many an adventure.

As well as the news angle, we also tried to produce relevant features. The French Foreign Legion were on the ground there and we did a feature on identical twin brothers who were serving – one with the Legion and one with the British army. They were nice guys, but you do not fuck around with the Foreign Legion. They are all psychopathic head cases. When I was shooting the guys, I kept noticing red dots all over me. I wondered what they were until I realised it was the other Legionnaires training their laser sights on me. Very fucking funny, guys. One of you trips over and I'm Elvis! Examining the role of women in the forces was a good fit for *The Mail*, too, so we put together features on the many serving women. *The Mail* was very good at heart-rending stories in those days: save the trees, save our seals, save the orphans – basically anything that would sell papers.

In order to generate more stories and get a better handle on what was going on, we hit the road and travelled around much of the region. We took the coast road to Dubrovnik, which was a relatively calm area at the time. We passed through a couple of checkpoints without incident and arrived at a lovely but completely deserted hotel in the New Town area to the familiar accompaniment of mortars. The hotel was sited on a cliff and we had a glorious view of the islands off the Dalmatian Coast. I thought, 'This is good. Where's the fucking bar?' Caviar, Parma ham and Dom Perignon were all available and we tucked in. I felt

> '*The Mail* was very good at heart-rending stories in those days: save the trees, save our seals, save the orphans'

like James Bond. We ended up by the pool in the evening, helping ourselves to the bar and watching the mortars fall. They couldn't reach the Old Town of Dubrovnik and they couldn't reach us. Didn't stop them trying, though. It was like a bad movie – or a great day out. We were in the middle of one of the most brutal conflicts in recent history, paddling our feet in the pool and swigging champagne from bottles (I couldn't find any glasses and, hey, I'm an Aussie).

Such moments of levity were few and far between. We were there to report. We visited Mostar, where the beautiful historic bridge had been destroyed. The huge refugee camps we visited were technically in safe areas. On my first visit to one of the camps I took a moving and evocative shot of a little boy through the barbed wire. He was dressed in pyjama bottoms and was crying. When I devyed the picture that night it almost broke my heart to see his face. Three days later, I went back to see what I could do to help him, but he was dead. The people there had just been broken, torn apart. The wailing of women was everywhere; it played in my head like a stuck record. The barbarity and utterly nonchalant rejection of the value of life could not have been more apparent. I personally knew journalists who were killed out there, and I always knew I could be next.

Still, I was a confident little bugger and wandered off on my own on occasion. The majority of our brief was to cover the activities of the British contingent of the UNPROFOR initiative, but I couldn't resist trying to get my own exclusives. Was this stupidity or getting the job done – who knows? There's a fine line between a genius and a madman. Sadly, I'm the latter. (You know what they say about curiosity and the cat. Well, I'm certainly a cat – a BIG cat. It's even the name of my home-town footy club. And didn't they have an amazing 2007, winning the flag for the first time since 1963.) Heading out one day in the 4x4 I became aware of a group of people down by a bridge. They were kneeling down, hands behind their backs and heads bowed. I turned down the dirt road towards them and then heard gunfire: someone had obviously just been executed. I slammed the car into reverse and got out of there fast. Had I been 50 yards closer it could have been a different story. Pushing too far – it's the story of my life. Luckily it hasn't yet caused the end of my life.

Though we witnessed much violence and saw the result of the 'ethnic cleansing' program that had been instigated, much of the true horror was hidden from the world. Even now many of the mass graves have yet to be uncovered. We didn't see any – no one saw a mass grave unless they were about to go into it or were the person doing the killing. That said, we did see queues of soldiers waiting to rape women, and people killed indiscriminately by the side of the road.

The fall of Knin was the last hurrah of the Serbian forces holding out against the Croats. There was something strangely orchestrated and organised about the happenings there. I'm convinced that the Americans were doing more than their remit suggested; we were actually bussed in by the US army and every single building in the town was on fire. We saw ruined churches filled with soldiers praying for the end of the war. That night we stayed locally and the following morning I woke up to find a dead guy lying in a pool of congealed blood just along from my room. I wasn't sure which side he was on, why he was there or who had killed him. But if he'd been after us, he'd got damn close. Eight steps from death. I counted them.

The Croatian forces had taken the city, but there wasn't much left and there were still pockets of insurgency. Notwithstanding, the celebrations had started and once again we had to be vigilant to avoid the 'friendly fire' of celebrating factions.

That first tour lasted six weeks, and then we got the call

to pull out. On the way back to Split, we went to a village to cover the story of a statue of Christ that was alleged to have started crying. I stood looking at this thing for two days, with my motor drive ready at six frames per second, shouting increasingly loudly at Dave. We were staying in a hotel and there was a local summit of some kind going on, either politicians or warlords. I have never seen so many Mercedes 500s. They were supported by even more black cars, overflowing with machine-gun toting guards leaning out the windows – it was as if the Corleones had come to town!

Dave and I did two tours in Bosnia, the first in July, the second in November the same year. Although what we saw will remain forever etched in my memory, the experiences were so intense that both tours have melded into one. The second tour lasted about four weeks, and involved a lot more press conferences and taking haunting shots of the ruins of beautiful buildings. The region was far livelier than I would experience it when I returned for the third time a few years later, but I felt relatively safe due to Dave's expertise.

Some time after I returned from the second tour, my brother told me he was concerned that I was being a little odd. He asked why I wasn't receiving counselling. His astute question hit home; I had broken down privately several times since returning. One night I had a strange out-of-body experience. I was back at the Russian roulette situation, but this time I realised I had been killed. I was looking down on myself, lying next to Mel in bed, and I knew I was on my way.

I didn't know where I was going, but I was on my way. I saw myself crumpled on the floor of the car and my body slumped out of the door as the shooter pulled it open. And I'm the kind of guy that doesn't believe in any of that crap. Of course, being a typical bloody Aussie I didn't ever go for counselling.

# A New Kind of Agency

**BACK IN LONDON,** away from the madness and murder of Bosnia, my mind worked overtime. I seemed to have the edge over my rival photographers and, to a certain extent, was generating more ideas and spreads than some of my bosses were. I needed both more artistic freedom and the chance to really go for it – and I admit I wanted to make some serious money. A plan came to me pretty quickly and I knew I needed Mel.

One night I came home and told her that I was taking her out for dinner as I'd had a great idea. We jumped into the car and ended up at a Mexican restaurant called Chiquito. I've got to say that the food was crap, but the conversation went well. I explained the thinking behind my idea to found a new kind of photographic agency, one that would be unbeatable in terms of scope and delivery. Though initially Mel was reluctant, she had confidence in my foresight. This is one thing that I believe I have a talent for – sensing what is coming down the track. I think it's an essential talent for any entrepreneur. I knew my agency was going to kick arse, but if Mel hadn't believed in me I don't think we would have gone ahead. PapPix was born.

As soon as I had generated the idea, Mel and I started work. She was very nervous about how we would fare in the business world. Neither of us had been to college, nor had we had any legitimate experience in the world of commerce. However, I was a good teacher and Mel rapidly picked up the skills necessary to edit and sell a picture – she took to it like a duck to water. Mel was a born salesperson. She used to hit the phones during her lunch break from the Shiseido counter at Harrods. The papers would send a bike to the back door of the store to pick up the envelopes of 10 x 8 images. I'm not sure Mr Al Fayed would have been too impressed if he had known what was going on – he probably would have wanted a cut!

We had to make it up as we went along, and we worked seven days a week. We would often get in the car and head away for the weekend, trying to produce great shots that we could sell to the papers. The first shots of some tigers and their cubs at a safari park made us five grand. Soon it became obvious that my hunch could really pay off – this could be seriously lucrative and fun at the same time. I was still working for the *Daily Mail*, but our trips away in search of images became regular.

Those were exciting days. We worked very well together, and it didn't affect our relationship dynamic. I remember one weekend up in Scotland at Culloden Castle where I gave Mel a friendship ring that she still wears today. We didn't get engaged as such, but we were certainly very serious about each other – I love the word 'courting'. Our relationship was occasionally tempestuous – Mel burned my diary when she found the name of another photographer, Jenny Goodall, in it, although there was absolutely nothing going on that she needed to be worried about. Mel also ripped a picture of an Aussie ex, Rachael, out of my portfolio. I was seriously pissed off as it was a cracking frame.

From the start the agency was designed to be the best, and soon we began to attract talent. We were getting everything. The *Today* newspaper, a new Murdoch publication, was a major client. Its editor, Richard 'Stotty' Stott was filling his paper with all of our new celebrity material. I got on really well with the paper's picture editor, Geoff Webster.

PapPix had a fresh approach and the money was certainly coming in. The agency was averaging about thirty grand a month – only two grand less than my annual wage at *The Mail*! Our overheads were very low indeed. Each set probably cost us around £40 to make. In those days the Wapping (News International) darkroom at night was a paradise to the likes of us. All the darkroom guys were on bungs (bribes), and any freelancers who were part of the club could get their processing done and pick up free film. The amount of money flying out of that place was unbelievable. It was busier at night than it was during the day. Our images would often be printed at News International and biked back to Mel at Harrods, where she would check them upon her arrival at work and then put them back on a bike to Wapping to be sold!

When I set up PapPix I was unhappy with the agency culture in the UK. Photographers seemed to be second-class citizens and I wanted to change that. I set up the business to sell images that I shot or that were shot by a freelance team who earned their money from a ratio of the sales revenue I brought in. This was good business on my part, but my royalty deals were also more than fair. I made a lot of people rich – I made photographers into millionaires. And I always paid more than the rest of the market because I wanted to give people a leg up. I know for a fact that at my memorial service there will be lots of people who will walk in thinking, 'I hated him, but he changed the business and helped me make lots of money.'

**'I made a lot of people rich – I made photographers into millionaires'**

By the time I set up PapPix, I had worked on every section of *The Mail*. I needed to be challenged and PapPix provided that outlet. Geoff Webster had just joined *The Mail*'s picture desk from the *Today* newspaper. In 1992, when I won all my photography awards – Kodak, AGFA, UK Press, you name it – Geoff had offered me a staff job at *Today*. I knew we would work well together, but moving from *The Mail* didn't feel right then.

I told Andy Kyle I had been offered a job and he made it clear that there were no staff jobs available, but that they didn't want to lose me at that point. The only other person I remember at *The Mail* winning an award during my years there was Mike Hollist, so I'm sure they wanted to keep me around – I had just won British Press Photographer of the Year, and not only was I freelance, I wasn't even British! Following the intervention of the editor, they offered me a staff job.

The freelance team, my peers at *The Mail*, were Mark Richards, Jenny Goodall, Steve Poole, Gavin Rodgers and Graham Trott. There was a lot of rivalry, particularly between Steve and me, but I revelled in it. The great thing about Fleet Street was that you could never be complacent or you were fucked. When I was offered the staff job, I should have turned it down despite the prestige. I only took it to piss off the others. I was a stirrer, but this time it wasn't too smart. The perk was the travel expenses, but financially my deal as a freelance who was willing to work all hours and take any job I could physically schedule was cut to pieces. Suddenly I had better job security, but I was earning a third of what I had been. Honestly, at the time I wasn't just doing the job for the money, but this was a big drop.

By the time Geoff joined *The Mail*, I had been running PapPix for a few months, combining it with my work for

❦ Sneaking into the Palais Garnier theatre with a 600 mm lens to capture the final moments of Nureyev's life on stage was a huge gamble, but it paid off. These were the last shots ever taken of the great star and they won me News Photographer and Press Photographer of the Year in 1992 and were also included in *Time Life*'s 'Picture of the Decade' series.

I shot this hand-held on a lens bigger than a bazooka at a 15th of a second. It was an impossible shot, but I made it work. →

I call this picture 'The Last Goodbye'. A friend touches the great man's face after his final production.

This is the last ever picture taken of Nureyev. He died three months later.

# Daily Mail

FRIDAY, OCTOBER 6, 1995     NEWSPAPER OF THE YEAR   35p

Daily Mail
INSTANT CASH
ARE YOU A WINNER TODAY?
PLAY TODAY: PAGE 66

# Rosemary West's steel-ringed cell on wheels

## Daily trip for mother accused of 10 murders

LOCKED in a steel capsule inside a blacked-out prison van, Rosemary West leaves Winchester jail yesterday on the short journey to court where she is accused of mass murder.

The 41-year-old mother of seven sat alone in the specially-constructed metal box, her only view of the outside world through a small window.

This morning she will make the same five-minute trip to Winchester Crown Court to hear Brian Leveson, QC, open the case for the prosecution in a trial expected to last two months.

The widow of Gloucester builder Fred West, she denies murdering ten young women including her eldest daughter Heather, 16, and stepdaughter Charmaine, eight.

Picture: DARRYN LYONS

This is one of my favourite shots and was a very important news picture at the time. Serial killer Rose West is locked in the cell of a police van at Winchester Prison and taken to court at the start of her trial.

Rose West arrives with a massive police escort. Among the photographers are two of Fleet Street's finest: Tom Smith and Steve 'Beastie' Burton.

# UP ON TOP

This is their story, well, at least as much of it as we dare to print . . .
**Right Said Fred** a fusion of sound and images, fluorescent shirts, leather trousers (ooh, too sexy!) and personal stylists. Iron pumping shaven head (well two out of three) deeply dippy dynamites.

Richard, Fred and Rob are not your typical stars. For a start, they are, after spending many years playing for other peoples bands,

Every so often there comes along a hit band, whose sound and image is totally and absolutely unique. It refuses to be filtered into a neat pop, rock, house, rap or any obvious music classification. Such a band is **Right Said Fred.**

With sound, lyrics and a look that is totally different to anything or anyone else.

"The point about our songs," says Rob, "is that they don't fit into any niche. They're not rap or house or obviously commercial. They're just irreverent and very funny. People like us because our music is so off the wall."

**Right Said Fred's** debut single, *I'm Too Sexy,*

'O' levels and Comprehensive in expelled from school Chelsea and Fulham for London. The brothers fat years ago, aged 67. Sad Their mother Betty, now Richard and Fred 80's. Richard, who is no was originally a bass p Mick Jagger, David Bow Fred, who writes t ivry. He toured with Jericho in 1989.

Over the years, tions of the media. R

◄◄ Getting creative with Right Said Fred. In one of my first studio shots, rather than standing them in front of a backdrop, I made them burst through it. The shot below shows me at *The Mail* picture desk.

Italia 90 here I come! This picture was taken in the stadium in Bari just before England lost to Italy in a playoff for 3rd and 4th place.

Darryn LYONS
DAILY MAIL
INGHILTERRA
44996-RM

Covering big news stories was part of my life at *The Mail*. I reported on both the great fire at Windsor Castle and the dreadful Clapham rail disaster.

I'm seen here with *Daily Mail* staff photographer Paul Fievez.

The scene of devastation after an IRA bomb tore a hole in the centre of London's financial district in 1993. I saw the plume of smoke from miles away and got in before the police cordoned off the area. I lost a colleague from the *News of the World* that day.

Chasing the breaking news, I hit shots
of the first flight into British Midlands Airport
after the M1 crash in 1989; Terry Waite after
he was held hostage in Beirut for five years;
and the aftermath of the IRA 'mistaken identity'
murder of Australian tourists in Holland. There
was no such thing as a 'normal' day.

↑ Boris Becker and Steffi
Graf are all smiles after
winning Wimbledon in 1989.
Double Deutsch!

Bill Wyman and Mandy Smith
were huge targets for the
papers, and I got a great shot
of them on their wedding day.

A HAPPY ENDING TO A POP SCANDAL

Happy honeymooners Mandy and Wyman. He said: I'm a new man'   *Picture: DARRYN LYONS*

# Wyman marries Mandy in secret

By BAZ BAMIGBOYE

THE bride wore black when ageing rock star Bill Wyman married his 19-year-old girl-friend yesterday.

The Rolling Stone guitarist tied the knot with model Mandy Smith in a quiet register office ceremony with only his son Stephen (seven years

older than the bride) and her elder sister Nichola looking on.

The service was a surprise prelude to a whirlwind weekend that began with an appearance on last night's Wogan show and will end on Monday

with their marriage being blessed in front of TV cameras followed by a star-studded reception for 500 in a West End hotel. 'It was the calm before the storm,' quipped Wyman, 52. 'But we both wanted a peaceful and quiet wedding.

And it set the seal on an affair that

Turn to Page 2, Col. 1

**AB's a big hit with Sue**

AUSTRALIAN cricket captain Allan Border (above) has won over the woman who was at the receiving end of his mighty six at a match at Arundel on Sunday.

Sussex housewife Susan Edwards was hit in the face by the ball, which sailed from Border's bat over the mid-wicket boundary rope during a friendly match between the Australians and the Duchess of Norfolk's XI at Arundel Castle, Sussex.

Border threw his wicket away two balls later to see Mrs Edwards and offer his sympathy.

*The Daily Mail* reports Border gave her a bouquet of flowers and a miniature bat inscribed: 'To Susan. In future, watch the ball but not quite so closely. Best wishes, Allan Border.'

Mrs Edwards said: 'I think he is a very pleasant man.'

Yesterday Mrs Edwards visited a specialist who confirmed she has a fractured forehead.
— LONDON BUREAU

◀◀ Having spotted him at the team hotel,
I reunited Aussie cricket legend Allan Border
with the lady who copped two black eyes
after one of his sixes ended up in the
crowd. And, yes, I bought the flowers!

Jason Donovan leaving the
High Court after winning his libel
case against *The Face.* →

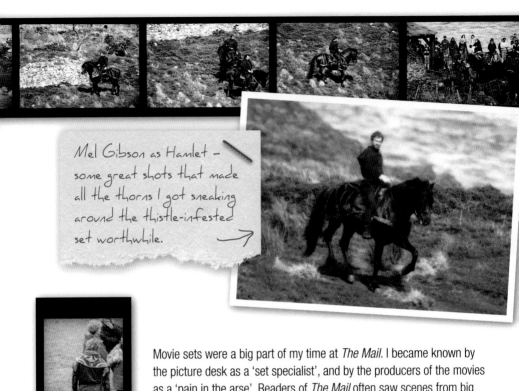

Mel Gibson as Hamlet – some great shots that made all the thorns I got sneaking around the thistle-infested set worthwhile.  →

Movie sets were a big part of my time at *The Mail*. I became known by the picture desk as a 'set specialist', and by the producers of the movies as a 'pain in the arse'. Readers of *The Mail* often saw scenes from big movies months before they hit the cinema screens. Giddy up!

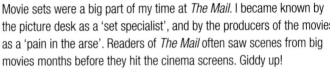

A great shot of Costner on the set of *Robin Hood*, taken on another one of those days that could easily have been my last!

*The Mail.* I had already tried to quit the paper on a couple of occasions to concentrate on running the business. The success of the agency was growing and Mel and I were working flat out. In order to keep me on *The Mail* team, Geoff and I did a deal that allowed me to go 'off diary' and produce a lot of excellent stuff for myself, but I also had to come up with two great sets each week for *The Mail* – a 'great set' was page three or a spread. Also, I was allowed to syndicate my own stuff. Geoff and I knew about this deal, but the powers-that-be didn't.

Webster was my kind of guy. He was really dynamic. I had enormous respect for him and worked bloody hard for him. Not many picture people end up in positions of real power, but he's now assistant editor of *The Sun.* When he first became a PapPix client at *Today,* he knew I would go to the ends of the Earth to get what he needed. It's unusual to have a business relationship like that. It worked because I knew what picture editors had to go through every day in the editorial conference. They had to fight their corner with the editor ten times over.

As I hit my stride in London for PapPix and *The Mail,* I was busier than ever. Ondrej Foltin, one of my old colleagues from Geelong, came to visit. Though we didn't get out and about that much as I was so busy, I wanted to show him what I did and we went papping together. We headed out for the day in my Range Rover and drove around West London while I pointed out the locations of my freelance guys waiting for action. These men would only get paid for shots that were actually sold, which meant I could have a decent team without overstretching myself financially. As we drove, I would get coded waves from guys at Harrods or San Lorenzo restaurant telling me there was no action to be had there.

We swung off down the Fulham Road and suddenly I shouted, 'Look, it's Jason Donovan! And he's fucked up!' He had a Range Rover, too, and I recognised the number plate.

> **'We swung off down the Fulham Road and suddenly I shouted, "Look, it's Jason Donovan! And he's fucked up!"'**

I pulled the car round in a U-turn, shouting at other motorists to get out of the way, and the chase was on. I was amping it up to add a bit more drama and got on the phone and called a couple of my guys to intercept Donovan. Eventually, the other Range Rover parked and I dived into the back of my car and started shooting away with the long lens. Donovan and his companions headed into a shop and I sent Ondrej in to check it out. He reported that Donovan did indeed seem to be off his head and was dancing on the spot. Eventually Jase and his party emerged from the shop. I got some killer shots and ended up exchanging numbers with the star and agreeing we would do some set-up stuff together.

It was interesting for Ondrej to see what my work involved. I always told him to travel with an Instamatic wherever he was in Oz and to look out for pictures I could use. I would phone him from the UK. 'Look out for Kylie,' I'd hiss, 'Big money! Big dosh!' He didn't really understand what I was on about. The paparazzi market was nothing in those days.

My school friends got a taste, too. Lewy came to visit with his girlfriend and got an eye-opener as to how things worked. They were staying during an infamous episode when I took a picture of a criminal who would rather have remained anonymous. The guy grabbed me and then smashed my car up. Lewy saw my expenses form for *The Mail*, which read: 'Three lunches, ten rolls of film, one car'!

One day, Lewy and I were out in the Range Rover when I told him to drive to San Lorenzo so I could prepare myself to get a shot of Princess Diana. We went up on the pavements, people running everywhere. Lewy was really starting to worry and thought we were going to crash. I told him I didn't care as long as I got to the restaurant in time to get the picture. Once we arrived I even threw him a camera; he stood where I told him to, at the ready. While I was finding myself a position, one of Diana's bodyguards came over to Lewy, said he knew why he was there and that he could take one picture and then move on. As the bodyguard imparted his message he moved his jacket slightly so that Lewy could see his gun. Lewy did what he was told. Meanwhile, I was operating on the fringes doing whatever I chose. Lewy was amused that I loved the thrill of the chase so much. He certainly could never imagine me working in a shoe shop.

Lewy also noticed that old habits die hard. He remembered from our East Tech days that I had always used a pen that could write in a choice of four colours and an A4 spiral notebook. The pen wrote in red, blue, black and green – maybe that's where the idea for my hairstyle came from! When Lewy walked into my office on that trip, he laughed when he saw that I still used the same stationery.

I was able to work at *The Mail* and run PapPix at the same time, and the secret behind this dual success was simple: I worked twenty-four hours a day. I worked my bollocks off. Nothing comes from nothing. These days everyone wants to be rich and they don't seem to associate that with work. I hate that word 'wish'. Fuck wishing – just do it. I have had that attitude all my life. If I had to work all day just to scrape by, I would. It's not about the money. I just don't want to have a minute of the day that I'm not a part of.

I proposed on Mel's 21st birthday, in July, at a surprise party I threw for her. I bought her twenty-one presents, one for each year of her life. My parents were over from Australia and I could tell that my mother thought I was being seriously over the top. I could have been with Princess Diana and my mother would still have had reservations; her expectations were very high. I guess you never want to let your baby go! She was also worried that we were too young, and in retrospect, she was probably right. My dad loved Mel immediately and she was instantly part of the family as far as he was concerned. He and Mel actually have similar personalities; they are both a little introverted but very warm. They don't make a big deal about things and just get on with life.

I had invited around a hundred guests to the party and we had a fantastic evening, culminating in my going down on one knee on the dance floor in front of everyone to propose. I cringe now at the thought of it, but luckily she said yes.

Within twelve months of my proposing in London, Mel and I were married in Geelong. Mel went over to Australia to plan the wedding with my mum, which I gather was pretty traumatic! The marriage took place on May Day.

There were around 130 guests and it was an emotional day. I had a pew full of ex-girlfriends sitting in the back row at the church. Funnily enough, they didn't seem too upset that they had lost out! Unsurprisingly, given the distance from the UK, my side of the family was dominant. Mel had only her immediate family there. Her parents and grandparents came over for it. Her grandfather, Hedley Pettitt (great name!), is one of the greatest men I have ever met. We have a very strong bond. He used to call me 'Wombat' and was the grandad I never had. He even built an Aussie-style barbecue complete with the Australian flag in his back garden.

The wedding almost didn't happen. Mel and I argued through all the preparations and most of the way through the day. The fact that I'd had a wild one with the boys the night before had gone down badly. The reception was at Rosnashane in Geelong and I had a wonderful time drinking with all my mates, which didn't impress Mel either.

One thing you can always say about a wedding is that it is a bloody good day out. It was expensive, though, not least because the cousin of one of my friends stole half of our presents and the cash box from the reception venue. My old buddy George Ramia was my best man and, to be honest, I didn't want to leave the reception for the honeymoon. My speech lasted for an hour. However, the day was over all too soon and we were off. We left the reception in a stretch limo and checked into the Menzies at Rialto hotel in Melbourne for our first night as man and wife. My sister Vikki and her kids turned up to see us the following day, and then we headed to Sydney.

Even as Mel and I had been making plans for our wedding, I'd been aware that work was going to play a large part in our relationship. The honeymoon started badly when Mel realised I was trying to sell some pictures in Sydney for the legendary Chris Barham of the *Daily Mail*, one of the all-time greats, a smooth, sophisticated craftsman who truly painted with light. He had once bedded Sophia Loren, or so he said. He was certainly a ladies' man who enjoyed success with many of the starlets of the day. The set I was selling for him in Sydney was an 'at home' with Robin Gibb of the Bee Gees, with whom he was great mates. I got a really good price for it from the *Woman's Day* title. Despite my getting twelve grand for the set, I think Mel felt I had my priorities awry.

We had a week in Sydney, and then I hired a 70-foot private yacht to take us around the Whitsunday Islands and the Barrier Reef. It wasn't plain sailing in any sense. Early in the trip the crew and I opened up the sails and the yacht took the wind and set off, causing Mel to fall over in the shower. We had a huge argument after that. Apparently, I told her I was going to divorce her before we had even returned from the honeymoon. All in all we were away for around a month, returning via Phuket flat broke, but ready to hit the ground running to grow our new business.

# Off to Battle

**Shocking scenes from a senseless war; 'why can't human beings just get along?'**

**WE HAD ONLY BEEN BACK** in the UK a few months before I had to dig out my passport and flak jacket. I was off to the bloody front in Bosnia again. I was a lot more prepared this time around and felt more confident as it was a slightly more relaxed environment and I was a veteran, after all. It was a very different experience from the first. A lot of the region was under control and the fall of Knin that I had witnessed had really been the end of the hostilities. This trip was about recording our forces' efforts and also getting into places we hadn't been able to reach the first time around.

For this third tour I was with a guy called Sean Rayment, a former Northern Ireland army boy who was now the defence correspondent of the *Daily Mail*. He was a really nice guy but things really seemed to get to him; he was a bit of Dr Jekyll and Mr Hyde character. We had a few run-ins, I have to say. Turning in one night, he went for a piss after me. Apparently I had left a sprinkle on the seat and he went mad and tried to beat the crap out of me. There was no electricity for lighting and it was the middle of the night – surely it was no big deal, I reasoned. This was right at the start of the trip and I thought I was in for a nightmare tour. Despite, or maybe because of his experiences in Northern Ireland, the poor guy lost it. Though we sorted things out, there was tension for the rest of the trip. He wasn't a good person to be around.

The first couple of nights we spent there were very difficult. The conditions were really against us and the atmosphere was a little strained. I had to rub my camera to get it to work, to warm up the battery. Those batteries became like a teddy bear for me. I had to heat them up however I could, and that meant sleeping with them.

We stayed very near the farmhouse we had used before; in fact, our lodgings belonged to one of Lucas's daughters. We were there for around a week, checking things out and getting all the equipment set up. The landscape was still beautiful, but this time we were there in winter and it was staggeringly cold, minus 10 degrees Celsius on a good day. It was a beautiful hell. There was an incredible sense of purity and death. There's no doubt that the snow covered a lot of bodies and an even greater number of mines and booby-traps.

This time around, our team was more autonomous and had less of a brief. We covered a huge amount of ground. I made sure that we hired the same model four-wheel drive that we'd had before, and we covered thousands of kilometres in it. If I could get that car framed and put on my wall, I would.

The war was drawing to a close and access was much better and more controlled, but it was still very dangerous. Checkpoints were still a big feature of travel, but they were mostly staffed by the NATO-led peacekeeping force (IFOR) personnel. The roads were all mined. Sean pulled over to take a piss one afternoon as we drove through Bosnian Serbia. He was about to walk into the woods when I told him to stay on the road. Forget about pissing on a toilet seat – if you stepped on a mine it would blow more than your cock off.

Throughout the trip, the roads and paths were frozen solid and we slid all over the place – not good when every second building is booby-trapped, from homes to schools to churches to village halls. One day I was looking for traps with a female IFOR officer when I slipped down an icy slope towards the footing of a house. Clawing at the ground, I managed to arrest my slide and came to rest an inch away from a trip wire that was attached to a land mine nestling in the snow. I remember saying to the woman, 'Don't move. I think I've found one. And unlike you, I'm not wearing the right gear.' I managed to crawl into the space under the house by way of a footing stump and get away while the mine was disabled. That particular model was one of the 'hoppers' that jump up and cut you in half.

We went up to a British army barracks one night to cover MP Sir Nicholas Soames visiting the troops. It was more of a photocall type of affair than true reportage; the politicians don't turn up until the job is pretty much done. But there were still plenty of loonies around. Despite the good rapport that Sean obviously had with the army, we went off on our own on several occasions. That said, Sean's connections meant that we had an in with the forces, and on one occasion we actually stayed in barracks over the border in Serbia for more than a week. It was fun but pretty hard. We were basically staying with the troops in a tin shed with our sleeping bags rolled out on the floor. I have to say that the food was good, though we did eat with the officers rather than the rank and file.

**'I climbed onto the back of one of the trucks and helped throw bread down to those who needed it'**

We followed a lot of tank regiments and helped them hand out food and other aid. I climbed onto the back of one of the trucks and helped throw bread down to those who needed it. It was a harrowing experience. These people were truly desperate. It was like feeding the ducks in Kensington Gardens with frozen bread, except that these were people. We were well off the beaten track and there was nothing left in these places – no windows, no doors and certainly no food. I had the latest thermal gear and I was still bloody freezing.

In one of the villages, I took a picture of an old woman with a scarf around her head. To look at her you would have thought she was 250; the lines on her face her whole story. We witnessed some of the refugees being ferried across a river by their countrymen and finally getting home. It was a powerful moment, not least because the soldiers who were responsible for all the devastation were on the other side of the river watching.

This army and its opponents had left death behind them everywhere. The landmine situation was massive and was Princess Diana's pet project, so we worked with the bomb-disposal guys. In one place there was a huge missile rigged to explode. We were doing a feature on a female bomb-disposal expert; the *Daily Mail* loved that kind of thing. I remember posing in front of around twenty landmines that were going to be destroyed in one massive explosion. I didn't even have a helmet on. There were some seriously big bangs on that trip, I can tell you.

The booby traps were pretty ingenious in a sick way. The most twisted one I saw was a rigged playground. Anyone kicking the ball that lay invitingly on the frozen ground or opting to take a quick ride on the swing would have been blown into little pieces. I heard recently that while the Americans are spending mega-bucks on laser sighting systems to uncover trip wires that are invisible to the naked eye, the Brits have found a cheaper and more effective method. They are buying cans of aerosol-powered party foam string for a couple of quid from

Woolworths and spraying it into a building. If it hangs in the air, they know it is being suspended on piano wire and that the building is rigged.

As well as explosions, there were also some very surreal moments. One day we saw an old woman, her husband and their son towing a huge frozen pig behind them on a rope. That was going to be their dinner whenever it defrosted, I guess.

We weren't just in danger from booby-traps and frozen pigs. We went to all the hot spots, including 'Sniper Alley' in Sarajevo. Dave Williams and I had been unable to get into Sarajevo on the first tour, but the danger had abated since then. I think that was possibly why Dave hadn't made the trip this time around – there was no fun to be had! However, if you wanted to get around down there you had to run the gauntlet. There were plenty of shooters. When we arrived, scouts were preparing the way because Woody Harrelson was filming the end of the movie *Welcome to Sarajevo*, which was pretty weird. The last scene in the film was shot in the hotel we were staying in.

I had plenty of hairy moments, not least standing still to make a call on the sat phone to get in touch with Mel, who was handling the first flow of sales for PapPix. I stood there with shells flying over my shoulder, discussing how much a set of shots of TV presenter Jonathan Ross might make. 'Let me just duck this mortar! OK, ask for eight grand,' I suggested. 'It might pay for my funeral.' 'OK, thanks,' she replied, hanging up. Running a paparazzi agency from Sniper Alley, Sarajevo, was no mean feat, though it would probably make for a funny film. Now there's an idea!

The final leg of the trip was into Mostar, which was incredible; there was still a lot of resistance there. The temporary 'peace bridge' had been put in place and it was fantastic to see such a tangible sign of recovery. We met a resident who told us of the casual brutality of families who had turned against their friends of many years, all for a cause that seems obscure now. The passion for death that was aroused over there is one thing that will stay with me forever. Some of those people loved it. Why the hell can't we get on as human beings? I couldn't stop asking that question, and I still can't.

On my tours to that region, I learned a huge amount. I learned not to get involved sometimes – we were there to report the news, not become it. I got into a strange mindset where nothing could shock me. My appreciation for life expanded and in business it made me realise that this isn't a dress rehearsal. There's no time. I pack a lot in and my energy levels are very high even when I'm dog-tired; I've got to live life to the full. My wartime experiences certainly brought home the fragility of life and how well off we all are.

DAZZA'S CASHED UP, BUT CAN HE KEEP MEL?

# THE FINAL PAGE

**WHEN MY LIFELONG BEST FRIEND,** Mario, visited us in London not long after Mel and I got married, I was really busy but he still got a taste of the action. I actually took him on a job for the *Daily Mail* to the worst council estate in Britain, located in Coventry. There had been a riot and we saw burnt-out cars; I took an amazing shot of a forlorn-looking little girl clutching a doll in front of one of the cars. Later we were challenged by a resident who had a rather large carving knife in his hand and we had to make a run for it. Who needs Bosnia when you've got Coventry?

Danger is an ever-present threat for press photographers. I remember all too well the London city bomb detonated by the IRA in 1996. Coded warnings had been received and the police threw a security operation around the whole area. A colleague of mine, a shifter on *News of the World*, beat me to the scene and managed to get through the police cordon. When the bomb went off, he was just 20 metres from the truck into which it was packed. He was found later with his camera embedded in his skull. I failed to get through the cordon, but I climbed forty-three storeys up the Natwest building, which was falling apart. Electrical cables were sparking and snaking all around me, but I hit the most fantastic shots. I was right above the crater and the excitement was palpable. Although London had become a war zone, the adrenaline rush I felt was just brilliant. I was truly alive.

**'Electrical cables were sparking and snaking all around me, but I hit the most fantastic shots'**

Those are the risks you take. Most people don't realise how dangerous the job can be. In my early days at *The Mail* I did a lot of night shifts and we would get coded warnings regularly. I would end up somewhere waiting for a bomb to go off and actually hoping it would so I would be the one with the glory of getting the shot. The alternative never really occurred to me. I got myself into ridiculous positions overlooking buildings and would have been in serious trouble if anything had gone off.

Of course, the dangers of the job were outweighed for me by the thrill of the hunt. It wasn't long after Mario's visit to London that I got a major exclusive. Actors Joanne Whalley-Kilmer and Val Kilmer were breaking up. They had a rented house in Pimlico that I'd been working on for a couple of weeks and I managed to get her looking really dishevelled and then him out on his own with the kids. I got page three of *The Mail* and also rang Mel at Harrods and told her to syndicate them for PapPix – we made about £30000. *The Mail*'s syndication arm made peanuts, because we knew what we were doing and they didn't. Our proactive approach meant that we made sales.

This success raised my profile, as well as plenty of management eyebrows. The shit hit the fan. Geoff told me to get suited and booted and meet him at the Royal Garden Hotel bar. He bought us a double G&T each and told me it was all over and we were both going down because of the deal we had reached. He had tears in his eyes. I'm an extremely loyal person – a real Leo trait – and integrity is everything, in life, love, everything. I'd worked my bollocks off for *The Mail*, got shot at for them, and now they were treating me like a dog. This situation just wasn't right. I had tears in my eyes, too, but I tried to keep everything in.

I told Geoff I was going to leave anyway and would protect him from any flak. He had done the right thing as a picture editor by trying to keep me on board. I had worked hard for him, and he knew it. The problem was with the managing editor, Laurence Sear. When he walked into the office you could almost hear the creepy organ music start to play and I always felt I was about to get battened into a coffin. Sear made sure I was threatened with legal action. Maybe I should have taken them on, but I fell on my sword for Geoff. All the staff photographers had been syndicating stuff for years – just look at GANS (Give Us A Neg Society). Many people routinely gave one set of negs to the paper and one to their agency.

I packed my stuff and walked out of the office in tears. I remember standing outside Northcliffe House looking up at the *Daily Mail* clock, crying. It was like a bereavement. I sat at home for a while and then called Mel, who told me, 'You're Dazza. You'll make it anyway.' I liked her confidence in me, but sometimes that's not what you want to hear. She was great, though, and gave me a lot of strength. I could almost see the *Daily Mail* offices from my house and I was sad that my time there had ended that way – with a misunderstanding over a situation I had thought was a simple one. I don't like walking away from any situation where someone feels I've done the wrong thing by them. I felt that the editor, Paul Dacre, who hadn't long been promoted from deputy to top dog, had valued me, but still it had ended like this. I know Dacre later asked Geoff and Paul Silva – who was number two at the time – if I was OK.

My time at *The Mail* had honed my talents. I travelled the world like a nomad, even if I only saw much of it through the lens. *The Mail* gave me some wonderful opportunities and threw me into some amazing events and locations, and I learned from it all. Once I got a taste for that life I was hooked. I remember floating in the swimming pool of that deserted luxury hotel in Dubrovnik wearing my flak jacket and drinking vintage Dom Perignon with the other snappers. Getting hammered while getting shelled – I can really recommend it.

Geoff sent someone from the picture desk around with some gear that I could borrow until I got myself back on my feet. I had dinner and fielded the usual thousand calls from people sorry to hear what had happened. 'Yeah, right,' was what I thought about many of them, but I didn't say it. I knew that a lot of those guys were delighted that the mad competitive Aussie was gone. I had friends at *The Mail*, but the majority probably rubbed their hands with glee. My bombastic nature hadn't worked well with some of my peers. I wanted the front and back pages plus a spread every day. I did a lot in my own time and made many of them look lazy and pedestrian.

Even though I got to work in such exciting arenas there was no doubt that my ambitions outstripped just working for the paper. Though we got on very well, picture editor Andy Kyle really struggled to rein me in, as is my history with anyone trying to manage me. He knew I was good at the job, but I don't think he liked my confidence. He invited me down to his cottage once, about eighteen months after I started. We had a really good weekend. I guess he wanted to remotivate me, and he certainly had concerns about me building a business on the side. My sideline wasn't exactly a secret on Fleet Street; nor was it ever supposed to be. While I was in a good position at *The Mail*, I also knew there was a niche opening up and, now that I knew the game, I was the man to fill it. The war experiences hardened my resolve.

In hindsight, of course, leaving *The Mail* was the best thing that ever happened to me, the best bad news I could have had. I have always believed that a man is not finished when he is defeated – rather, he is finished when he quits. No one needed to put pressure on me to achieve. I knew what could be done. I do not accept failure – it makes me mad. But I turn that anger inwards and it motivates me to get the best out of myself and my people. I'm a doer, and there's nothing to be gained by playing at being the hurt party. Get out there and make things happen! I thought, 'Fuck it. I'm freelance now. I'd better get to work.'

My days at *The Mail* were done. I was finished, and truly out on my own. It was time to devote everything to PapPix and really give the industry a kick up the arse. I knew I was taking a gamble, but, like a punter buying scores of tickets, I stacked the odds in my favour by working every hour I could to ensure a steady supply of images. I was good at what I did, and I was tenacious. Strangely, that weekend, my first back as a freelancer, I made my entire year's salary at *The Mail* in two days.

At about 11.30 that night, I decided to get out of the house and go and cover the door at Browns nightclub. I hit the road on the scooter and headed to town. There were a couple of guys there, but I gave them the old three-card trick, telling them I was knackered and had heard there would be no one around tonight. I jumped back on the scooter, took a turn round the block and, when I returned, they had fallen for it and left their pitch. For the first time ever, I was the only snapper there. These days it wouldn't work because there would be twelve of them there when I turned up! Maybe it was fate; I don't know. I turned things around, a bit like in the movie *Sliding Doors*, which has always been one of my favourites. My philosophy is that you have to constantly put yourself in a position to win, and maybe that was borne out that night. If I had stayed at home moping, crying into my beer, and hadn't got off my arse, things would have been different. I think that an aggressive attitude commands respect, though it does get me into trouble.

Terry, the doyen of doormen, tipped me the wink, suggesting that I wouldn't be wasting my time. He was a great 'spotter' and a real goldmine. He had an excellent rapport with both the celebs and the paps – a class act, you might say. In a lot of ways, along with Jake Panayiotou, the owner of the club, Terry was the face of Browns. Soon singer Mandy Smith walked in with actor Sid Owen. I didn't get a good shot then, but knew I would get something when they came out. Sure enough, a couple of hours later I got a fantastic shot of them leaving together. Sid even cheekily poked his tongue out at me. He was a huge star in *EastEnders* at the time and she had been off the scene for a while, so it was a great result. The shots, for which I was paid twelve grand and a dinner, ended up as a splash in *Sunday People*. The editor of the paper was Len Gould, who had come over from *The Mail*, where we had been very close. We had worked on the Pamella Bordes story (she was the former Miss India who became the intimate acquaintance of several MPs). Len was a real newspaper man with true flair and talent, a strong influence and almost like a dad to me at *The Mail*. He knew what hard work meant and was a canny Scot, always happy to praise people when it was deserved.

That evening I also nailed celebrity hairdresser Nicky Clarke, which was a belter. I got him being breathalysed; he had obviously had a few when he came out of the club and as he put the key into his car's ignition the Old Bill turned up. I was on the spot to catch all of the action, and as the boys in blue moved in, I papped him. There were a couple of other photographers there; I suspect one of them had tipped off the police. Nicky didn't actually move the car, but the law states that if you put the key in, you're fair game. It was a good set of images and a great tabloid story. I sold the images to the *News of the World* for about fifteen grand – six months' salary in one night. Giddy up!

When I moved on from *The Mail*, PapPix had been going as a sideline for about a year. One of the real spurs to getting things moving in a more intense way was the discovery that our syndication had not been done equitably. We realised we could do better ourselves, so we took on a manager and decided to grow up.

Our place in Muswell Hill had a tiny front room that we used as an office, but we had outgrown the space. We were turning over £30000 a month – phenomenal money that was equal to my annual wage at *The Mail* – and were well ahead of the game. No one else was really doing what we were doing.

In 1993 we set up a proper office at 9 St John Street in London's Clerkenwell district. Moving PapPix from our North London home after a year or so of success felt like a big change and a real initiative. When we took over the building, it was a completely empty concrete shell on the corner of London's meat market. There was a spiral staircase to reach the office. I had just signed the lease for £9000 a year when I realised that we wouldn't be able to get any of our equipment up the narrow staircase. Nice one, Daz! I'm such an impulsive little bugger. To load the filing cabinets and printer in, we had to go round the back of the building and gain access to the cellar by opening a door, then carry them through a meat cold-storage room to reach the emergency stairs. With all the carcasses hanging down it was like a scene out of *Rocky*, so I did a spot of shadow boxing on the way through.

In creating our work environment, I called on Dad's experience as an architect. I certainly wasn't born with a green thumb like Dad was, but on his advice I put plenty of greenery between the front and back offices and used lots of dark wood that reminded me of the Australian jarrah tree, plus some slanted pine for contrast. It was just like our ceiling at home in Geelong.

We trawled the UK looking for cheap printers and got a second-hand Noritsu for around fifteen grand. This was money I had already saved up. The machine would have set us back forty grand new, which wasn't an option. I kept to a strict budget, and that was hugely important. We were, I believe, the first agency to be digital. Everyone else was working with transparencies at the time and we were buying scanners and Macintosh computers. This was a major innovation; I knew we had to harness the best technology available if we were to make our mark quickly. I didn't understand what the fuck it all meant – I am very old-school as a photographer, though not as a businessman – but I saw which way the wind was blowing. It was that foresight thing again.

I started to grow a team, beginning with a guy called Mark Rogers, who worked the occasional weekend, and then John Gordon. I had met John in front of San Lorenzo; he'd walked up to me and said he needed a job because he had no film and holes in his shoes. I had given him some film and some cash and he became a regular freelancer.

In John I saw the same talent that I had. He could be

aggressive and upset people on the street, but he got results. Many of the other snappers were actually scared of him and he had dust-ups with some of the doyens of the industry. He had talent, but it needed to be moulded; he had to become more professional. Always in the mix, he knew where to be and when. He often got great shots of Princess Diana as he knew her routine. When I hired him, he and a mad Spanish guy called Raphael were working for a guy called John Shelley who was apparently paying them £10 a picture, which was ludicrously low. I knew that with the quality they were bringing in, I could give them a much better deal and still do well myself. John worked his arse off and in no time he went from rags to riches with me. He was soon earning a Premier League footballer's salary. He could smell a story and was an outstanding spotter of even the most discreet or carefully disguised celebrity. He got more exclusives than anybody else and at one stage out-shot everyone else on the street.

**'We were basically running a sweatshop – an orphanage of misfits, including me'**

The year we moved into the Clerkenwell building, Mel and I took a break at Christmas. When we returned we found that John had spent his holiday painting the office. The improvement was immense. PapPix was truly a team effort; everyone was proud to be involved with building the agency. We were 'the photographer's agency' – which was the slogan on the PapPix letterhead.

Our IT team was pretty unconventional. Once we were established at St John Street we started to use a guy called Jim, who was from somewhere in East London and had a couple of truly notorious brothers. He was on a government re-employment scheme and he was cheap, but he had a pretty good feel for computers. Truthfully we didn't have the facilities to be offering anyone training of any kind. We were basically running a sweatshop – an orphanage of misfits, including me. In hindsight, maybe I should have got a real expert in, but Jim did a good job. He could fix anything, even if it sometimes didn't stay fixed for long. He was a grafter and worked very long hours, probably because he either didn't want to go home or didn't know what he was doing. But I liked him; he was yet another of life's great characters. I even sent him out to New York later on to help Mark Rogers out at BIG USA.

Something else I had managed to miss on my recce was a cheap porn cinema above the office, full of dodgy geezers. We never really saw them arrive or leave. One weekend I was heading to work to process some of John's shots when, from the car, I saw a plume of smoke. It didn't concern me too much and I continued to the office and started work. Pretty soon, though, I heard sirens and realised that our building was actually on fire and there were bodies falling past my window from the cinema above. Realising I was in the middle of a major news story, and knowing that ambulances were already on the scene, I grabbed a camera, threw open the window and started hitting images. I called John in to back me up. There was water and smoke coming from all directions, but I stayed put. I didn't want the police or emergency services to spot me and move me out of position. It didn't register that I could be burnt to death.

Before too long even I had to bow to the inevitable, though by this time I had got some excellent shots. I was rescued by the fire brigade and the true extent of what was happening became obvious. The subsequent investigations showed that fourteen people were killed and the fire had been set by a disgruntled former punter who ignited a bucket of petrol he placed inside the front door of the cinema.

I was able to cover all of our expensive equipment with plastic sheeting so it was undamaged. Fortunately all the negs and the Macs were kept in the basement and there was a solid concrete floor between them and the main office, so they too were protected. The water damage was minimal, as was the interruption to our activities, though we had scaffolding and temporary signage on the outside for almost a year while repairs were carried out.

The business began with a dream, but it started to fly very quickly. Most businesspeople will tell you that if your business is growing you should take it easy and let it evolve; don't let it burn like wildfire. I let it burn, and I loved it! Pretty soon the results I was getting were ruffling feathers. We had started using full-size prints to sell our images while everyone else was still using tiny contact sheets. I remember doorstepping

Diana one morning with some of the real Fleet Street photo divas. Julian Parker, who used to run UK Press, mocked me for making large prints to show our images: 'No one will ever go for it; it will never work.' It not only worked, we blitzed everybody.

# BIG DEVELOPMENTS

**WHEN THE NAME 'BIG PICTURES'** came to me, I was still doing night shifts for *The Mail*. I was sitting in my second-hand Range Rover Vogue SE, bought with my Bosnia expenses pay, trying to think of a good name. I wanted it to have an impact. I considered 'Storm', 'Life' – bold words. Then it occurred to me that everyone on the road always asked each other, 'What's the big picture?' and it just clicked. I didn't ask anyone else about it. The logo was created by one of the night-time graphic guys at the paper and me – thanks, Chris. I wanted to use all the colours that make up the spectrum of light – obviously essential to photography – and he just knocked it out.

BIG has always been a big company run by little people. We struggled in certain areas. For example, I'm not a numbers man. I'm a photographer and an entrepreneur, not an accountant or a number cruncher, and I should have invested in numbers people earlier. I couldn't think of anything more boring, to be honest, but believe me, numbers people are crucial and it's hard to find good ones. Strict financial controls are imperative. It is the first piece of advice I give to anyone starting a business. I should know; I've been there. Successful entrepreneurs say that you have to listen to people, but I also say if you don't have the right people then don't listen!

When BIG started to grow we had people working with us on placements and internships, anything to get cheap labour and keep overheads down. Some of these people were brilliant. I had been struggling and failing to find people from the UK, so recruited Kirsten and Stefan from East Germany; both were amazing on the Macs and a huge asset. They saw the future: Stefan became a photographer and is still working with us today, and Kirsten was with us for quite a while.

We needed a bigger space as we were up to about nine members of staff from the original four. Kevin Anstey had joined us from All Action very soon after we moved into St John Street, and he became a very important part of the operation even though, disappointingly, he ended up leaving us to set up the short-lived Star Images Agency. The pressure of space was undeniable, and Kevin pointed out a perfect replacement. The building on Clerkenwell Road had two sitting tenants on three floors, which left two floors for us while their rent covered the mortgage. It was an ideal situation, and the way I thought business should work.

The two biggest transactions of my life went through in a single week in 1996. I made inquiries about the property on Clerkenwell Road only to be told that it had just been sold. Undeterred, I bought it on the turn for £550 000, upping the price by £30 000. The guy who had just bought it made that as profit in just a day. The same week, my dog, Amber, found a new home in Kensington for Mel and me. I had bought Amber from a puppy farm in Ireland and brought her home in a Harrods hat box that dwarfed her. That dog obviously inherited the Lyons battling gene; she was critically ill for the first few weeks of her life, but pulled through. She has kept me sane, and also seen some things that no dog should ever see!

The house that Mel and I were sharing was so tiny that its kitchen was smaller than the galley on my yacht. I was out walking Amber one day when she disappeared into an almost derelict garden. The gate was open, and I let her run around in there because I couldn't be bothered to walk her properly. Looking through the window, I could see that the house had been partially renovated, but not finished. The following day I inquired about the property at the local estate agent, despite the fact that there was no 'For Sale' sign. They told me it was in fact available for purchase. One of the directors of the Gulfstream private jets company had bought the place for his son, only for his son to tell him that he wanted to live nearer his friends in Chelsea – honestly, the way some people live! The asking price was around half a million, but it was blue-chip property. I knew that if I could raise the money it would be a shrewd purchase, though when Mel saw it she didn't like it because the walls were yellow – must have been a girl thing. However, I'd made my decision, and I knew we would repaint the rooms.

There was no way I had the money to get the purchases through, but somehow I had to make them happen. I was very lucky the way things panned out. The vendor of the house bought our old place for a reasonable price and I was away. I had just lost my gold card because the bank manager had taken exception to a large cheque I had paid out to a casino, but luckily, my company was fairly cash rich and I was able to secure the purchases in the company's name rather than my own. It was a balancing act and a gamble; I used the house to secure the office and raided the VAT fund to afford it. It was a hard time, but the company was on the up. I was on a roll at the tables and winning. No matter how big the risk, I wanted a slice of the action.

**'I was on a roll at the tables and winning. No matter how big the risk, I wanted a slice of the action'**

BIG moved into the basement and the ground floor. Our IT man, Jim, came too. He would often come in with various bits of dodgy equipment for us to buy. He was connected.

With David Williams, chief reporter at the *Daily Mail*, in Tusla, northern Bosnia. Behind us is the 32-kilo satellite phone we used to send stories and pictures back to London. It was powered by a generator that ran on black-market petrol. The phone was a prize target for snipers and car-jackers.

Growing pains in a new Europe – half a million protesters demonstrate in Prague, November 1989.

Holding a standard British Army SA80 rifle with my camera gear, flanked by two British soldiers, in Vitez.

Hitching a lift on an RAF Chinook helicopter from Zagreb to Banja Luka, the Bosnian Serb stronghold. Chinooks regularly fired chaff and flares as decoys for heat-seeking missiles.

These graphic shots were taken in a tented refugee camp in Tusla. Thousands of desperate women and children had fled here from the so-called UN 'safe haven' of Zepa.

These babies and toddlers were in a house for orphans and infants separated from their families in Travnik, central Bosnia. Such was the desperation of parents to ensure the safety of their children that some were 'given' to friends who were able to take them to safety through the frontlines.

Three Croatian militia fighters toast their latest success in the Croat-held town of Prozor. Frontline positions were constantly changing, and it wasn't unusual to see Muslim and Croat checkpoints within a few hundred metres of each other.

🔺 A soldier prays in the devastated shell of a church at Guca Gora in the hills above Vitez. This small town was the focus of brutal attacks by mujahadeen fighters (many of them veterans of the conflict in Afghanistan) who fought alongside the Bosnian Muslim army.

🔺 An anguished Bosnian woman cradles her baby in a makeshift camp on the outskirts of Zenica. She was one of the survivors of the Srebrenica massacre, where thousands of men and boys were slaughtered by Bosnian Serbs.

A Romanian woman mourns her husband, who had suffered an agonising death in the torture chamber behind her.

⬆ A grandmother and child take a cautious step in Timisoara, Romania's *securitate* stronghold, during the 1989 revolution. Bodies were piled high in the square and a sniper's bullet could have struck at any moment.

⬆ One of the little girls who had fled Srebrenica is treated by a Bosnian doctor in a tented camp near Tusla. The women and children had walked to freedom under Serbian fire, but the Serbs only aimed to terrify, not target, the refugees.

⬆ This Bosnian Serb had been living in Krajina, a Serbian enclave in Croatia, and was killed by Croat militia as he made his way up the stairs to my room.

He also helped me sandblast the whole of the interior, which was a filthy job. I was truly grateful for his help. If someone is a worker, not a skiver, then they have my respect forever.

We had the reception area done out with £30 000 worth of fittings, and it looked amazing. We even had our logo on the welcome mat – hey, wipe your feet on BIG Pictures! The rest of the office was fitted out on the cheap. The back office was pretty threadbare, as was the library in the basement. Image was everything at this point. We were the biggest and the best, but we still had much to prove. At the time we were running a photo development lab for the public and it really looked the part. My printer was running out images for the papers to look at with a view to buying them, and Jim's wages were basically paid by the work we did for the public.

The sitting tenants were an interior design company and a trade publication firm. We were able to put their rent up a couple of times, but after a few years I wanted their space to establish a BIG photo studio. I was tempted to look at other buildings, but decided to stay put. The configuration of the building is now completely different from what it was when we bought it. The ground floor and basement are a restaurant and bar paying good money in rent, and we have the rest of the floors. We have a beautiful view across London, taking in Sir Christopher Wren's St Paul's Cathedral. When buying property I always look for a million-dollar view; these places are always more expensive, but they appreciate by more.

Almost immediately after we tasted success with BIG in the UK, we went into the USA with Mark Rogers at the helm. He had been with us as a weekend freelance right from the start. We'd become very friendly and I felt he was the man to make it work over there.

I agreed that he should get moving on the idea, and in 1995 we put together a small team and I sent him and another guy, Phil Coburn, over to New York. We had a little office in Queens, overlooking Manhattan. The whole thing was self-financed and Mark had 20 per cent. He was a great snapper, great with people, but not a great businessman. I regret not having had a trained business manager there; I think BIG USA would be huge today if I'd had one. But you've got to take the lows with the highs. Business is all about learning, often the hard way.

I loved New York. As well as the agency I had a share in a place with a guy I met out there. Noah had put the Ice Bar together and it was looking excellent, but he had run out of cash and couldn't stock the bar. He and his partner had maxed out all of their credit cards already. I never saw my involvement in the bar as a business venture; I was just helping a mate out. That place was a real success for quite a while, and a lot of fun, though it became a victim of 9/11.

Mark worked really hard for BIG USA. His girlfriend, Stephanie, joined him and they started to have some real success, running a team of fifteen. We were making a lot of money and reinvesting it, and were able to move the business to downtown Manhattan. Unfortunately the business was hit by a series of disasters. First, due to the relentless hard work and a painful separation with Steph, Mark seemed to lose his spark and energy. We renegotiated the deal to make the split more equal and then suddenly the whole venture hit the skids. He was confused and came to see me as a predator rather than a partner. Always be patient and never be greedy are my golden rules of business. The whole thing came crashing down, and he left under a cloud. We had lost the trust factor.

I was at crisis point myself, too, because not long after BIG USA launched I had bought out a company called Profile Press in Australia for $1, taking on a lot of debt. BIG was their main contributor, generating about 60 per cent of their income. The company was renamed BIG Australia and within six months, had turned around. Meanwhile power struggles in the US office and dodgy staff members on the make destabilised the company, and when 9/11 happened, that pretty much did it for BIG USA.

If you have offices overseas you need them to be run by people you trust like blood. It was an uncontrollable situation and eventually there was no option left but to close down the company. I should have had someone in there to handle all of this, but these are the lessons you learn.

I had brought Kasey Drayton into BIG Australia some years earlier. Kasey had worked as a journalist with the *Geelong Independent*. Though I had headed off to the UK and Kasey had also left Australia, to study in South Africa, we stayed in touch. When she returned to Australia in 1997 I contacted her and told her I was starting a photo agency in Sydney and asked if she would be interested in working for me there. She told me she knew nothing about photos and wouldn't know whether to sell something for $200 or $200 000. I just laughed and told her she'd pick it up.

Kasey started work at BIG Australia when it opened in February 1998. She began at the bottom, working in the library, and learned the business. Her joining me was a vote of confidence, really, because she wasn't certain what she was getting into. She was a bit wary because she was leaving her family and everyone she knew, but she told me that she'd decided to give it a go because my enthusiasm was infectious. I made it sound so exciting – and it is an exciting industry to work in – but it was an alien world to her. I would tell her about being camped out somewhere trying to get a shot of Prince William at kindergarten or whoever and she just wouldn't get it.

The media in Australia operates very differently from the UK, and I tried to encourage some of the practices that made BIG work in London. The local industry needed a kick up the arse and we were the ones to do it. I knew that celebrities and paparazzi would work together in any western country. I stated that we weren't going to undersell our pictures; we introduced a minimum price and the whole industry picked up on that approach.

Kasey is now the head of BIG Australia, and under her

the company is going very well. She will say that I'm a very loving guy, but I can be difficult to work for. She told me once about being in the car with her husband when I came on the line. The phone wasn't on speaker but her husband could still hear every word because I was really letting loose about something. I know that when I visit the Sydney office they have to mentally prepare themselves. Anyone who hasn't met me is given a briefing before I get there and warned not to take anything personally. Some people just don't get me. In fact, at times I don't even understand myself! I spurt out ideas like a machine gun fires bullets. Kasey says that she has never learned shorthand and that she really should in order to deal with me better. She says that I tend to use volume rather than punctuation. I know that sometimes she thinks, 'Go home, Darryn, so we can have a rest!'

**'Anyone who hasn't met me is given a briefing before I get there and warned not to take anything personally'**

The business has diversified, but I still manage to keep the focus – though obviously these days Kasey and her team have a very large degree of autonomy. They don't bother me with the mundane, though of course I keep an eye on the profit/loss figures. Kasey knows that if there's a crisis, she will be able to find me.

While BIG Australia is now working well, opening offices abroad has never been a happy experience. This was proved yet again by BIG Scotland, which was started by Stuart

Morton, an employee at board level and a great buddy of mine at the time. In years to come that relationship would sour.

Stuart came to me and told me he was leaving as he was tired of London. I didn't want to lose him to *News of the World* so I suggested that we open an office in Scotland. How much happens in Scotland? Not much, as it turns out. It only lasted about eighteen months despite a good start; Stuart wanted the offshoot to be as successful as BIG UK but underestimated the amount of work that was required. He did his best, but was a spender, not a builder, and in the end he left under a cloud.

We brought all the business that BIG Scotland was doing back under our roof in Clerkenwell and closed the Scottish office. Once again, it's an example of my business credo: always be patient and never be greedy. Many people don't understand that when you start a new business, most owners don't get to take a wage. I didn't take a salary when I started off and I didn't take one for eight years. Of course, my living expenses were paid through the company, but I reinvested everything. It's a long game.

BIG UK has always been a strong business, and in 2002 we were approached by Getty for a buyout. Getty came in and looked us over, did due diligence and were really interested. Terms were discussed, but in the end they came to the UK and started their own thing. It was a temptation for me to sell, but I didn't really want to let go at that stage. There's no doubt that I could have brought a lot to their table. I'd say they're the most important people in world photography today. I've always said that BIG is 'maybe' for sale. Everything is for sale at a price.

We have a secret, key element that we use to run BIG, and it works. A rival outfit, Action Images, started a celebrity wing called Star Images and hired most of my staff out from under me just after I started. They tried to take me out, but they flopped within six months. They didn't have that key element. And I'm not revealing it here! Although the same thing could happen again, in all honesty it wouldn't affect me. The people at BIG who know the secret are people I'm not afraid of losing. The success is not just down to me; it's a combination of things. Staying ahead of the game for as long as we have is no mean feat. These days I have more competition than ever and I am still beating them all. I never worry about what they are up to. I just concentrate on being the best – and I think we have been since we started.

# Roller-coaster Ride

## Paparazzi entrepreneur hits self-destruct button

**FORMING MY OWN PICTURE AGENCY** made me a success commercially, but it came at a price. Mel and I still work together, but our marriage hit the buffers. I was working full time at *The Mail*, all over the country, if not the world, and also running PapPix, though technically I didn't really work in the business properly till I left *The Mail*. If I'm honest, Mel and I didn't see a lot of each other. She would probably say that I was never there. During the first year of our marriage, I was abroad for *The Mail* for a total of thirty-two weeks! After that year, I could hardly bear to get on a plane. I don't regret the opportunity to cover those stories and record the greatest events of my lifetime as they happened, but I know it affected our relationship. I was a rising star at *The Mail* and the world was my oyster. I will admit, too, that when it came to work I couldn't say no.

The business was 24/7 and so, even when we were at home, there would always be sporadic phone calls at all hours from the lads we had out on the road. Mel treasured the little time she had to herself in the first hectic years – she used to drive herself to and from work just in order to get a little space. Of course, we had arguments. Nothing serious, though it added pressure to our relationship. But we coped really well. On one regrettable occasion I actually sacked her, but I apologised and re-employed her within about half an hour!

When the problem that would eventually split us up came along, I didn't see it at the time, but looking back, all the signals were there. Mel's lover (unbeknown to me) had been with us from very early on. He was my protégé and a mate. I even sent Mel and him away to follow Betty Boothroyd, then the Speaker of the House of Commons, in Cyprus for a week. There were rumours, but while I was a little suspicious, I didn't believe them. I am the trusting type, after all. One day I thought I saw them in Mel's MX5 flying past Harvey Nichols on Knightsbridge, but then thought I must have been mistaken. This mate spent a lot of time at our place, but he was a friend so I thought there was nothing in that either.

On one critical weekend, Mel told me she was heading off to see her parents. I spoke to Mel on the Saturday afternoon and she said she was out shopping with her mother. Perhaps my instincts had been sharpened by working with the best investigative journalists in the world, namely Dave Williams and Paul 'Hendo' Henderson, but suspicion got the better of me. About ten minutes later, I phoned Mel's parents' number. Her mother told me in a very strained voice that Mel wasn't there. It didn't take long for her to fold, and the whole truth emerged.

On the Sunday morning I told Mel to meet me at the BIG office. She arrived and I asked her thirteen times to her face if she was seeing anyone. Each time she denied it, but eventually she realised that I knew and she admitted everything. I felt awful because she had violated my trust. I had been totally faithful to Mel throughout.

Everything was a huge mess. Mel was being vile to me, I think to try and get me to finish the whole thing so she didn't have to face up to the guilt. She was never a big decision-maker. I remember her trying to run away from the bank manager when he asked her to sign the loan agreements to purchase the BIG building on Clerkenwell Road – because she didn't want the responsibility.

Mel and I spent a lot of time trying to decide what we were going to do. Much as I was tempted to do something dramatic, I knew I had to keep calm and be a gentleman. My family values kept me on the straight and narrow. After a couple of weeks,

I suggested that she join me on a trip to Australia just to get a change of perspective. Ironically, despite all the difficulties, it was one of the best holidays we ever had together. The weather was pretty bad, reflecting our situation perhaps, and that brought Mel down. We were both quite tortured but making the best of it. We got on really well as mates, but we weren't a couple any more. We knew we were better off as friends, and had been way too young to get married, but still felt we had to try to stay together for our families' sakes. I told her that I still loved her and didn't want to lose her, but that she needed to be sure what she wanted. Mel stayed in Australia for three weeks to try and sort herself out, while I left for the UK to look after the business.

**'I told her that I still loved her and didn't want to lose her, but that she needed to be sure what she wanted'**

We stayed together for a couple of weeks when she came back to the new house at Kensington Court, but she decided to find a place of her own and I didn't fight it. As part of our separation terms I bought her a flat in North London. While we were no longer a couple, she stayed in the business and her lover continued to freelance for me. He was a good operator and it made no sense for either of us to end a mutually good deal. I guess a lot of people would have seen it differently. Some people advised Mel to take me to the cleaners, but actually there wasn't much of a business at the time. In fact, if she'd wanted to take on half of the debt at that point I would have been a very happy man.

At times during the divorce process the atmosphere was very difficult in the office for us and for the staff – I know Mel found it difficult to return to her new place at the end of the working day instead of the place that had been 'our home'. I didn't find it easy, either. We had to adjust our lives, but we did it because we wanted to continue being friends and continue working together. After about eighteen months everything fell back into place and we started to meet up at weekends and socialise again.

I have never regretted marrying Mel, but I regret the journey we went on when it all went bad. I guess we were still very young and perhaps Mel hadn't seen as much of the world as she would have wanted, but it was a good marriage. There were times of tension, but we got through them and we're still here today. We were together for seven years. I was very much the leader and Mel admired my verve and energy, but she became a great operator in her own right and she still is. The whole experience cut me to my heart and didn't do much for my trust in people afterwards. But we are all mates now. I think people are quite envious of our relationship these days. Mel and I really are like brother and sister.

Despite all the drama in my life, I became involved almost immediately with a girl from a casino around the corner. I congratulated myself for moving on, but of course I hadn't. That was the start of my descent into the world of sex, drugs and rock'n'roll.

By now I was well established in the media world and a fixture on the party circuit. On Prince of Wales Terrace in London there's a little hotel called the Gore, and I ended up in the bar there one night in late 1999 slightly the worse for wear. The friend I was with was close to mega-band Duran Duran, who were there on a social night. The boys were in full party mode. We pitched in with them and started sculling shots. It was a spontaneous evening of mischief. Given what was going on I probably wasn't the most obvious guy for them to have around, but I was up front with them and told them what I did and assured them that I wasn't working that night. As the night turned into morning, Roger Taylor, his lovely wife Giovanna and a few of his mates joined me back at my place and we kept on going. Everyone was totally out of it; it was a seriously big night. Giovanna ended up leaving with a cuddly koala toy that I insisted she take.

At the time, the whole incident made me laugh. Mario's sister Angie had been a Duran Duran freak (Mars and I had been into Spandau Ballet), and here I was drinking with them. It wasn't so long ago that I would have been sitting with Mario in Geelong having just walked past Angie's room, which was papered with the guys' faces. That night was a real introduction to the rock star lifestyle. I felt it suited me.

From then on I locked into serious party mode, and to an extent was on autopilot at the business. Though there were some days when I didn't make it into the office, which was unheard-of for me, I was generally putting in the time the business needed. If I wasn't in the office, I was networking furiously in the bars and clubs of London as if there was no tomorrow – and our fortunes started to brighten even as my health started to fail.

I discovered the 'white stuff' on a mad weekend in New York. Back in London I kept going in the murky end of life. There were arseholes all around me and I was binge drinking, hitting the casinos – everything I could do to damage myself. I really hit the self-destruct button. I had huge wins at the casino and then lost it all. I remember the morning following one particularly huge loss, I sat at home watching Paul Lawrie win the British Open golf; what he made that day in prize money equalled my previous night's losses.

Looking back on that period of my life, I see six months of hell. I was living in a 'white cloud' of my own creation. Sometimes it had a silver lining, but generally my days were like thunder. One afternoon Dave Morgan had to come over from BIG to look at my computer and found me hiding behind a tree wearing my flak jacket and helmet, yelling for him to 'get down'.

I knew I was depressed – and I was a long way from home. My family and best friends were in Geelong. I really felt I had no friends in London that I could trust. I went to the doctor for the depression and got a prescription, but I threw the tablets away after a week. They made me more depressed and weaker and I knew they weren't for me. I found out later that during the break-up with Mel, Mum, Mario and George

Ramia had all independently wondered about coming over to be with me, but they all reached the same conclusion – Daz is invincible. So it seems I'd covered it all up really well.

It was a terrible time. I had people trying to blackmail me over addled conversations I couldn't even remember. On one occasion I ended up in bed with twelve women and I didn't know any of their names. I went to Australia at the height of the madness and my mate Mario couldn't believe what he was seeing. I'd get smashed off my head and drag him off to the casino, where I would lose loads of money. He kept screaming at me that I was stupid and I should give the money to charity rather than throw it away.

I lost my marbles and a lot of money. It was a very expensive lesson, and I don't regret it. I still have photocopies of the huge cheques the casino wrote to me to cover my winnings framed on the wall in my house in Geelong. Naturally I ended up giving it all back to them, with interest.

During that period my uncle and aunt came over to visit me in London. We came back to my house after a wonderful lunch at the OXO tower and Uncle Max decided to wander around my garden. He discovered two G-strings and a bra hanging off one of the trees and thought to himself, 'This little nephew of mine has done all right!' but my aunt was less impressed. She told me that nothing she heard about me amazed her any more – but they had no idea about the true extent of my madness at the time.

There were a lot of hangers-on. Daz usually paid the bill;

in fact, he always paid the bill. Sometimes even now I don't go out because of those people. It's certainly more of a London phenomenon than anything I've experienced in Australia; perhaps that's because there is more equality in Australia. There are rich and poor in both places, of course, but in Australia the differences between the two seem less marked and people are willing to buy a round. If you haven't got money in London it can be a brutal city.

Despite our differences, Mel was very concerned about my behaviour. I was out every night caning it and very often didn't make it to the office, and she and everyone else thought I was going to get myself into real trouble. I was depressed and getting in deeper. One morning I woke with my pillow soaked in blood from a nose bleed, unable to move. When you've never had a nose bleed before that's pretty scary. That was it for me. I told myself that unless something changed I was going to lose everything and die. I was hugely proud of

**'My mother opened the door and I looked into her eyes and told her I had been taking drugs. She was devastated'**

myself for reaching that conclusion, but I still needed help. Mel came round and told me that the police were onto me, which was a lie, and she packed me off to Australia to sort myself out. I know she felt a little guilty that our break-up had affected me so badly, but she knew that I could turn things around. Her decisive action proved to be one of the greatest gifts a friend has ever given me. It was almost biblical.

I remember walking up the drive to my family home. My mother opened the door and I looked into her eyes and told her I had been taking drugs. She was devastated and burst into floods of tears, but I told her not to worry, that I was over it. And I meant it. I went cold turkey. I was there for just over a month. It was all about surrounding myself with love and putting my life back on track – an antidote to the way I had been living in London. We had Christmas in Sydney that year and they were there for me when I needed them. That's what mums and dads do, and mine certainly supported me. Most of the time I didn't want to talk about what was happening. I don't think I could believe it, and nor could my family. I had my closest friends around me, too. They had all been worried about me. I had scared Mario when I was going through the break-up with Mel – I kept ringing up when I was at the bottom of the pit and telling him I was going to kill myself. Mario didn't have a frame of reference for the drugs thing, but he was there for me.

I don't wish to glorify that time in any way, but I learned a lot that has helped me to deal with the rock'n'roll lifestyle I live now. There was a heavy price to pay for that wisdom. I know I could have died. My advice to anyone starting out on the same path is simple: 'Don't be so fucking stupid.' I've seen people ruin their lives with drugs and I don't condone them. I feel blessed that I had the guts to fight my way out. If that period turns out to be the worst part of my life – and I hope it does – then I will consider that I have done very well. It gave me real perspective. It sounds clichéd, but it's true: it is only when you have been in the deepest valley that you can know how magnificent it is to be on the highest mountain.

Though I needed that break, I was never tempted to stay in Australia. I had unfinished business in the UK and responsibilities to my staff, and I've never been one to shirk my responsibilities. I got myself straight, came back and turned a small company into a medium-sized one very rapidly. I increased turnover by 100 per cent and I did it with a degree of finesse that had hitherto been lacking. I was back and I was ready to work.

# Lifting
# the Lid

**WE WERE ON THE VERGE** of something massive and I knew it. I felt like I had a crystal ball, and in it I could see the rise of celebrity. Editors and readers were sick of doom and gloom news. Celebrity – pure escapism – was poised to fill the gap.

I genuinely believe that the modern era will be remembered for the cult of celebrity and, of course, the paparazzi who fuel it. I helped to create that boom and yet I do not feel like Dr Frankenstein now that my creation is rampaging across the globe. I have a very healthy take on the whole industry: I would rather wake up and see Britney Spears checking into rehab with a shaved head than bodies lying dead in ditches in Bosnia. I have seen both.

Famous celebrity snapper Jason Fraser has been quoted as saying, 'In the great scheme of the news, there is no doubt that photographs of celebrities seem trivial. But that's not to say they don't have a place. It's escapism. Newspapers are there to inform but also to entertain.' He's right.

A great paparazzi picture is someone looking either amazing or unbelievably bad. However, we are just the conduit between the star and their audience. We have changed the media and therefore society. We supplied wholesale images at exorbitant rates and people couldn't get enough. That appetite has fuelled an incredible number of magazines, and more and more are being launched. Ten years ago people told me the bubble was going to burst, but it can't unless we bring in draconian publicity laws that would cripple a multimillion-dollar publishing industry and shoot down Hollywood. We satisfy people's craving for knowledge of the famous. Fame used to be a by-product of talent, but that's not necessarily the case any more. With reality shows, the number of 'celebrities' has increased to fill the pages of all the magazines.

**'I would rather wake up and see Britney Spears checking into rehab with a shaved head than bodies lying dead in ditches in Bosnia'**

The press has a rapacious need for celebrities now. When

I came to the UK *The Mail* had two pages of world news, but you don't see that any more. It's celebrities that sell papers. Understanding the press is as important as anything else in a star's life. Get that right, and you can make it.

Let's face it – celebrity is a bit of fun. I do not feel that the world of celebrity trivialises the more serious news. People relate very differently to both, as they should. Celebrity gives the world a sprinkle of showbiz and opens the window onto a world that people can aspire to. Without idols, many people wouldn't have anyone to look up to or anything to live up to. I think anything that can inspire someone to get up and do something, to earn the money to buy that handbag or to express themselves differently by getting the latest haircut, is a good thing. I also think the world of celebrity cheers people up, and I am happy to be part of that process.

Celebrities are often presented – both by themselves and their representatives – as perfect, flawless beings. Looking good goes with the job. I am not a film star or a rock star, and I look like shit because I can. Critics of the celebrity obsession claim that it can lead to poor self-esteem because the general public cannot compare themselves favourably to the stars and celebrities. But that is where I come in. For me, paparazzi show us the other side of the coin and offer the real deal, with no subterfuge. In many ways, we are the antidote to all the bullshit. We offer a reality check and bring honesty to the world of celebrity. We have shots of John Travolta sporting the biggest man boobs in the world and a couple of big-name actors with their willies out – and they are tiny! These people are just like you and me; they look like shit. Have you seen Cameron or Brad up close?

Brand culture has grown out of the perceived celebrity lifestyle and it is huge business. It's grown so big that people have forgotten what some of our celebrities actually do. Victoria Beckham is almost inactive in any specific commercial field these days other than being really good at being Victoria Beckham, and yet that is enough to guarantee her place in the pantheon of stars. Now a multi-billion-dollar industry, celebrity informs every aspect of our lives, from what we wear to where we holiday to what we think.

If someone becomes a global box office smash, then in media terms they are as important as the President of the United States. Richard Nixon said that it is the responsibility of the media to look at the president through a microscope – though they go too far when they use a proctoscope! There are days when I look at people in the public eye and see a potential sale rather than a human being. That frightens me. In many ways I don't take the business seriously: paparazzi goes with showbiz like popcorn goes with watching a movie. The demand is massive and we supply the goods. On occasion we create the celebrities, and in many cases we provide the exposure that can sustain their careers. I give them their oxygen. I think the public sees things in much the same way as me. People love the naughty element in what we do. I'm sure most people agree that we've got more important things on this planet to worry about than one of my guys getting a picture of Britney with a shaved head or Angelina Jolie's wrinkly newborn.

The market has moved on from the cheesy 'at home' shoots; people are not fooled by shots like that anymore. They know that most of the time the stars are not even at home, but rather in some stately residence. People want reality, or at least a convincing version of it. Celebs *do* look like crap occasionally. Don't we all look like that when we roll out of bed first thing! The publications themselves just want the images; they don't care how they are generated. We get calls every day from picture editors panicking because they have nothing to take into the morning editorial conference.

Most stars, I believe, are fair game. Though I do take a moral line on occasion, I believe in the old adage that if you live by the sword you die by the sword. It's not fair for people to think that once they have achieved the fame and success they desire (a process helped along by the media) that they can opt out of the paparazzi game. I truly believe that celebrities have a duty to the public who have afforded them their success. One previously highly litigious superstar couple found this out recently – they have denied gagging orders by judges pointing out that generally they were all too willing to be papped and had in fact colluded on innumerable occasions.

Celebrities on the whole are fairly happy to have their picture taken, especially the old guard. These are the people who realise it is a symbiotic relationship. They give us the shot and we splash on them just as their new film opens. Hollywood A-listers will either tip you off or arrive on the right scene at the right moment. Often the snapper won't even realise that the stars know he is there; he'll just think he's hit lucky. That kind of behaviour could be seen as a defence mechanism or just playing the game. A prime example of working the game was of course Diana, Princess of Wales. She was a hustler and I worked with her on many occasions – she even turned up on my doorstep once to complain that some shots I had taken weren't suitably flattering. Royalty doorstepping the paparazzi was certainly unusual – and let's face it, she would have looked good in a garbage bag!

There are stars who take another route. Rather than having relationships with photographers, they have people – often themselves – who leak their location or planned movements so they can ensure that their public profile doesn't dip and that they look their best in the shots. David and Victoria Beckham were masters at this in the early days. We once caught David on a hotel balcony in his underpants. You can't tell me that he didn't know he was being photographed – he happened to be wearing his Police sunglasses just after signing another million-dollar contract. He has great management: she's called Victoria! There were ten photographers there, but all the nationals used our shots to keep their guys out of trouble, avoid any issues with the Press Complaints Commission (PCC) and make sure they didn't hurt their chances of getting the next interview. We took all the heat and ended up making a donation to charity to soothe everyone's ruffled feathers.

To be honest, I think celebrities are stupid if they don't have an official and unofficial public relations team – the latter being someone like me. I think it's an extremely important way to control their image. We work with a lot of public relations and management companies to ensure that we show the stars in a positive light. For example, when Oasis hit the music scene, Noel Gallagher was in Ibiza dropping his trousers for the camera while Liam was in the south of France throwing beer cans at Kate Moss and the hordes of waiting press. To be a rock star, you have to create a rock star persona. Those pictures of the bad boys of rock'n'roll hit the papers the day of their album release – I saw the queues at Tower Records and thought, 'We've pulled it off.' They weren't bad boys at all, just playing a part, and they did it very well. The only problem for us is talking people into embarking on these stunts.

Very often what a celebrity has printed on their T-shirt can decide whether the shots get into the papers or not; of course, the stars are all too aware of that. That's why Britney may sport one that says 'Rehab' or 'These boobs are real' – whatever will work. In fact, there's a shop in LA called Kitson that specialises in printing slogans onto blank shirts for celebrities.

I do think that once you have sold images of yourself you

are fair game. If you sell images of your wedding, then you can't claim to be haunted by seeing yourself in the papers. As stars get more famous, publicity seems to drop off – I guess because it takes less effort to get into the papers. Celebrities forget very quickly who helped them become so famous when they've reached the position where they don't need publicity. They are desperate to know you on the way up, but they hate you on the way down. Suddenly they become the experts and it is at this point that they can make fatal mistakes. Once again, I would mention the words 'patience and greed'.

It takes real effort to get the genie out of the magic lamp, but once you've freed it, it's almost impossible to get the fucker back in. Some celebrities are isolated by their lifestyle. Actor Telly Savalas once said that he'd lived all his life in a bubble and missed out on a lot. Some celebrities miss out on being normal. Is fame worth sacrificing your happiness for? No. Is it worth it to satisfy the ego? Yes. For the first three months, celebrity is great. Everyone wants you and you go to the head of every queue. But after that it becomes a nightmare, a chore. The D-list love it all the time because they never have enough success for it to become a poisoned chalice.

**'For the first three months, celebrity is great. Everyone wants you and you go to the head of every**

There have been examples of shots we produced that I considered fantastic and totally newsworthy, but that I have not sold because they would cause distress to the subject. For example, I had long discussions with PR Matthew Freud about two topless shots of German supermodel Claudia Schiffer. A rumour circulated that I had the pictures; within five minutes *The Sun* was on the phone, but Matthew and I ended up doing a deal.

We were promised access to her wedding in return for not selling the pics, but in fact this never came through for us, which was sad. I could have put the images out onto the market to spite them, but I didn't. We've got pictures of Janet Jackson naked doing all sorts of strange things by a swimming pool. The privacy code has been tightened up, but I do now believe that I have matured and that, to an extent, 'An Englishman's home is his castle'. I try to protect that privacy. There have been several sets I haven't put on the market due, believe it or not, to my morals.

There are many rumours about the pictures that never get seen. People talk in hushed tones about the contents of '*The Sun* safe'. It's rumoured that some of the great stories lurk in there, unloved, taken off the market by large wads of cash or surreptitious sacrificing of another, less important name – or just sorted effectively due to political expediency. I'd bet that *The Mail* has a similar safe. I'd love to see what's in there. Perhaps Fergie and Paddy McNally allegedly 'sharing' a bottle of champagne in the bath . . . all sorts. It's fun to guess. One legendary set of images shows a famous British television actress naked on the back patio of a house, smearing dog food all over herself and setting her two Alsatians to work.

It's an open secret that someone has a set of topless pictures of Princess Diana. They were apparently bought off the market by the owner of *Hello!* magazine to keep them out of circulation. Years later, BIG Pictures nailed the first set of Victoria Beckham topless with David, and we were discreetly approached by their agents and asked if we would like to sell the negatives. Naturally, we declined. It wasn't just about the money! I have seen pictures of Jemima and Imran Khan on their honeymoon; Clive Howes of *The Standard* showed me. My God – Imran is a legend! Those pictures were allegedly bought off the market by Jemima's father, Sir James Goldsmith, for more than a million pounds.

**'These days if you took cocaine with two circus clowns and then had lesbian sex you could be famous!'**

I may have been instrumental in creating the wave of celebrity that has swamped the modern media, but I still despair that so many people nowadays just want to be famous. Not for a talent necessarily, just famous. The notion of celebrity has been debased. These days if you took cocaine with two circus clowns and then had lesbian sex you could be famous! Every second person is being approached to sell their story. On the scene in London I know for a fact that there are professionals operating, girls who go out to shag famous guys just to sell their stories. It is very lucrative, whether they sell the story or it gets bought off the market. I do have an issue with entrapment and would not generally get involved with such deals. On occasion I have used my influence to negate such stories. There is a fine line, of course, and I have made a lot of money out of selling stories of that ilk, but I do not believe in wilfully destroying people's lives for the sake of money.

All these truths about the nature of celebrity mean that when BIG Pictures is out there papping the stars some will claim that, to an extent, we are imposing on their privacy and causing them some kind of distress. My answer to that is simple: if you can't hack the job, don't wear the hat. All jobs come with a downside, and if allowing the public some access to their lives is the only downside to celebrity, it's a small price to pay – especially when that access gives them the publicity they need to perpetuate their careers. That is a lesson you can learn from many of the real stars, the big names who are unfailingly courteous and understanding. A smile costs nothing. While we all have bad days, I don't understand why some celebrities display such a lack of grace. It's a question of style. Many celebrities have money, but don't have any style. People say the same about me. Ha ha ha.

Some people just know how to play the game, and it is often the biggest stars who are the most decent people and the easiest to deal with. My fellow Aussie, Kylie Minogue, is a prime example. Despite being a regular target, she has only ever pulled over and threatened to call the police on us once.

If you could hold anyone up as an example of how to play the game and deal with the paparazzi, then it would be Kylie. She understands the working of the media and knows when and how to give us shots, as many A-listers do.

These days BIG is concerned with more than just image capture. We are in the business of news creation, of making people famous. We build celebrities almost from scratch and not only sustain their level of celebrity, but move them to the next level too. We have many celebrity clients on our books and we take that part of the business very seriously.

Celebrities are just human, of course; everyone makes mistakes and if they are caught out then the chances are that BIG will already have a system in place to deal with it. Very often we will have a relationship with the photographer who hit the shot and we can negotiate the pictures off the market and into oblivion – or at least into a deep safety deposit box. I rarely destroy images as insurance is always useful! If we don't have an existing deal with a certain snapper then we are quickly able to broker one. We've done that for model/actress Victoria Silvstedt (who was caught very much with her pants down by at least three photographers), Claudia Schiffer, and plenty of big stars.

Confidentiality deals represent a win–win situation. They allow us to control the flow of images, either by releasing favourable images or by blocking or buying up poor ones. A celebrity today needs someone to manage the media for them, no question. Obviously the advent of the Internet means that pictures can go around the world almost instantly, so it is important to deal with someone in our position who can stop that happening. BIG negotiates with the photographers holding the contentious images and we agree on a price per territory to remove them from the market. Because we know the way the market works, we are able to achieve that quickly.

BIG Pictures has worked with some of the biggest names in the world, and there are some clients who I cannot mention in this book as I have a non-disclosure deal with them. These stars don't want the hassle of working against us, but they do need the exposure that BIG can generate. A lot of the images that BIG sells onto the market come into our possession as a result of reciprocal access deals. Either we've approached the celebrity directly, or their management team has come to us looking to do a deal. It can be very difficult to get through the door of some management companies, but once they understand what can be done they are very accommodating. On very rare occasions, a star is switched on enough to realise that image is everything and understands what we can do in terms of creating a positive image – literally – of them, and we then deal direct.

A friend of mine told me recently that she had been driving past my office in Clerkenwell with Kylie Minogue, who – and she's a girl from just up the road in Melbourne, remember – said, 'There's the friendly paparazzi.' I must say that really made me feel proud. Thanks, Ky. Good to see us Aussies sticking together. BIG is very proactive and I would rather be known as the 'friendly paparazzo' than the unfriendly one – and it makes it easier for everyone if there is collusion. If I had my way, we wouldn't need to pap anyone! This is an expensive business to run; the BIG travel budget is around £1 million a year. It's no wonder the papers are cutting back on their photography – they can't rival our output. The celebrities can deal with us for self-protection; we dominate the market and if we are on their side they are safer than otherwise. People like Pammy Anderson are smart. Our guys covered her wedding in 2006 and she invited them onto the boat! That's class.

Because of our success rate, we are approached by all sorts of people and we are very choosy about who we work with. With some of our clients, all of the money they earn with us goes to charity; others want every penny for themselves – often the wealthiest are the tightest! My dream clients would be Prince Harry and Prince William – though Harry is more fun – and Brad Pitt and Angelina Jolie.

We put together a plan of action for our clients, carefully pitched to achieve whatever their objectives are. Often we will begin with a studio shoot to start a supply of great images and follow that with some set-up shots and pap shots. We have been known to shoot a star at their house in an amazing outfit they are planning to wear to a premiere, and have the pictures

Fergie and Diana at Epsom on Derby Day.

⏩ The BIG Pictures Royal Archive is one of the best in the world. This shot was taken after the Queen Mother presented shamrocks to the Irish Guards on St Patrick's Day, 1998. The shot below was taken on the palace balcony during an RAF fly-past.

BIG Pictures

Another day, another Royal Wedding! Prince Edward marries Sophie Rhys-Jones in 1999.

# Following in mother's fashionable footsteps

**So smart: William** *Picture: DARRYN LYONS*

**So stylish: Diana and Harry** *Picture: STEVE DOUGLASS*

DIANA dressed for winter, Harry for summer ... and a smart new look put spring into William's step.

The colourful contrast of royal styles was on view yesterday as the Princess and her sons left home on an extra-special morning for the two Princes.

Diana's striking outfit of Western-style calf-length suede skirt, riding boots and wool polo neck jumper was the perfect blend of pretty and practical to beat the chilly weather.

But Harry, eagerly anticipating his fourth birthday celebrations, was oblivious to the breeze. In cool cotton madras-checked Bermuda shorts, Polo Club sweatshirt and with socks round his ankles, he looked more beach boy than birthday boy.

William, meanwhile, was proudly parading his new red and grey uniform for his first term at Wetherby School, Notting Hill Gate, West London. Diana and Charles dropped him off there before taking Harry to his nearby kindergarten — where a royal aide later delivered a tray of cakes and jellies to be eaten in between party games.

And when school was out, no one was left in any doubt about just how grown up the little Prince has become.

He emerged from his class clutching a large paper cutout figure 4 — which he proudly waved as he was driven home.

My first big scoop as a freelancer! While everyone else was at the front door, I was at the back.

➤ Shenanigans in the race queue during Prince William's school sports day at Wetherby pre-prep.

← The famous spanking incident. A huge scoop — everyone else had packed up, so Jim Bennett and I got the only shots.

I happened upon another exclusive while nosing around Kensington Palace — some great shots of Harry's birthday party. Here the guests are taking a minibus ride while Diana looks on, laughing.

Prince Charles and Princess Diana with William and Harry at the V J Day anniversary march in the Mall.

Ken Goff/Big Pictures

🔺 I always thought that Diana, the loving mother, was ahead of the pack and this picture proves it!

A moment of happiness for the royal family – the Queen Mother's birthday.

Harry at the Hohne barracks in Germany – his first official public engagement – in 1993. The shot below shows him in a police helmet at 4.

The Queen Mother, accompanied by the Duke of York, leaves St Margaret's churchyard where she'd been visiting the Royal British Legion's Field of Remembrance.

William's first day at Eton.

Ken Goff/Big Pictures

Big Pictures

Big Pictures

Big Pictures

Diana with her lawyer Anthony Julius during her divorce negotiations.

⚑ Princess Diana at the Serpentine Gallery, June 1995. In the shot below, she tries to avoid paparazzi photographer Mark Saunders in London.

Charles looking to the heavens for help on the day he split from Diana. This shot won me the AGFA Press Photographer award.

The Princess loved being photographed, and manipulated the photographers every day, but alas, we all get out of the wrong side of the bed occasionally. These pictures show Diana on her 'off' days, but I think she still looked terrific, even in the middle of a scream.

One of my favourite BIG Pictures images of Diana, taken by the photographer Ken Goff during her state visit to Hong Kong.

over to the newspapers before the client is anywhere near the red carpet.

Obviously the contracts we sign set out the breakdown of revenues and stipulate a minimum number of shoots or set-ups that we need access for. We have requirements and expectations as regards exclusivity, but if someone gets papped there is not much we can do about it. The client gets a sales report every month that shows what has been sold and to whom. Each client will be somewhere on a sliding scale of percentage return on all sales. The splits in profit vary, but often the stars will be paid nothing as they are just in it for the publicity – and of course we have clients who pay us to be on our books. Generally, we bear the costs of shoots and set-ups; these are recoupable before a dividend is paid.

The money that can be made is enormous. One of our clients made a quarter of a million pounds in a year – and this person is certainly not an A-lister. You have to open a lot of supermarkets to earn that! For the really big stars, the sky is the limit. Despite what people think, most celebrities have no money. They have a brief moment in the limelight – during which they pay around 20 per cent commission to their agent and 40 per cent tax – and then disappear. To return to the limelight they need a lifestyle and that is why they are often very happy to work with us.

Sometimes partnerships may be short-lived or come about by accident. On occasion, we have hit shots of a star unawares and then their representatives have come to us offering to arrange an exclusive set-up to generate better shots in order to get the first set off the market. We did that recently with the actress Tamzin Outhwaite, who we papped on her honeymoon; her cut went to charity. I am happy to agree to deals like that because the better my product, the happier I am and the more the pictures sell for. If a celebrity is going away for a holiday they don't want to live in fear of being papped and so we will do a deal for a morning's access and then the job is done and they can be left alone to enjoy their time off.

People expect us to work with models and glamour girls, but our reach is far greater than that. BIG gets calls from people close to the Hollywood A list, huge music stars, it can be anyone – a lot of our contracts have come through my networking and my own raised profile.

BIG has ongoing deals with many celebrities that bring handsome returns on each side. Sometimes stars aren't even aware that their management team has a deal with us; they might be against the paparazzi or just can't understand the benefits. Some managers don't want their clients to miss out, others just like the kickbacks. On a couple of occasions I have received an email from a celebrity manager telling me that they will ring me at a certain time to shout at me in front of their client to maintain the illusion. I'm fine with that – business is business.

People need reassurance, and to be able to trust their instincts, because when you're famous everyone wants a piece of you. Of course we make money from our relationships, but when we do well, our clients do well too. Loyalty can go out of the window in this game, especially when the stakes go up. And that's a mistake. It's usually the brightest people who realise that the best approach is to stay humble and true to the people they know and trust.

**'When you're famous everyone wants a piece of you'**

Often we will follow the celebrities to secure the stories, but sometimes they come to us. One day a girl called Daisy Wright rang the buzzer at the BIG office and asked to see me, looking for advice. She had been embroiled in a scandal involving actor Jude Law while she was in his employ as a nanny. Fearing that the story was already out, she had been encouraged to sell her side of the story, but things had not developed as she had hoped.

Daisy had arrived in New Orleans with Jude's elder son Rafferty the same day that Jude's girlfriend, the actress Sienna Miller, had flown home to London. Daisy told me that she had never heard of Jude Law prior to working for him and that he wasn't her type – she generally went for black men. What transpired was a complete surprise. Jude and Daisy went to a concert that night and things developed from there. Their relationship was made up of stolen moments when the kids were in bed and the other staff weren't around. This went on for six weeks until Rafferty asked someone why Daisy had been snuggled up with Daddy. Jude told Daisy that whoever ended up with her would be a lucky man; there is no doubt in my mind that he felt he was missing something.

Once the news broke, Daisy had a real dilemma. She knew that if she stuck to the 'official' story that there was nothing going on, as Jude had suggested she do, that Rafferty would essentially be branded a liar. She was unwilling to allow that to happen. When the details began to emerge, Daisy made a decision that she now regrets; she decided to sell her story. Luckily I was able to generate interest within the media and set up an interview that allowed Daisy to set the record straight – to tell the story in a more balanced way. I also used my contacts to cut deals and secure her extra work and contracts, from which she has made great money.

BIG Pictures also negotiated a deal with singer Charlotte Church and took her down to the south of France to our yacht. She was keen on the control aspect of being involved in a set-up, particularly as she was moving into the world of pop, where image is everything. Charlotte and her boyfriend, Welsh rugby star Gavin Henson, were to be shot together. My former driver, Robin, picked them up from Wales, and after an overnight stay near London we flew them out to the south of France and got to work. Though they were very sweet, the trip ended up being a bit of a nightmare for BIG as they were spotted by some of our rivals. Charlotte and Gavin had decided that they wanted to sail to 'paparazzi central', Monaco, where they were easily identified. Marty, my picture editor, was down there with them and he copped it pretty hard from me as the exclusivity was gone. Despite that, we still had by far the best images and managed to do quite well out of the set-up. The couple were really pleased with the images we released, and they got some excellent coverage from it. Charlotte's career has since taken off, and she now hosts her own entertainment show on Channel Four.

Very often we will be contacted by lawyers acting for stars who want to buy pictures off the market – often for more money than we would be able to sell them to a paper for. Easy money, I guess, but it's a bit boring. I prefer to give people a laugh! We just took a set of a well-known model off the market. Personally, I don't know why she bothered. It is fairly well known that she supplements her income from modelling by moonlighting as a high-class hooker, so I'm not sure why these innocuous pictures bothered her so much. Not that I care.

If the stars are rich enough, you'll get a legal letter fast. Sometimes we have to pull the pics and make a donation to charity – great examples were the shots we hit of Elton John cleaning his windows in a nightie, and David Beckham posing in his undies on the balcony of his hotel. It's a shame, but I don't enjoy protracted legal fights. They are a diversion and very expensive.

Legal letters are part of the business, unfortunately, and

they can cause us real worry. If I ever see a letter on high-class legal stationery I know we are in for a tough time! Chances are it will be one of the firms that looks after all the big names and likes to earn its money.

Despite being associated with him for years, BIG once got a legal letter from London club-owning legend Peter Stringfellow. We'd caught a shot of him, in fairness not looking wonderful, in a g-string that even I wouldn't have had the front to climb into. I was a little bit upset at the time to receive word from his lawyers, not least because I spent a fortune in his club and we had done a lot of business together. I sent back a letter saying that surely they weren't serious, and it's all been forgotten about now. Stringy is, without question, one of the good guys and one of the people that makes London the town it is.

Working as a celebrity photographer is a job like no other – part superstar, part slave. I've been invited to attend some incredible events, but I've also stood in the rain outside countless mediocre parties waiting for something – anything – to happen. You get to do something different every day, and to spend your time recording the antics of the good, the bad, the ugly and the beautiful. The game is about contacts, networking and schmoozing, relationships and planning. It's fucking hard yakka. You get a lot of grief. Shooting the stars is literally a hit-or-miss affair. I remember shooting presenter Chris Evans when he was huge on TV in the UK. He was in the process of stumbling out of Browns nightclub, and as he came towards me, the mystery girl he was with flashed her boobs at me. I saw it through the lens, which meant the shutter wasn't open, so I knew I had not captured the image. That shot would probably have made me twenty grand at the time, but that's the way it goes sometimes.

Celebrities are getting more savvy and increasingly know how the game works in the studio; they know it is easy to trim off the pounds with a little computer time – or a lot, if you are Kirstie Alley. I hear it all the time: 'Airbrush that! Lose that!' We've taken shots of celebrities who will come in and literally sit there and have a go with a PhotoShop application themselves. Completely shameless, guys. I call it techno lipo.

I know both sides of the game, of course – studio and street. I used to do both quite well – but I preferred the pap side because there was more of an adrenaline rush. It was just more exciting. But because I came from a newspaper background I had to be able to cover everything. I trained myself in the studio. While more creative, studio photography could be mundane – though when I have more time I would like to return to it. I've seen many paparazzi photographers who are also great studio photographers, but rarely anyone who has made the transition in the opposite direction. Maybe it's because studio photographers are too pampered to want to hang around on street corners – I'm not sure they would know what to do.

In the studio I prefer not to go too heavy into lights; I'm a big fan of available light, especially window lighting. Of course, you have to know the female form very well – and I've enjoyed my research! If you are going to produce a memorable image, there has to be a great relationship between subject and artist. It's no good having someone just standing there. They have to be relaxed; I always make sure they have a couple of glasses of wine beforehand, or whatever. In a studio you really have to get on a roll and get a vibe going. It's all about sex. Sexual chemistry gets the best results, which is why so many photographers date their subjects. The eye is everything, but you have to be feeling the intensity. The sexier the model is, the better the pictures will be – so never shoot your friend's grandmother in the studio!

The great photographers have huge talent, of course, but it's all about access. Someone like Mario Testino is a wonderful artist who enjoys unparalleled access. The celebrities want to be photographed by people like him. I've seen shoots by him that I consider very ordinary, but his images of Liz Hurley, Diana and Robbie Williams surround me in my living room.

I love much of Testino's work, and on one occasion during a London Fashion Week I made him a cup of tea at my house. I was in my living room and glancing out of the window when I saw some gorgeous women gazing in. I went out to suggest that they either come in or move on when I realised the great man was there too. Testino told me he had never seen his work displayed in such a way and asked if he could come in and look around. He actually told me that he wanted to come back and do a shoot at my place, but sadly it never happened.

The access enjoyed by someone like Testino, however, has to be earned. Norman Parkinson, David Hamilton, Lord Lichfield, Rankin and Annie Liebowitz have produced incredible work. Of course, many of the big names have excellent assistants who are there to organise anything complicated and make sure that the lighting is perfect.

People always talk about whether photography is an art or a science. On the road in the old days you literally had to be a chemist to develop your images, but I think in truth it's a bit of both. To get a great image you have to feel it. You have to live it and love it and almost look into the future before you take it. Where paparazzi shots require the capture of a heart-pumping instant, a studio shoot is more controlled and measured, although a few palpitations in the studio always help. You've got all the time in the world to fuck up the shot in the studio, whereas on a pap assignment you may have one-thousandth of a second to capture that million-dollar shot.

**'To get a great image you have to feel it. You have to live it and love it and almost look into the future before you take it'**

I think that digital technology has made photographers lazy. Show me someone who can make something look great on a negative – just one – and I'll show you an artist. In the good old days, say the 1940s, the leading Hollywood photographers had to make people look good by using their own nous and employing great lighting. They were simply more talented. There are still various tricks that a decent snapper can use. For example, I always shoot up, from lower than eye level, because it slims the cheeks and enhances the profile. Cheekbones and long legs are everything when it comes to shooting women. Every woman wants to look fantastic and I can make that happen – though not many of them look fantastic when you wake up next to them in the morning after a few drinks!

The process of photography does change the way people look, though. I've photographed celebrities over many years and it's bizarre when you see them in real life. Some people just draw the camera to them. Being photogenic is certainly a gift that many huge stars have. For the rest there's airbrushing and PhotoShop. One thing I have noticed about big stars is that they often have big eyes and large mouths. Just look at Julia Roberts or Angelina Jolie.

It is vitally important that everything within my business empire is perfectly presented. First impressions count in my book, and if you can make everything look perfect, then the rest of your plans will just fall into place. Of course, if your subject is *not* perfect, there are a few tricks of the trade you can use to make sure that the finished image looks the part. The women you see in the magazines are obviously not as beautiful in real life. The amount of airbrushing that goes on is unbelievable. Some of the studio guys work full time on retouching. I would say that anyone you put in front of a camera can look amazing once the computer has been to work. I promise you – real is not real and what you see is not what you get.

Whether you're a model, an actress or a rock star, image is everything and people will do whatever they can to manipulate it. The public do not realise how much control the stars have over their image. There have been several situations with stars where there have been complaints about the illusion and the reality. They can be on the cover of a magazine one day and then papped the next day looking two stone heavier. That's why many of the stars can't deal with the paparazzi. The stars like to deal in fiction, with doctored images, and what we offer up is fact – warts and all.

The 'approval' issue is massive with celebrities these days. Whenever possible, the stars will try to control which pictures are used and, of course, which are not – though it never ceases to amaze me which images they think make them look good. We lost a contract with Dannii Minogue once because she didn't like the images we had signed off jointly with her management company. Naturally, we got the blame. As a photographer you have to sign your life away. The guidelines are stringent because very often these people are paranoid and insecure. Truly they are a breed apart – they are the only ones who can't see their beauty. Sometimes I look at stunning models and wish they could be more relaxed about themselves and their image. They live in a house of mirrors and it really affects their life. Having dated several, I am a man who knows!

# Adventures with the Beautiful People

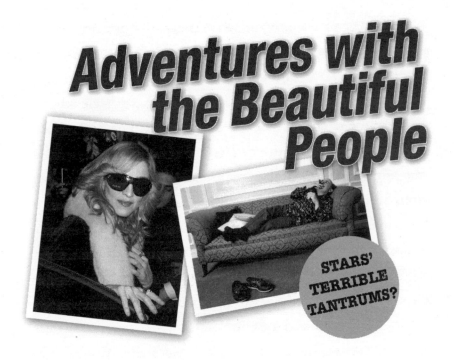

STARS' TERRIBLE TANTRUMS?

**OVER THE YEARS,** I have dealt with some of the biggest names in the world. I've nailed some amazing shots, but there have been some really strange times too. At the *Daily Mail* I used to be sent out on a lot of film sets, and these locations were always fraught.

When I was sent to cover Mel Gibson on the set of *Hamlet*, I turned up at Heathrow with tons of equipment and the kind of lens that could pull focus on someone if they were on the moon. As I sat killing time in the departure lounge, I noticed that my boarding pass designated me as occupying seat 1A. Upon boarding, I realised I would be spending the flight sitting next to Mel Gibson himself. Obviously I didn't mention that I was going to be trailing him for the next few weeks! He was in seat 1B, and it's probably the only time I'll outdo Mel.

Mel Gibson truly has star quality, and I have found that whenever I recount the story of my short journey with him, people start to think I'm gay – because I have to admit that I found myself getting lost in those incredible blue eyes. I don't get star-struck – and people who do really piss me off. The stars are just doing a job. But this was like looking at a hypnotist's pocket watch. I couldn't tear myself away. We didn't really speak on the flight, but I did get him to sign a British Airways sick bag for Kelly Ryan, a reporter I had worked with at *The Addy*. I knew she was a Gibson fan. I think the autographed bag is still stashed away in a box somewhere – sorry, Kelly!

Once the plane landed, I knew I would be pursuing Gibson across Scotland, so I made myself scarce pretty quickly. I met up with our Scottish team at our designated hotel and got everything ready for the incursion. The film set was located near Inverness, and the job would be tough due to the terrain. There was very little natural cover for me when I was working. The whole area was like a golf links, very flat, and I had a lot of gear with me. Each day I wore full camouflage, including a beanie hat with sticks, leaves and the odd thistle poking out of it, and smeared my face with mud to try and blend in as I snuck from thistle-infested swamp to tuft of grass. I'll never forget pulling all the thorns out of my arse!

I wasn't too sure what the Hamlet story was about –

literature wasn't my strong point at East Tech – but for Mel Gibson it seemed to involve a lot of charging around in a black robe and for me it involved a lot of trudging around. I got some great images, really striking shots of Gibson and his men waving their swords around. The first night I settled in at the hotel bar and had my introduction to the wonderful world of Scottish whisky. The following morning I was feeling pretty tender – Mr Glenmorangie had done me in.

Security was tight and every so often their tactics would work and I would be captured and marched out of the vicinity. The process of creeping in would then start all over again. Press photographers were still shooting on black and white in those days and once I hit anything decent, I would have to go through the slow process of transmitting the pictures to the newspaper through a temperamental wire machine.

The results from that set were good and, in fact, Gibson has always been a good gig for me. I also covered the filming of *Braveheart*. I stayed in a little B&B and really did my homework, even managing to get a copy of the script. We had good information on the location and, to be honest, when Mel Gibson directs a film the set is like a small city. Foolishly, I attended an initial press conference and he immediately recognised me as the guy who had nailed all the pictures from *Hamlet*; fixed grins all round. Gibson is by no means a lover of the paparazzi, though I'm not sure why. He even made a film called *Paparazzi*, in which we came out fairly badly – I hope the movie wasn't about me! Maybe the experience of me staring into his eyes so intently on that plane gave him the inspiration to kill us all off in the movie.

The *Braveheart* set was wonderful. By getting up very early I was able to cover the four miles to the chosen vantage point without drawing attention to myself. In any case, I needed to walk off the enormous breakfast of haggis that the old lady who ran the B&B forced down me. Happily, unlike *Hamlet*, this film was set in the highlands, so there were plenty of places to hide and I really enjoyed myself. I got a fantastic shot of Gibson jumping off his horse. His kilt came up as he jumped and I nailed a shot of his bare bum – though I saw it happen through the shutter as well, which usually means the moment has passed. Thank God for six frames a second.

**'His kilt came up as he jumped and I nailed a shot of his bare bum'**

My experiences on sets really drilled into me how boring film work can be. Everything is shot from a minimum of five angles and at least eight times. Gibson was really good and could nail a shot pretty quickly, but working with Kevin Costner must be murder; he would reshoot time and again. Pretty dull for everyone, particularly me – once I had my shot I wanted to move on to the next thing. Actors are so lucky with what they do. They can fuck something up nineteen times out of twenty and still be considered a star.

On that *Braveheart* job, I flew Mel (my wife, not the star of the show) up to join me for a weekend. Once I had finished my day's work, we checked into a really nice hotel. In those wonderful days of expenses, a decent hotel-and-restaurant guide was an integral part of my kit. There was a lovely big yellow cottage located just opposite the hotel and the morning we arrived, Mel Gibson and his wife and family moved into it. A strange coincidence.

While covering a Kevin Costner film set could be torturous, I did scoop a famous shot of him and Morgan Freeman on Hadrian's Wall during the filming of *Robin Hood, Prince of Thieves*. I had herded a conveniently available flock of sheep into position, and hiding in among them gave me a decent, if smelly, vantage point over the action. Security men were camped everywhere, but it was difficult for them as there were lots of public footpaths legally allowing access.

Whenever I worked on a set, I had to be careful when and where I jumped up. I needed to get the shot, but I also didn't want to appear in every frame of the film. In fact, in the final cut of this film, during the scene when Robin Hood fights Little John, if you know where to look you can see me in my yellow jacket. I'm very proud of that. On this occasion I was forced to bide my time among my woolly friends for an hour and a half. Finally the moment arrived, and as soon as I heard 'Action!' up I jumped and walloped the shot as the sheep scattered in all directions. I heard shouts ring out and I sprinted off. In the end I had to cover about three miles to get back to the car.

At one point during the filming I was trampled by a herd of wild goats. I was trying to get a shot of Costner filming a scene in the tower of a castle, but I couldn't get close. The only point I could hit the shot from was a pheasant breeding ground. There were ground nets everywhere and I kept getting tangled up. Reaching the position I wanted, I popped round the corner just in time to see thirty goats running at me and had to throw myself to the side so they wouldn't flatten me. What a way to goat!

I tramped around the highlands for over a month. I kept hoping Andy Kyle would let me come home, but I was producing good stuff on a daily basis so I sealed my own fate. Overcoming challenges and security on film sets was fun, but I did care about staying alive, and *Prince of Thieves* was the job I nearly died on. Down in a valley, Costner and a co-star were re-enacting the famous battle in the river between Robin Hood and Little John and I wanted one last shot, as usual. The scene involved Costner being knocked into the water. They were on about take sixteen and I couldn't work out why they needed to keep shooting it. A popular idiom is that something is as easy as falling off a log, but Costner couldn't seem to do it.

There was only one vantage point that would enable me to get the shot I needed and it involved scaling a very high, very steep bank overlooking the action. It was pissing with rain, and as I was focusing on composing my shot through the lens I didn't look at how safe my footing was. The instant I slipped, I knew I was in big trouble. I was off on a high-speed slide, my progress being sped up by all the kit I was carrying, including a 1200-mm lens that seemed to weigh a ton. Off balance and out of control, I careered down the slope and towards the edge of the precipice, trees smacking me in the face and every other part of my body.

My heart was in my mouth and I clawed desperately for some kind of a handhold because I knew damn well that I was heading for a 200-foot drop down Aysgarth Falls. I thought I was Elvis for sure. Just when I thought my number was up, the very gear that had knocked me off balance in the first place saved me. The tree cover was beginning to thin out as I rushed towards the edge of the cliff when my 1200-mm lens snagged in a fork between two sturdy tree branches and the neck strap brought me shuddering to a halt. I lay on the sodden ground with muddy rainwater flowing into my mouth and just laughed, thinking 'It's good to be alive.'

**'I careered down the slope and towards the edge of the precipice, trees smacking me in the face'**

I reached round, grabbed the lens from the other side, pulled myself clear and got back up. My neck wasn't in good shape, which was no surprise as I had almost hanged myself. The last thing I did before deciding that I really needed to examine my priorities was bang off the shot of Costner. At least I hadn't gone through all that for nothing. Seriously cut up, and sporting bruises from top to bottom that I would have for weeks, I knew it was time to go.

By the end of the film I was well known to all of the cast and crew. I think a lot of them found my antics funny, but I guess extra reshoots cost big money. On one evening I even found myself eating in the same restaurant as Costner and the producers. If looks could kill, I certainly wouldn't be writing this book. I guess to the film crew I was the worst irritation known to man. I was forever popping up – between trees, sheep, deer, even Irish wolfhounds. The security were onto me though. One day after I'd finished shooting, I came back to my car – parked a few miles away – and found it vandalised: broken windscreen wipers, slashed tyres, the lot.

I thought it was a good film in the end, though to me Alan Rickman as the Sheriff of Nottingham was the real star. I loved eavesdropping on his scenes and a lot of them didn't make the final edit, which I thought was a shame. I'm sure Costner would have had a bit to do with that; one can't have another actor stealing the show!

Once I'd done a good job on *Robin Hood* I was considered a film-set specialist, and when BIG started, I made sure that we continued to work the sets. I even covered the set of a Charles and Diana film, where I got some excellent stuff at a stately home up in the Borders. The Americans went potty over that film; I thought it was a heap of shit.

A lot of the film business – and of course the general entertainment business – is run by public relations specialists, or

PRs. They are in with the newspaper and magazine editors and often there is a deal done to get things into the papers, or indeed to keep things out. The PR company that represents Working Title films in the UK is Freud Communications, and they were paranoid that someone would get a shot of the 'lesbian kiss' twist at the end of *Bridget Jones: The Age of Reason*, the sequel to the hit debut. We had received a tip from an insider and just about hit the shot. It wasn't great, but it was certainly good enough.

Naturally it wasn't long before PR guru and Rupert Murdoch's son-in-law Matthew Freud called me on the mobile; ironically, I believe he had received a tip from *The Sun* picture desk, with whom we had already had a brief conversation. He was desperate to buy the picture off the market until two weeks before the release of the film; we settled on £20000. I think the film tanked anyway. In hindsight we would have made more money selling the picture there and then, but it's about building relationships.

The scope and scale of film sets allow for drama in every sense, as two of my BIG Pictures guys found out. Stewie Morton was over in Morocco with Pierre Pham Van Suu covering the filming of *Alexander*, starring Colin Farrell. They had delivered some wonderful images on their first day and were looking for a killer follow-up. Positioning themselves carefully to get shots of one of the big battle scenes, they found themselves staring down some serious trouble when the massive cavalry cavalcade they had been papping suddenly turned and charged in their direction.

It wasn't much fun being in the way of 2000 charging horses and chariots and it was no doubt seriously scary, particularly when they saw it all coming at them through a long lens. They managed to throw all their kit onto the back of the truck they were using and hightail it. Neither of them was too keen on going back to the set the following day. Stewie and Pierre had pissed the crew off so much that I think director Ridley Scott decided to have some fun with them by ordering a full-scale cavalry charge!

Covering a film set takes stamina and sometimes a bit of ingenuity; luckily I have a crazy picture editor at BIG called Martin 'Leaverage' Leaver, who is a mad film-set man. I received a tip from a good source that Jordan (aka Katie Price) was going to be filming *Footballer$ Wives* (it came from her manager at the time, Dave Reed, in fact). Martin checked out the stately home where filming was to take place and drew a complete blank. Due to the extensive lawns surrounding the property there was nowhere he and his team could hide themselves away.

Then came a stroke of pure genius and invention. The team came back with some amazing pictures, which they had nailed from a vantage point nobody would have suspected. Martin had headed off to a garden centre and bought himself a few large rolls of turf. Overnight he dug out a low trough in a garden bed at the front of the great house and placed the turf on top. Then, just before first light, he and another guy slipped under the turf, leaving only a tiny ripple in the 'lawn'. They lay there all day snapping away quite happily, even though it was pretty dark and damp under there! We made all the papers the next day with huge spreads.

Martin's creative approach reminded me of my own. I've crouched in a dustbin for a whole day on jobs and once spent a day in the back of a dumpster. I had all kinds of disguises available to me, a real collection. Years ago I nicked – well, 'borrowed' long term – a British Telecom tent that I could put up to allay suspicions, and I had a whole array of hard hats and official uniforms.

A purloined British Gas uniform came in handy when I was sent by the wonderfully larger-than-life showbiz editor Baz Bamigboye, with whom I worked very closely at *The Mail*, to check out a tip. He had heard that all of the surviving Beatles were getting together to do a one-off TV interview from George Harrison's house. I headed off and got down there early in the morning and decided to 'check the gas meter'. In those days there was no such thing as privacy laws relating to photography and there was a lot of freedom. I remember Sir David English saying in my early days at the paper that he wanted me assigned to a particular job because 'Darryn will knock down a hospital door if he has to, to get the picture'. It was true. Now under the PCC it's a totally different story.

Just as I was getting myself ready, the gates to the property swung open and the first McLaren F1 road car that I had ever seen cruised out past me. It looked like solid burnished metal and I couldn't see who was driving, even through the lens. I walked in as the gates were closing and started casing the joint. At the front, off to my left, was a black tent surrounded by a lighting rig, but I couldn't get anywhere near it. Seeing a side door, I knocked and told the woman who answered that I was there to check the meter. She immediately asked which meter I meant and I could feel my fear rising. In these situations when I find myself somewhere I shouldn't be, I am always very nervous; there is so much that can go wrong, and the adrenaline really pumps. All I wanted to do was get the picture and get out. I knew I had to keep a cool head; I don't know what I would have done if I had been caught. I muttered something unconvincing about the gas and she waved me inside, suggesting that I start looking.

I began wandering around the house, which was beautiful; it had once been a priory. I heard someone coming and I panicked a little. I opened a cupboard and, when challenged, told her I was looking for the meter. Seeing my uniform, she seemed to accept this and wandered away. Seizing the initiative, I headed along the hallway, through a door at the end and out towards the black tent. As I worked out what line to take to my objective, I saw Paul McCartney's car arriving. It was an old-model Mercedes with blacked-out windows and strange mag wheels – not at all what I would have expected. The number plates read 'MPL', the name of his company. Shortly after, Ringo's car appeared and I got into position.

All of a sudden, the crew came out of the house and unfurled a huge black tarpaulin around the whole set-up. Every angle was protected. They were smart – though I don't know why they were so paranoid as I hadn't been rumbled. With my plans foiled, I had no choice but to leave without the shot. If only I'd arrived at the same time as McCartney, I might have been better placed. Missing such an amazing picture was hard to accept, but in hindsight I believe that morally what I was doing was wrong and so in a way I'm glad I missed it. I'd fire one of my guys now if he fraudulently accessed a private property. Images taken under those circumstances are unsaleable – unless, of course, they're in the public interest. Let's not forget Mr Prescott who, as acting prime minister, spent an afternoon playing croquet with his staff at his grace and favour estate in the Surrey countryside. An Englishman's home is his castle and all that, but privacy goes out the window if it's a public interest issue.

Working with people you respect and like is a privilege. When Baz Bamigboye discovered that the paper had landed an interview with actor Danny DeVito, he asked me to head over and shoot the star in the Mayfair Hotel. I love Baz. He is the prince of some tribe in Africa, a consummate schmoozer and a pleasure to work with. And he married an Aussie, which makes him doubly good! DeVito was a pleasure too. I walked into his suite with a camera and a head full of ideas. He asked me what I was after and I told him I wanted to get a shot of him sitting on the toilet, reading a newspaper and smoking a cigar. He just said, 'Whatever you want.' We got some amazing shots including one of him lying back on a sofa, cigar in hand, with his slippers arranged neatly by the sofa. He couldn't have been more cooperative.

Not everyone is as professional, of course. As a fan of Eddie Murphy I was very pleased to be sent to the Dorchester to shoot him. Right from the off, though, things didn't look promising.

**'I told him I wanted to get a shot of him sitting on the toilet, reading a newspaper and smoking a cigar'**

I couldn't believe the acne he had. He was a real short-arse, too. I towered above him, and I'm 5 foot 7. It seemed the only words to pass his lips were, 'No, I'm not doing that.' I received the same response to every request I made. Eventually I told him that if he wasn't doing it, then neither was I, and walked off. I could hear him shrieking as I disappeared. I did get bollocked, but he was a complete prick. I used to love him on the big screen, but he wasn't what I thought he would be.

I suppose that's why the profession is called acting. Murphy seemed to be a prima donna, to say the least, but maybe he just got out of bed on the wrong side that day.

While people like Murphy made me question why I was in the business, I did get to meet some of my heroes too. After starting BIG Pictures, I found myself attending some very worthwhile functions as well as the usual celebrity haunts.

I took a table at a gala event for the Number One children's charity, which a good friend of mine, the fashion entrepreneur Robert de Keyser, is heavily involved with. Each year they have a huge auction and this particular year (2004) I went potty. I bought an autographed U2 guitar for £8000 and a day at the cricket in Ian Botham's box for £3000. When I wrote out the cheque I didn't know who I was going to be sharing my day with, but it turned out to be Piers Morgan, then editor of the *Daily Mirror*, TV presenter Jamie Theakston, celebrated actor Peter O'Toole and, of course, the legendary Ian 'Beefy' Botham.

We had a wonderful day at Lord's Cricket Ground; I went with my accountant at the time, Mahendra. All day long, legends of the game would pop in to say hello and the booze flowed. I turned up with a collection of white cricket balls to be signed – I haven't changed since I was a kid! O'Toole looked really aged but was in fine form and he, Morgan and myself argued over who would be in our all-time World XI. O'Toole wrote his team of the century out on the back of a napkin, which I think Piers Morgan walked away with, and he signed my ticket for me – sadly, the company I sent this memento to for framing managed to lose it. By early afternoon, we were already so drunk that I was bowling O'Toole napkins and he was gamely batting with a knife from the table. Theakston was at silly mid-off, Morgan at long on and I think Botham was keeping. Sandwiches, pastries and tea were being brought out and ignored, but the wine and champagne were going down very nicely. O'Toole played a wonderful pull shot that took the cream topping off the cakes. Great shot, ol' man!

BIG Pictures had actually turned Jamie Theakston over only a few weeks previously, and he was initially very cautious around me. But the drink soon removed any awkwardness. He is an exceptional cricketer and got very high up in the amateur game, so we had plenty to talk about. After the match, he and I went to a pub in Primrose Hill and chatted up women (this was obviously after I'd split with Mel). It was a hot summer's day and from there we headed over to Notting Hill. There were girls everywhere and Jamie was much in demand, having just split up with actress Joely Richardson. Mel turned up at some point with our dog, Amber, as she had to head off somewhere herself, so I ended up toting a dog around the pubs of West London. Luckily, Amber likes a drink and can slurp up a pint quicker than most men I know. She and I left Jamie to it at about three in the morning and headed home. Booze, cricket, Hollywood legends and women – it doesn't get much better than that.

That day at Lord's was a fantastic experience, but it wasn't the only time I found myself in the orbit of my cricketing idols. I was staking out Browns nightclub one night in the early '90s, all on my own, when I spotted two guys leaving very quickly. To my amazement I recognised Dennis Lillee and Jeff Thomson; they had a gorgeous brunette with them and I got a slight nod from Lillee – who is, of course, God – that told me not to take the picture.

I didn't know what the story was – probably something perfectly innocent – but there was no way that I wanted to run the risk of compromising the guy who had meant so much to me through the years. At one stage there had been no one else in my life apart from Dennis Lillee! That night at Browns also reminded me of the time I sat in the notorious MCG Bay 13 with my father, watching Thommo bowling. Though he is unquestionably one of the all-time greats, that day the crowd was chanting abuse at him as he'd put on a little weight and wasn't bowling anywhere near his peak. The public can be very unforgiving. 'Who ate all the pies?' was the chant after lunch.

Though the paparazzi often have a bad reputation, there is a code of conduct that I adhere to and expect my staff to respect. Lillee and Thommo were off limits. There was no need for me to debate the rights and wrongs of it. Despite what some people may believe, I know where to draw the line, as I did when my skipper phoned up and told me that Simply Red singer Mick Hucknall had chartered my boat in the south of France. I refused to pap him as he was on my boat and I didn't want to abuse that arrangement. The opposition got him, of course. Excellent shots, too – another 'Who ate all the pies?' story, as Mick had put on a considerable amount of weight.

Some people in the public eye seem not to understand the balanced relationship that has to exist between them, the media and their public. Every pap hates Jude Law and Ewan McGregor because they have none of the style of the old school stars, yet they think they are a class above the rest of us.

Many celebrities seem to think they represent a step forward in evolution. It's interesting that since both Law and McGregor have become litigious, their careers seem to have stalled. They very quickly forget where they have come from, and I, for one, can't wait to see them returned there.

As a photographer, I have been in a position to record the foibles of the fickle celebrity world, but have also been granted access to the more rarefied world of royalty and politics. Many people are not lucky enough to see behind the curtain in the theatre of power and I count what little access I have enjoyed as a real privilege.

Early in my career, I was sent down to the House of Lords to cover the opening of parliament and record the Queen performing her duty. I loved seeing the corridors all decked out in gold. Being the son of a man whom I consider to be the best architect in the world, I really appreciate great buildings. It was a privilege to be there – it is a beautiful chamber and an honour to be allowed in. Being an Australian, it was amazing for me to be so close to the Queen and see her robes – I loved the white and black of the ermine fur – and the astounding wealth that literally covered her. And I wasn't surrounded by sheep this time!

Andy Kyle was obsessed by the royals. I remember how excited he was when I happened across Prince Harry's birthday party as I was nosing round Kensington Palace, and when I got some fantastic shots of William being spanked at a school sports day. All the planning and strategy in the world can't beat being in the right place and hitting at the right time. Jim Bennett – the greatest royal pap I ever met – was at William's school with me. On this day, Jim and I were the last to pack away. A lot of the other guys saw what was happening with William, but all their gear was back in their bags. Jim and I nailed the shot. He had a better shot of the spanking, but I had the tears – we just hit at different times. Like I've said before one of the rules of thumb, even now with the incredible shutter speeds available, is that if you actually see the moment through the finder, you've missed it. Ten per cent of a great press photographer's talent lies in taking the picture; the other 90 per cent is being in the right place at the right time to get it. Persistence, patience and hard work are the watchwords. Sometimes you just have to wait – wait till the crowds have gone, wait till the melee has died down, wait till it's right. Above and beyond the call gets results. Jim made a fortune with that picture, but I was just on a shift and made sod all!

While I was a monarchist for a long while, there was one particular set of images that, if I had sold them, would probably have caused me to be executed in the Tower of London. I walked into the office one morning and Mel laughingly called me over and said that I had to check out the pictures that had just arrived from our agency in France. Prince Charles and Camilla Parker Bowles (who at the time were lovers) were on holiday over there in a private villa and one of the paps had got a shot of Camilla topless. I couldn't wait to see the images – some kind of sick fascination, I guess – but I knew immediately that they would get any paper into serious trouble with the PCC. The shots the pap had stolen were of Camilla as she slipped into her swimsuit. They were actually very sweet and romantic images of a couple very much enjoying their time together. I knew they were worth either loads of money or nothing. That's often how it works in this industry.

I got straight on the phone to Andy Coulson, who at the time hadn't been in the editor's chair at *News of the World* for long. 'Andy,' I said, 'I've got a fucking corker!' He couldn't believe what I was telling him and we agreed to meet the following morning at Simpson's-in-the-Strand, which is the embodiment of the establishment in Britain and not the place to whip out shots of the future king of England's wife topless. We ordered kippers and English tea and all the trimmings and sat down to chat. As the waiter, who was at the very least seventy not out, was pouring tea for me I pulled the first print out of the envelope. I just couldn't resist. The tea went all over the table, and he scurried off as fast as he could go. I can imagine the conversations that went on in the kitchens and backrooms that day – Camilla could have given Jordan a run for her money in the fame stakes!

Andy blanched, then laughed and told me there was no way that the paper could use them – though he did take the prints away with him. I laughed and told him I knew that would be the case, but that we would both dine out on the story for years. With Camilla, any picture desk looks for the opposite of what we used to look for with Diana. Only shots of Camilla looking dreadful are likely to make it even today when she is more widely accepted, whereas with Diana no picture desk would service a shot of her looking anything but radiant – to be honest, she always looked good in our pictures anyway. It's a shame, really, but that's business. Not many people know that Camilla's grandmother was once a royal mistress, too – so she was keeping a tradition alive.

Royalty and politics may not have been the spheres that made me famous, but I have always had a keen interest in them. I was quite affected by the death of John Smith, the Labour leader who died suddenly from a heart attack in 1994. On the day the sad news broke, I headed down to Westminster Green to get some of the reaction and of course get a feel for what people were saying about who would succeed him. The place was full of journalists and camera crews. I was waiting for my *Mail* journalist partner to park the car when, off to one side, I saw a man all on his own, heading away from the action. Something about him drew me, and I had a premonition that this man was going to be the next prime minister. I had no idea who he was and debated whether I should photograph him or not. I decided that I should and so basically papped him, much to his surprise. He laughed and said, 'Thank you', and headed off. I wish

I had put money on the rise of that man – one Tony Blair, the MP for Sedgefield.

Though I admired Blair as an operator, I am a Tory through and through and when I came to the UK, I was certainly one of 'Thatcher's children'. I have two signed copies of her autobiography, although I have to confess I have never read it. I believe we all need to strive to make our space in this world; inherited money is no guarantee of wealth, and they say that every third generation loses it. Good – it leaves some cash for me.

Naturally, not all politicians are as amenable as Blair was that day. One of my guys had an absolute nightmare with Bill Clinton when Clinton was touring Australia. Shane Partridge, a real bruiser of a guy, was assigned to the job of getting a frame and the debacle that unfolded brings a smile to my face even now. Shane was always a walking disaster and in some sort of trouble, though he is now very successful in LA. He needed a lot of consoling and managing. (Funnily enough, a lot of the best snappers do – they are a sensitive breed, rather like actors. I was never sensitive, but I always liked a pat on the back.) Having weighed up the various options, I decided that Shane should try to get a shot of Clinton jogging. In order to beat the security team, he arrived in the park at the crack of dawn having done his surveillance, and hid himself in a dustbin. As Clinton appeared, Shane leapt from his hiding place and started hitting pictures. In a fraction of a second, he was being absolutely pummelled by Clinton's bodyguards, getting a real working-over. He was relieved of all of his gear and sent on his way. I thought it was hilarious, though I guess Shane was lucky not to have been shot – *very* lucky, given that every gun in the President's security team was aimed at Shane's rather large head!

# ST TROPEZ

**BIG HAS ALWAYS DONE** a lot of work in St Tropez on the Côte d'Azur in summer. I love the place because it is a hotbed for celebrities and also because it is the biggest small village in the world. In the winter it has a population of 5000; by the middle of July it attracts 150 000. The weather is also fantastic. The place reminds me of home – I'm not sure if it's the sun or the blue water – and I always feel relaxed when I am there.

I went down to St Tropez in 2001 in the middle of a cold and blustery English winter to meet a couple of estate agents. I was looking to buy a property for the business, as working there so often was costing us a fortune in rent. I looked around the whole area for three days before finally being able to view a property I'd seen in the brochure and immediately liked. It was a beautiful 600-year-old stone cottage, right on the harbour, and as soon as I saw it I made an offer and got it. The house has been great for the business, and for me. A simple but very romantic building, it's the kind of place that, if you walk a woman through the door, you are guaranteed to *faire l'amour*.

The first year that BIG operated from the property in St Tropez was very interesting. War almost immediately broke out between us and the French paps who had previously had the run of the place. It was like Britain versus France with an Aussie thrown in as General MacArthur! The French paps, especially Eliot Press and Angeli, had a stranglehold until we got in on the scene. Previously we had been syndicating their material; now we were taking them on in their own backyard. The dirty tricks were unbelievable. There was a lot of bitterness and we endured sabotage, break-ins at the house and missing gear. In our first year, we really kicked their arse. Now they have seized a little of the initiative back, but it is still a great hunting ground for us. As in all competition, the best pic wins the day. That's just the way it is.

Every Easter the BIG management used to go out there, ten or twelve of us in a two-bedroom place – a tradition that seems to have fallen by the wayside. We would basically run the company for a week from there. These days I doubt I would allow things to be operated in that way. It was mayhem – huge drinking sessions, intra-office affairs (though not me, of course), all sorts.

In 2003 I decided that our set-up was good, but that if we had a boat we could actually get out there among our quarry, get better positions and probably have more fun. I also realised that I could charter the boat when we weren't using it. So that was that. I took on a huge commitment and purchased a two-storey 60-foot Sunseeker Manhattan with a jet rib on the back. I invited the BIG team to join me on its inaugural voyage; I was so proud. It was a wonderful weekend, though it pissed with rain.

**'I can sit there with my binoculars, a glass of bubbly and a nice chicken salad and wait for them to come to me'**

Right from the off the boat was a huge success, though we've had some dodgy skippers in our time. We use it a lot for set-ups, where we make the yacht available to celebs in return for a set of shots. For a couple of years I also leased a private jet and the two worked particularly well in tandem. I often went down for the weekend; the harbour was a four-minute drive from the private airfield and we had a full-time skipper and hostess. It was an expensive habit, of course, but I wouldn't have swapped it for the world.

The boat has been an excellent business tool as it hands us the keys to the celebrities' playground. We are out there with them, though they don't necessarily know it. It's the ultimate paparazzo camouflage. We monitor boats, but we also know where people are staying. I can sit there with my binoculars, a glass of bubbly and a nice chicken salad and wait for them to come to me. The scoops we've landed have been endless: everyone from Kevin Costner to Brad Pitt and Jennifer Aniston. We've had some amazing exclusives. One summer Elle Macpherson tethered up next to us by coincidence and we got a great set of her. I turned up on the yacht to a *Vanity Fair* party at the Hotel du Cap and, assuming that a seeming high roller like myself must have been invited, they just let me in. Richard Young and Dave Bennett were the photographers who had been invited exclusively, and their jaws dropped to the bottom of the Mediterranean when they saw me. Truly this was 'lifestyles of the rich and famous' and I was living it – and also working hard. A dream combination – but remember the three Fs in business: if it flies, floats or fucks, rent it. This is a golden rule, but one I have enjoyed breaking.

I love St Tropez. It's probably the greatest place in the world for people-watching, and that's what I am – the people watcher. People fascinate me: all shapes, all sizes, all colours, boobs, legs, you name it. There's a cafe called Le Gorille and I often install myself there and just watch the world go by, not only watching for celebs but people generally.

Spending time in St Tropez makes me very happy and I have made some good friends down there, notably my Mr Fixit and confidant, Olivier Maassen. He and I met seven years ago in the restaurant that he used to run near my house. I was a big fan of the place and was in almost every night. I was probably their best customer and after the first couple of visits I didn't even bother looking at the menu – Olivier would just ask me what I wanted to eat. He began to order in my favourite wines and would often join my guests and me at our table. Olivier and I quickly became friends. There was no way he could miss me, dressing the way I do. Even in St Tropez I stick out like a sore thumb – though Olivier tells me that I was the first in the resort to dress in such a flamboyant way. He had no idea what line of business I was in – we just got on and started to stay in touch when I was not in town. He introduced me to everyone in St Tropez and I became a kind of honorary local.

We had not seen each other for two years and then in 2005 I met him by chance in the clothes store that he now runs in the main square. He had sold the restaurant and moved on, as all good entrepreneurs do. These days whenever I am heading to St Tropez I phone ahead to Olivier and he arranges everything I might need. The fact that I don't speak French can be a problem. Without the language I am at a disadvantage. St Tropez is a town that runs on gossip and I have learned to be a little more tactful than I would otherwise be.

This is also the kind of town where it is easy to get ripped off. Most businesses in St Tropez only operate for four months of the year, so they are keen to make as much money as possible. Olivier is always there to check bills and ensure that we get what we pay for. When I bought my house, he was away on business and he still kicks himself because he thinks he could have got me a better deal. He has in the past warned me about over-tipping in restaurants and clubs. He is very protective of me and makes sure that no one takes advantage of me. Once he even got into a fist-fight on my behalf with someone who was getting in my face on the street outside a nightclub.

The Palm restaurant was one of our favourite haunts and a few years ago we would be there every night. It's a superb restaurant and they treat me like a king.

After the Palm we would head off to the Papagayo club and continue the fun. The owner of the club is one of Olivier's friends and always looks after us. We have had some insane nights in the private room – I remember partying there with Olivier and fifteen girls, ten of whom were naked. There was one crazy Russian girl in particular who was not scared to express herself.

**'I remember partying there with Olivier and fifteen girls, ten of whom were naked'**

Despite the fact that Olivier works all day he has amazing stamina and is out every night. He can get by on two hours' sleep and sees maintaining a high social profile as an essential public relations exercise for his shop. Often when he is working I will be hanging out at the cafe next door and we'll chat and smoke together during the day. Olivier knows a lot of girls in St Tropez and most of them seem to be very much in the mood for some adult fun.

Olivier is extraordinarily well connected and in a town like St Tropez you need to be. He knows everybody. If I want girls, champagne, whatever, he can arrange it. Freeing up a table in a fully booked restaurant is another of Olivier's specialities. He is very comfortable around the stars who visit St Tropez. They may be global celebrities, but he is a celebrity in St Tropez! I am very well known there myself these days and have even had a couple of fans of the *Paparazzi* show outside my front door waiting for autographs.

My nights out are now less frequent, but they can still be as full-on as ever. Olivier and I are very close and can talk about anything. We know each other's secrets. Olivier says that the best time that he has ever had with me was when the two of us shared a quiet meal aboard the boat and just chatted. That's a measure of the man. He and I have plans for a business together. We're going to shake the town up!

It was through Olivier that, on Good Friday 2006, I met one of the legends of erotic photography. David Hamilton resides in Ramatuelle, a village just behind St Tropez, and Olivier mentioned by chance that this hero of mine was a friend of his father. Naturally, I jumped at the chance to meet Hamilton at the bar of his usual haunt, the beach club Cinquante Cinq. He has photographed many of the most beautiful young things on the planet and published scores of books, one of which I bought at the age of seventeen. I have always loved the quality and texture of his work; he has a wonderful way with the human form, especially nude females.

Hamilton was drinking black sambuca and was full of great stories. He was fantastic company, a true eccentric. After several drinks he drove me up to his place in Ramatuelle, where he has lived since 1962. Apparently he made a trade with the owner of the premises – Hamilton traded the woman he was with for the house. He got a good deal. The place was full of his works, stacked up against every surface – one of the best filing systems I have ever seen. I met his latest mistress, who looked all of sixteen, when she returned from school! Hamilton really gave me the urge to get out and take pictures again. It's been too long since I got behind a camera; perhaps I have been too busy building businesses.

**'It's a tough job, but somebody's gotta do it'**

# Glamour Girls

**THE FIRST TIME** I worked with Jordan, the surgically enhanced UK glamour model whose real name is Katie Price, was in St Tropez. Her manager, Dave Reed, and I were great mates and we decided to head down there and do some sets. When I walked up to Jordan/Katie at the airport she was stony-faced and quite definitely hung over – she loved her vodka in those days. She kept the steely expression up until I greeted her with a cheery, 'G'day, you cunt!' She pissed herself laughing and declared that she was going to like me – why, I'll never know. That was the first time I had met her and since that moment we have had a great friendship. She's very brazen, with thirteen different personalities, but she's a wonderful, lovely girl.

We had one of the best weekends of my life: me, Dave, Jordan and a glamour model called Jerri Byrne who Dave was 'representing' at the time. Though we partied hard, in two days I shot fourteen different sets of pictures; that's 1268 frames. Katie was a dedicated worker – she knew that every frame was money – but my main memory is of her standing naked on my boat singing. She's got a fantastic voice.

At one point on the first day Katie was completely naked and posing on the back of the boat. The water around us was full of French teenage boys, all desperately treading water, trying to keep themselves afloat and simultaneously take shots with their disposable cameras. Hilarious, to say the least! They couldn't believe those breasts. Three bottles of champagne

**'She walked up to the sheikh's table, grabbed one of his bottles of champagne and downed it'**

and vodka had gone down by this point – and that's three of each. Those poor guys trod water for the best part of an hour; it's amazing none of them drowned – but what a way to go. What a girl.

We staggered off the boat – Katie literally falling off – and went to a restaurant that was also playing host to an extremely important Arab sheikh. Despite the fact that she wasn't wearing a lot – she generally didn't – Katie decided that she wanted to dance. She walked up to the sheikh's table, grabbed one of his bottles of champagne (a Dom Perignon '63, I seem to recall) and downed it. Before I knew it, she had headed back to our table and grabbed me and we hit the dance floor. In truth, we hit it pretty hard because we were so pissed we couldn't stand. I ended up lying on top of her, my face between those magnificent pillows. 'Not a bad life,' I remember thinking. 'Giddy up! I've died and gone to heaven.'

The following day we had monstrous hangovers, but Katie is a true professional and we got some more sets done. That night we headed to the Palm for dinner and then, after a few more bars, we moved on to Papagayo for yet more Grey Goose vodka and Cristal champagne. Dave and Jerri had reached their limit by this point and headed back, but after the club closed Katie and I somehow ended up on a billionaire's 200-foot mega yacht in St Tropez harbour. There was a party in full swing and she wanted to join in. They had armed guards all over the boat, but it's extraordinary what a set of tits like hers can do. The owner spotted her pretty quickly and tried to get her into a bedroom even quicker, but I played chaperone and made sure she was OK. Not that she gave a shit. In fact, she could probably get herself out of any situation. She's a very intelligent woman, though she does play dumb a lot.

Not only did Katie want to party, she wanted to DJ and sing. She took over the sound system and held court to great effect. It was all pretty spectacular until she dropped her bottle of vodka into the system and blew it up. Had it been anyone else, they would probably have been shot – but she got away with it. Katie always does. It was, however, definitely time to go. I realised that I would be carrying her. She may be beautiful, tall and slim, but I had to carry those boobs as well!

We staggered back, cracked open another bottle of vodka and set the world to rights on the back of my boat in front of the Capitainerie, watching the carousel on the shore sparkle. I remember Katie talking about her dream wedding; she promised that it would be a real-life fairytale affair. (She wasn't wrong. I would have loved to have been there. While a lot of people have decried her and Peter Andre's wedding as a huge stunt, I'm sure there is something there. Whoever ended up with her had to be prepared to accept that Katie would always wear the trousers. I guess Pete is fine with that. As far as I'm concerned, he's a top bloke.)

Finally we got some sleep. After breakfast the following day we did another couple of sets, at Katie's insistence. She is a trouper. Both BIG and Katie made some pretty decent money out of various shots – though I dented my profit margin by buying her a Chopard watch and ring for about twenty-five grand at the airport. Anyone getting to know that girl falls in love with her personality.

I don't really see her these days, but if I bumped into her I know we'd pick up just where we left off. We're both very busy people – busy building our empires. She is a master at reinventing herself. Her new management has taken her in a totally new direction, one that will ensure far greater longevity. Back then we all knew what worked: 'Tits out, back of a boat, thank you very much.'

She invited me to Peter's first gig after he appeared on *I'm A Celebrity, Get Me Out of Here,* and I took my sister Vikki, her husband Raoul and their kids Sarsha and Oliver, but it was very crowded backstage so we didn't hang around. Katie is still a very good friend of the company and there's no doubt she is the best glamour model of all time. She knows how to play the game and has done incredibly well. She has become an icon of celebrity and the doyenne of photo shoots and will always be my number one.

Some people love to play the game with the paparazzi and it can become a real cat-and-mouse scenario, often with a lot of laughs along the way. Early in my career I spent a lot of time covering Mandy Smith, the model and one-time 'child bride' of Rolling Stone Bill Wyman. I used to doorstep her all the time because she lived in Coniston Road, around the corner from my £45-a-week bed-sit. She used to wind the snappers up and you could never tell what would happen.

On one memorable morning I went round to her house very early, well before anyone else, and knocked at the door begging, saying I really needed a picture. A couple of minutes later, up came the sash window on the first floor and out came Mandy and her magnificent mop of blonde hair. She was amazing. Everything was perfect: the light, her eyes, her teeth, her hair. I hit it on a 180 mm telephoto lens and ended up with a truly iconic image, a beautiful picture of a beautiful girl, which *The Mail* ran right across page three.

It was a great exclusive for us as this was the day she announced her engagement and no one else got anything. It was also very early in my career and caused a real stir at the paper. There's no doubt in my mind that Mandy wanted someone to get a great image to go with the story. I was always trying to stay ahead of the pack when it came to her; I remember going around once on Halloween and papping her when she gave some sweets to kids trick-or-treating.

Hers was a regular doorstep in those days; she was huge. I used to panic about getting shots of her. We'd all be there: Nigel Wright from *The Mirror*, Aubrey Hart from *The Standard* (a real pain in the arse who whinged about everything), Tim Cornell from the *Daily Star* and Ted Bath, a freelance snapper for *The Telegraph*, a wonderful old gentleman.

Mandy loved to play hide-and-seek with the press in her heyday. It could be a real pantomime. I chased her on the back of a motorbike after her wedding and I remember shooting her years later when she was with footballer Pat Van Den Hauwe. I met Mandy herself recently at a launch event for *The Magazine* in Manchester, a venture in which at one point I was going to invest. I ended up giving her a lift back to London afterwards and we had a good chat; it was like talking to your sister. She's such a sweetheart and told me that she wished we had known each other at the height of her fame as we could have made a fortune together. Too right!

Sometimes working closely with people can sour a relationship. Model Sophie Anderton was one client of ours who seemed to lose control of the game and caused an initially fruitful connection to come to an end. Sophie came to me after she had been through a terrible relationship break-up with Aussie goalkeeper Mark Bosnich and had got herself seriously embroiled in the bitter world of cocaine addiction. She seemed to have turned her life around and was now seeing a guy called Mark Alexiou, who was involved with running the Pangaea nightclub. At the same time I was getting involved with the Attica club in London, and I met Sophie there. Mark Alexiou is a lovely guy and he coped amazingly well with Sophie; I wouldn't have a bad word to say about him. I told them I could help them turn around her image if they signed up with me. Coincidentally, at the same time Mark Bosnich approached me, and we have in fact done set-ups with him in Dubai to try and help him sort out his image. I feel that he was a victim of circumstance to a degree.

Visually, Sophie is a stunning woman. She's an excellent model and could have been one of the world's greatest, but she can be scatty. If anyone needs a manager it's her, and she's been through several. She talks at 150 miles an hour; I'm not sure if that's a layover from doing so much charlie. We were close friends and I never once saw her take drugs. She was virtually bankrupt when she came to me, despite owning clothes that probably cost close to half a million pounds. I remember her discussing organising an eBay clothes auction with Mel. She should have done it, but I gave her an advance against her first earnings to save her home and car from repossession.

We enjoyed each other's company and before long we did a deal and drew up a twelve-month contract. The first set-up we did was in one of London's parks, with Sophie relaxing doing yoga. Do you think Sophie had ever done yoga before? Not that I knew of. We sold it for good money to the *Sunday People*, who ran it as a double-page spread. Bang! We were off. She was on a percentage and was going to do well out of it. I got her a big fashion deal with designer Jeff Banks, loads of free clothes, and we even went off to the Maldives on a *Sunday Mirror* shoot, which was fantastic. We ended up with around fifteen sets of pictures from that trip. We were making great money and it was all the right image – at the time she was involved in making her own documentary and described me as the best thing that had ever happened to her. She was back, big time.

The honeymoon was over pretty quickly, however, and we soon began wrangling over the contract. Sophie actually claimed that she had thought the split between us was the other way around, despite the figures being crystal clear on the contract we had both signed. That kind of attitude saddens me. Someone – I believe it was Jason Fraser – offered her a sweeter deal and she was off. Hey, that's competition and I'm fine with it. I couldn't start giving her money that I knew I was never going to make back.

She did a couple more set-ups and that seemed to be it. Short term, I'm sure they made more money out of those two shoots than they would have made with me over the same period, but look at her now.

I started working with Abi Titmuss after another chance encounter at Attica. I was enjoying one of then boss Marios's Saturday-night dinner parties with some real movers and shakers. Marios was a wonderful host. He loved women and loved spending money. Abi was at the club, we got chatting and I offered her a deal. Lots of other people wanted to get involved as she was on the rise, but we met up again over dinner and sorted out an arrangement. She was about to sign a deal with another agent – a colourful character and a wonderful salesman who told people he was somehow involved with the *EastEnders* TV show and was starting a talent agency. He made everyone a lot of promises, but then disappeared for a while, split from Celebrity Pictures and eventually reappeared.

After our initial conversation, Abi met up with me with her recently appointed PR, a good girl called Sam Mortner, from Taylor Herring. They sat down with me and I explained how things would work and that I would turn over a quarter of a million pounds for Abi in her first twelve months with me, just from pictures. Sam was very protective of Abi, but she was fine once I had explained how it all worked. Abi would be on 30 or 40 per cent, which was a good deal, and we agreed we could do studio shoots too. She was about to take off.

The first set of shots we did was of her with some girlfriends down in the south of France. We worked really hard and shot eight or nine sets, all manner of shots, at all hours, day and night. Next I took her to Barbados and St Lucia to get some more sets done and we had fun. She's a very bright girl and very ambitious.

She made a lot of cash, particularly compared to what she had earned as a nurse – I reached my target for the first year, and the second year was even better. When I had been simply dealing with her PRs everything was fine, but the dynamic changed. If I'd been able to sit down with her, things could have been sorted out, as our arrangements had always been conducted personally. I was upset and warned her that eventually we would fall out over it. The contract kept being renegotiated and it got to the point that it wasn't worth me working with her any more. Despite the

**'We worked really hard and shot eight or nine sets, all manner of shots at all hours, day and night'**

fact that I had put a lot of heart and soul into her and really created her press profile, I was frozen out.

Sometimes people don't realise that what we do leads to more work and makes the job of management much easier.

**'Sometimes people don't realise that what we do leads to more work…'**

Many of the girls I've taken amazing shots of have proved themselves great sports and also to have very capable business minds. Rachel Hunter impressed me greatly when she hit London to shoot a big Ultimo lingerie campaign. I was trying to get in with her management and we set up a meeting at the Dorchester. It went really well. We just chatted. I sorted her out with some sleeping pills as she was dead on her feet after the flight from LA, and told her I had bought the Lamborghini that used to belong to her ex, Rod Stewart, and that it was now garaged in Geelong. I told her I had often wondered what went on in the passenger seat. 'Not much, darling,' she told me, laughing. We got on really well; she's a Kiwi girl and I'm an Aussie boy. She told me she had been near Melbourne very recently and had been surfing off Torquay, not far from Geelong. Shame I missed it – it would have made for some wonderful shots. She was a lovely person, a genuine busy mum, on the phone to her kids throughout her stay. Following our meeting, we did some pictures in Battersea Park and afterwards shopped for stuff she misses when she's in the States.

Another Antipodean export with whom I had great fun was Elle Macpherson's sister, Mimi. She was signed through BIG Australia to be the face of Foster's beer as I knew her from Australia. She was a great girl, a real crack. It must be difficult to be the sibling of someone as successful as Elle. Mimi arrived right in the middle of my insane party period after I had split from Mel. My driver and I picked her up from the airport and she headed back to my place to get changed. She was here to party and I was ready to go. We got on really well and I have to say that I think she's got an even better body than her sister.

Mel, Melissa Kelly from BIG Australia, Mimi and I went out to the Atlantic Bar and by the time the food arrived, Mimi and I weren't interested. We just wanted to drink and party. Mel and Melissa left us to it and we kept raging despite the fact that Mimi had an all-day shoot the following day. We ended up back at Elle's London home – she was away at the time – in the flat that Mimi had beneath Elle's main property. It was eight in the morning and we had an hour to go until the start of the shoot. Mimi wasn't worried. She grabbed some more champagne and told me to come upstairs while she got ready. We went into Elle's bedroom – realising another ambition of mine! All around the walls were beautiful black-and-white shots of Elle, each one showing a different section of her body. They were amazing and very arty – they looked like the work of Rankin or one of the other greats. Mimi stripped off and ran into the shower, which was quite a sight.

We then got her to the shoot, which was a long one. By the end of it she was exhausted. Due to the partying, dealing with her was hard work, but good fun!

# SUPERSTARS AND MADMEN

**HOT PICS OF A-LIST COUPLES**

**EXPERIENCING CELEBRITY** is like opening a gate to another world. Always exciting, often hilarious, it's fun to gaze in wonder, but you need to remember that the whole thing is like a house of cards. On occasion, this crazy existence will just reach out and pull you in and the only option is to hold on and enjoy the ride. One of the funniest twenty-four hours of my life unfolded when I was sent by *The Mail* to cover legendary actor Jack Nicholson on one of his famous London nights out and I ended up getting rather closer to the action than I'd planned. The resultant images made a splash for *The Mail*, who produced a double-page spread called 'The 24 hours of Jack'. I didn't see the feature until it was a couple of days old because I was recovering.

The shift started at a show at the Whitehall Theatre (now the Trafalgar Studios). Nicholson was partying there with Simply Red's Mick Hucknall, of all people, watching some sexy show. *The Mail* photographers' room had received a tip that Nicholson would be heading to the theatre and so when his car arrived I was waiting, camera in hand. The limo stopped at the front door and it became obvious that the car was bouncing up and down. After a brief pause, the driver gunned the engine and drove off around the block, returning to the same spot a few minutes later. Finally Jack emerged, leaving his friend in the car.

By slipping the doorman a few quid, I managed to sneak backstage and bang off some shots of Jack before returning to the kerb to snap him getting into the car. He wound the window down, leaned out and said, 'If you're going to follow me around all night, you might as well be comfortable. Get in.' He was already off his trolley and we had a great night. The first port of call was a restaurant, though I don't recall him eating, and then we went on to Browns nightclub. After half an hour he came out of there with a girl and took her back to the Connaught hotel where he was staying. Later he emerged from his suite and headed back to Browns again, before returning once more to the Connaught with another girl. And then again.

I thought I was a goer, but I've never seen a man with Nicholson's energy. The final shot of the series run by *The Mail* was taken by John Gordon of PapPix, because I had flaked out by that point. John's shots showed Jack half-naked, looking truly exhausted, grabbing some fresh air from his hotel window. This was a true life lesson. I was a young man wanting to be a playboy and Jack – other than perhaps Hugh Hefner – was the best, the master party man.

Nicholson is a pro who knows the game. He is a movie producer's dream because he knows how to play the press, is a great showman and can always generate interest in his films. He even managed to turn the turkey that was *Wolf* into a hit in the UK by making sure that pictures of him dropping his trousers and diving off a yacht with his backside hanging out hit every national newspaper and made him a talking point on the day of the film's release. I bumped into Jack recently, walking round St Tropez. He was shouting, 'I'm the greatest!' over and over. Ironic that he played a nutter in *One Flew Over the Cuckoo's Nest*; it seems that he is one now!

Covering the antics of nutters is all part of the game, of course. When Michael Jackson arrived in London in the late '80s/early '90s, every pap was off on a mad chase. *The Mail* team hired courier bikes to shadow him around town and my brief for the whole week was to perch on the back of a huge motorbike and follow him. My mate Ken Lennox got the first shots of him after his latest round of plastic surgery – fucking horrible. Lennox ended up picture editor at *The Sun* and now does his own PR thing. He is one of the greats.

Jackson was kooky, but heading down to Ozzy Osbourne's mansion near Beaconsfield to photograph his wife, Sharon, was even more of an eye-opener. She was wonderful and very accommodating. Little did I know that in future years we'd become great mates, exchanging Christmas cards and gifts. We walked through their mansion looking for a suitable location for the shots and the place was unbelievable, full of cats and dogs. I asked her where Ozzy was and suggested that maybe we could do something with both of them. Sharon told me that wasn't going to be possible as Ozzy had been out all night and wasn't in the house. He was apparently out in the woods in the grounds of the house, dressed up in combats, equipped with night-vision gear and God knows what. As she was telling me this, over her shoulder I could see this crazy character who looked like he'd just walked out of Iraq running across the lawn behind her. Complete fucking nutcase, but you've got to love him. He's one of the world's great characters.

Musicians have always been favourites of mine and I have had great commercial success working with them. I got some fantastic exclusive shots when the Spice Girls were in Bali in 1996. I also got arrested. I had called in a few favours and tracked them down to the Four Seasons hotel. I headed out there with a small support team and we hired an old Chinese guy and his wooden canoe, borrowed some of his clothes and a coolie hat and headed out to sea. We were getting some fantastic stuff and it was all exclusive, as none of the other agencies knew the girls' location. Action shots, topless shots – we were hitting the target. Then, suddenly, we got busted like never before. The security team working with the band had called in the Indonesian navy, who arrived in a bloody destroyer!

The first whiff of the impending disaster came when some gun-toting military personnel sped towards us in a high-powered jet rib. I've rarely been so surprised in my life. The navy guys turned us over to the girls' security, which was when things became a lot less funny. They kicked the shit out of me, really tore into me. Luckily, just before I was collared I had managed to stuff the exposed film into my undies. I gave them some blank film, instead, to stop them kicking me. Later, I also slipped away from the security guys

**'I got dragged off to a filthy jail cell. Just me and two hookers – no change there!'**

for a second and was able to palm the lot to my junior, Adrian Turner, who was on the beach watching with an open mouth. He cleared off sharpish and I got dragged off to a filthy jail cell. Just me and two hookers – no change there! The Australian Embassy lawyer who turned up to see me was dressed in a scruffy creased black suit and a comedy tie. He was no joker, though; he not only got the charges against me dropped – all for a bottle of Jack Daniel's and US$200 cash – but charges were actually laid against the Spice Girls' heavies. They weren't laughing quite so hard then. To top it all off, the *Sunday People* splashed on our exclusive pictures.

The Spice Girls were huge business for BIG Pictures and we have had excellent commercial success with images of them collectively and on their own. One of the best deals I ever did was to pay six grand for a set of pictures of Geri Halliwell from a guy out in Windsor. He had a full set of nude images of Geri that had been taken prior to the Spice Girls hitting the big time. She was in a forest completely starkers. He got in touch with me through an intermediary, Mark Saunders, a great royal photographer who used to haunt Diana. The pictures of Geri went out for minimum reproduction costs of a couple of grand a time (though we did some exclusive deals initially) and they made a packet. It was a picture agency's dream – the pictures got used and used and used again. Six grand was a lot of money then; we certainly made a decent profit. We should probably put them out again now: 'This is what she used to look like'. I used to have a bit of a thing for Geri; I liked her attitude. I am really impressed by women who truly know what they want, 'what they really, really want', even though they will always wear you out in the end.

Victoria Beckham and obviously David are still very important for us. I have had mixed thoughts and emotions about Victoria over the years. I think she's very savvy and her style makes her one of the greatest ever. I don't think she's naturally the best-looking girl, but she makes the best of what she's got. And there's no doubt that she is the brains behind Brand Beckham. She created David's career and has been brilliant in that, but has been prone to manipulate the media to keep the spotlight on her. One editor has told me straight to my face that he can't believe a word she says any more. Possibly she thinks that getting busy behind the scenes adds to the results – but I wonder if she realises that it can actually upset the plans put in motion by her team of advisers. I think her first PR, Alan Edwards, did an incredible job, but that her activities undermined his and the situation eventually became untenable. I think she should probably allow herself to trust her team – in life or in business you can't do it all yourself.

The initial pictures of David Beckham and Rebecca Loos together came as a shock to me. I was in Café de Paris in St Tropez having an early-evening rosé on a Friday night when a phone call came in from my Spanish agent who was working out of Madrid. He told me he had amazing images of Beckham and a girl that had been taken at a nightclub the previous evening and asked if I wanted to see them. Damn right!

Telling my contact to get the images over immediately, I placed a call to Joe Sene, my CEO, to forewarn him. A few minutes later he came back to me. The images were stills that had been taken from video footage – video paparazzi were becoming increasingly common, and Spain had loads of them. The images showed Beckham with a mystery girl at the club and then leaving in the early hours of the morning. Nothing explicit was happening between them in the images, but obviously he was very hot property, so I got straight on the phone to Andy Coulson, editor at *News of the World*. He was immediately interested, but asked to see the video itself the following day. His team duly saw the footage on the Saturday morning. It was obvious to everyone who saw it that something was going on between the two – it was the look of love – but we didn't know exactly what, or indeed who the girl was. Coulson knew I wanted five figures for the shots – not least because my agents were adamant that we should only sell for a high figure. Realising it was a 'take it or leave it' deal, but that it was Saturday and therefore time was against us, we agreed to keep talking exclusively, but that the pictures would be held over to be considered for the following Sunday.

On the Tuesday, I headed over to see Andy and we did a deal. The pictures ran that Sunday. *News of the World* was really gunning for the Beckhams at the time and none of the papers had anything much for that weekend. We all knew that just a sniff of a Beckham scandal could shift shitloads of extra copies. Many of the papers the following week took great delight in mocking the 'scoop' when the Beckhams revealed that the 'mystery girl' was merely David's personal assistant, Rebecca Loos. Of course, it turned out later that there was more to the images than that.

People often joke that you can't believe what you read in

the papers, but actually, in my experience you generally can. The papers have to be very careful. They don't want to get sued – this can be serious stuff. For the *News of the World*, these pictures were the start of a six-month investigation that led to the eventual uncovering of the affair between David and Rebecca. We gave them the seed, but they searched out and nailed the story. Once it was in the bag they had to approach us again to use the pictures, and every other paper had to buy them as well to follow up the story. *News of the World* had a field day and our pictures helped them set the news agenda.

The Beckham/Loos story was a big hit for BIG Pictures and I found myself getting rather closer to the story than was usual. Rebecca became famous as a result of her work with the Beckhams and her involvement with David. A while after the story broke, a good six months in fact, the dust settled and I met Rebecca through Max Clifford, who was handling her publicity. I felt there was a lot of money to be made by doing set-up pap shots and studio work, and I discussed this with Max. He's the kind of operator who flogs the whole lot to the paper and lets them get on with it – it's an old-school approach, but it's been very successful for him. I look at things from a different perspective and in this case I felt that a lot more could be done. I wanted to get involved. Max was very receptive and allowed us to run with the idea. We did a studio shoot for Rebecca, and I also interviewed her for the Australian celebrity gossip radio show I was involved in. There was

▲ This is my all-time favourite image of the Princess, taken on her yachting holiday with Dodi Al Fayed aboard the *Jonikal,* moored off St Tropez.

♟ Diana gave us an abundance of great pictures in the last two weeks of her life, all of them on her yachting holiday with Dodi. Even Harry picked up a camera and became a pap!

This picture of Diana and Dodi was used widely.

The love boat.

A lovely moment between a mother and her son. This was the last time her boys would see her alive.

Big Pictures

⚑ Diana meets Nelson Mandela on his first tour to London after
his release – two people who touched the hearts of the world.

➤➤ The Princess travelled the world and
is seen here with Mother Teresa in New York.

KCS Press/Big Pictures

➤➤ Diana is helped into the Mercedes by bodyguard Trevor Rees-Jones, watched by Kes Wingfield (right) and the Ritz doorman.

❦ The wreck of the Mercedes in the now infamous Alma tunnel is loaded onto a police truck for forensic examination by French police.

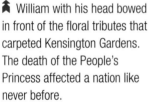 William with his head bowed in front of the floral tributes that carpeted Kensington Gardens. The death of the People's Princess affected a nation like never before.

*Me outside the Alma tunnel where Diana died. Ten years on, I spent the day reflecting on those events and reading every inch of graffiti that covered the tunnel.*

Big Pictures

Big Pictures

🔺 A father's eyes say it all. Prince Charles at Diana's funeral with sons
Harry and William. Diana's brother, Charles Spencer, is on the left.

something about her, and we clicked straight away. She's got a wonderful personality and told me I was a great interviewer. There's nothing like pandering to my ego!

Following a wise recommendation by Max, Cheryl Barrymore (entertainer Michael Barrymore's ex-wife and ex-manager) was looking after Rebecca on the management side and we got on really well. Cheryl was a lovely lady, though with a lot of baggage. I really felt for her. She had made Michael Barrymore the star he was and suffered horrendously when he eventually came out after their marriage. It was unfair for her to be in the public eye and she handled it well. I thought Rebecca was doing well, too.

The studio shoot didn't set the world on fire, for whatever reason, though I have to say I wasn't delighted with the results my guy got. I liked this girl's brain and I can see why David fell for her. She's very switched on, very intellectual. I forget who phoned who, but she and I met up pretty soon after that. We started doing pap work with her at night and I started going out with her. She's not what people think. There's a lot that went on between her and David that hasn't come out (and won't) – much of it very funny.

There's no doubt that Rebecca was put in very difficult positions, if you'll pardon the pun, and had to make the best of them. I think the same is true of Faria Alam, who I also know is not the woman that she has been made out to be. She's a really sweet girl and the affair she had with England football coach Sven-Goran Eriksson when she was a secretary at the Football Association gave her an infamy in the UK that she never expected. Public perception can be way off the mark. When I was judging Miss Great Britain, Faria was also a judge and when she walked out on stage some people booed. I thought that was terrible. The judging panel was made up of some real characters, including Christine Hamilton, the wife of the shamed MP Neil who was jailed for perjury, the mad aristo Lord Brocket, footballer Teddy Sheringham and Alex Best, wife of legendary soccer star George Best – but Faria was the one singled out. I don't know if girls like her regret doing the kiss and tell, but it can be tough on them. They certainly don't seem to have any regrets financially; both Rebecca and Faria have bought properties from the proceeds of the sale of their stories.

Some people just seem to attract headlines and not always for the right reasons. BIG Pictures knew British TV presenter Paula Yates, Bob Geldof's ex-wife, very well. We did a lot of deals with her and she occasionally rang me for advice. A lot of the time she didn't mind us getting shots of her; she would even pose with her daughter Tiger Lily. I remember following her and Michael Hutchence one day when they were shagging in the back of a black cab – the chassis was bouncing up and down! We used to get shots of them having naked picnics on their roof. They were so crazy, so bohemian, but you had to love them.

Paula rang me one day right after Michael died. She said, 'I want to talk to you because I have all these beautiful memories and I was wondering if you could send me some of your pictures.' We did an album for her and she carried it everywhere. I guess that shows another side of our business – whatever people think about the paparazzi, we do keep a record of people's lives. Paula and Hutchence were absolutely the hot couple at the time. I remember I was in Sydney when the story broke that he had died and I couldn't believe it. I went to the funeral; there was a huge sense of loss in Australia. I did take some pictures on the day, partly to capture the end of their story as I had the beginning.

**'We used to get shots of them having naked picnics on their roof'**

People always described Paula as difficult, and of course she was – but in an endearing way. Other celebrities in far more favourable situations make life unnecessarily difficult for both themselves and the paparazzi.

One of the most enduring figures in the celebrity pictures industry is Tom Cruise, who for many years made no secret of his loathing for people like me. I find it amazing that he has managed to stay on top for so long. There have always been whispers about him, but ever since the earliest days of Hollywood people have loved to gossip about the biggest stars. Image is everything and deals are brokered at every level within the industry to make sure the wheels keep turning.

I was covering the Ivy one night when Tom and Nicole Kidman were in. Upon arrival, their driver pulled up right next to the wall so there was no chance of getting a shot. It was the same story on the way out and so there was a chase. I can't understand why people won't just pose for a second; almost all chases happen because people won't cooperate. The police were absolutely on their side and that angered me – what we were doing wasn't illegal.

There were lots of rumours about what was going on between Tom and Nicole while they were over in the UK filming *Eyes Wide Shut* with director Stanley Kubrick. Apparently they were fighting constantly. Our source was actually one of their security guys, an ex-army man who knew one of my snappers, Nick Towers. He fed us top-notch information – gossip about Kidman really going mad at Cruise and verbally abusing him. The happy couple were staying in a mansion in Holland Park and Cruise reportedly spent a lot of time in the kids' playhouse at the end of the garden. This was all hearsay, of course, but all the rest of this guy's information stood up. We got loads of exclusives and great shows in the papers.

I once had personal experience trying to get shots of Kidman and Cruise when Mel and I were in the Whitsundays on a sailing holiday. We were aboard our boat, a 47-foot Bénéteau called *Big Pictures*, when we happened to come across Kerry Packer's huge yacht – a converted Arctic icebreaker. He and the Cruises were very close friends and they were all aboard, but for once they managed to spoil *my* holiday! I wasn't sure whether I should attempt to get a shot, but I couldn't resist trying; the temptation gnawed away at me. Mel and I wasted a whole day watching them, but they didn't even appear on deck.

The following day, Packer's boat slipped its moorings and headed off. We took off after it and tailed it for a day but still no luck. At that point we gave up. I needed to relax and actually have a holiday. To be honest, I couldn't believe that anyone could be in a stunning location like that and not even come out on deck from their cabin. Cruise had another boat that he kept moored up near Hamilton Island. I knew which one it was, but it had a special tarpaulin rigged over the boat's name to protect his identity.

As Cruise's career has progressed, I've seen a real change in the way he deals with the paparazzi. He used to hate or fear us – I'm not sure which – but now he seems far more approachable. Perhaps he feels he needs us more now. He even invited some of my LA guys to a photocall recently while he was on an outing to the park with his kids.

A similar situation, in a way, has arisen with Angelina Jolie and Brad Pitt. Initially it was impossible to get a shot of them together, and when we did we made a fortune. Now the golden couple are trying to kill the market by flooding it with images.

A combination of sources passed us information that enabled us to get the first shot of Brad and Angelina together, and the sources were paid very well for their trouble, taking a percentage on each sale. The original source was someone very close to Angelina on the business side and the information came to us through at least one other middleman. All we were told initially was that she was going with her adopted son, Maddox, to a resort in Kenya. We didn't know for certain that Brad was going to be there until he actually arrived. She arrived first and my guy, Ray Field, hit a couple of very average shots of her at the airport. Very soon afterwards it became obvious that Brad had arrived separately and we realised we could be on to something massive. One of the locals told Ray that the couple were there. Once we knew that, I sent Simon Earl out to join him.

The sources the national newspapers use to bring in their scoops are often the same as ours. Most of our contacts are drivers, doormen, security staff or family. The sources for many of our scoops are the people who are so trusted by the stars that they are deemed above suspicion and beyond reproach. My advice is simple: guys, look closer to home. It's often the brothers, the mothers, the drivers or the secretaries. Many celebrities simply don't realise that our tips often come from their inner sanctum. I've had some serious laughs over the years about the identity of our informants; some of them are absolute belters! I maintain these relationships by offering a percentage or straight payments. I pay out, so why would people go elsewhere with their information or images?

On the day Pitt arrived in Kenya, the couple appeared with Maddox on the beach for ten minutes. Ray hit that and we thought it was going to be followed by a lot more spectacular frames. However, it was the last time we saw them. There were fifteen shots in total and only one was very good – this was just a reflection of the situation, not Ray's talent. It was hard sitting behind a desk when I would have loved to have been out there having a crack myself. The couple apparently spent the rest of their time in and around the pool, or in their room shagging. On one occasion, Ray was told, hotel staff ran into their room as they thought the two were being attacked by wild animals. Red faces all round – either she's a screamer or he is, or maybe they are both wild!

Up until our shots emerged, the rumours had been rife. The pair had just finished filming *Mr and Mrs Smith*, an ironic title given that they had started using aliases when checking into hotels. We spent a lot of money putting the whole plan together and needed some success. Prior to the job I had been away for six weeks in Australia and maybe hadn't had my eye on the ball as much as I should have. The business needed an influx of cash and those images came at just the right time – they more than doubled our normal month's business income.

'On one occasion, hotel staff ran into their room as they thought the two were being attacked by wild animals'

We embarked on a marathon selling session. There were

bids coming in left, right and centre, from around the world. In the UK, Richard Wallace at *The Mirror* wanted the shots but in the end couldn't raise the cash. I was having my hair done throughout all of this and Runar, the creator of my wonderful mop, couldn't get a thing done as I wouldn't sit still. The office was in a frenzy. The atmosphere was electric and the tension was palpable.

Joe Sene had recently left BIG to go to the *National Enquirer* as picture editor and I tried to get hold of him but failed. For old time's sake I would have preferred to deal with Joe, but I knew the editor, Paul Field, too as he had been at *The Sun*. Paul offered me US$100 000 for the first publication rights. I wasn't sure what to do, but decided to sit tight. Mel was negotiating the UK magazine rights and made around eighty grand sterling.

From the States, *Us* and *People* magazine were on my case about first usage rights for the pictures, and despite the offer from *The Enquirer* I decided to open out the bidding and wait. I had already decided to sell direct and not put them through our usual agent, Malibu Media. The calls started to jump incrementally. The figure was now hovering around US$250 000.

Towards the end of the day, *People* magazine thought we had a deal in the bag, but I wasn't confirming. By nine o'clock that night I had received a firm offer from Peter Grossman at *Us* magazine that was too good to pass up. He asked me what figure I would accept to take the pictures out of the auction and guarantee a sale. I told him half a million, a figure I derived by just doubling where we were at the time, and he said he'd come back to me in five minutes. An hour later he came back and said that they would pay and that I should end the auction. I closed the deal there and then.

I had held my nerve and considered it a fair price – albeit a record for a pap set sold in the US. Also, I had two dilemmas that tempted me to close quickly: firstly, I couldn't be certain that no one else had the shots, and secondly, I couldn't be certain that in the three days before the magazines could print the pictures more shots would not emerge. I told *Us* magazine to wire the money; the only account that could take it at the time was an Australian one so I got on the phone to Mario. It was over.

In the UK the pictures ended up as a *Sun* exclusive, though originally it was going to be a shared deal between them and *The Mail*. At the last minute *The Mail* pulled out; I was really pissed off, but they are a good customer of the agency and I had to let it go. On top of those sales we had reproduction and electronic rights, so we earned across the board. The editor of *People* magazine went crazy and promised he would never work with us again and never buy another picture from us. Of course he has – these things are said in the heat of battle. That's the way it is with the biggest pictures. It's going to be hard going, but one rule in business is don't take on the Americans. They're fucking good, and they'll beat you every time.

I booked the Ivy for the management team and uncorked the champagne. I was exhausted, and had probably smoked 100 cigarettes. We had a wonderful night and finished up at Stringfellows, a well-known lapdancing club.

This was a huge success for BIG, though of course it crossed my mind that the couple had known they were being photographed. There's no reason why I would care if they knew or not. I have a suspicion that Angelina wanted the story of their union out in the public domain and Brad didn't; obviously I can't prove that, but if it were the case then I am delighted their team chose to come to me. Very indirectly.

Jennifer Aniston is quoted as saying that the first she knew about the affair was a phone call she received from a friend in the UK who had seen the pictures. So, Jen, I'm sorry because I do love you. I think Brad and Jen were probably the golden couple that no one wanted to see break up – apart from maybe Angelina and my bank manager.

Of course, not all our stakeouts and tip-offs pay off. Four weeks later I was going insane in the office over the agency blowing £16000 on a trip to Guadeloupe that didn't produce a single picture for us. Someone had better information than us and we got beaten. The targets? Brad and Angelina again! Later, I sent a team to Cyprus for two weeks to cover a celebrity couple who were reportedly holidaying there, but again we got nothing. That was Brad and Angelina as well.

It's a strange business in that regard. The upswing when you get the shot can be huge, but so is the disappointment when you fail. Of course it is a form of gambling – and you'll never make a mint in the casino if you stick to the $5 tables.

# The People's Princess

**I HAVE WORKED WITH** hundreds of celebrities the world over and, whether I am a fan or not, it is indisputable that they all have something that makes them special. One modern celebrity, in my eyes and the eyes of the world, simply shone. I refer, of course, to Diana, Princess of Wales.

Diana was a regular doorstep for me and many of my colleagues at the national newspapers. I would often be found at the gates of Kensington Palace. There was a real 'Diana circuit' in London; Beauchamp Place in Knightsbridge was a favourite haunt for her and she spent a lot of time at San Lorenzo and O Fado restaurants. The Harbour Club in Chelsea was a fixture too; the press pack would lean six-foot ladders up against the wall there from seven o'clock in the morning trying to get shots of her going to the gym. Often there would be up to twenty-five of us hanging around. That job was in the diary of every paper, every day. It was a full-time business. A couple of royal-only agencies appeared; truly it was Diana Inc.

She generated a lot of cash for a lot of people. In the early days we were getting minimum reproduction fees of £750 an image, and everyone was paying it – even *The Times*. One good picture could generate thousands of pounds, and Diana was generally accessible.

**'Most of the royal family look like the back end of a bus! Not Diana'**

Often she wanted to be photographed and would stop her car to allow people to catch up. I think she wanted it all on her terms, though, and it never works like that.

Everything Diana did was recorded with pictures. We used to say it was for history's sake, but of course it was just for the newspapers' sake. One of the most beautiful princesses ever to grace the earth, she attracted the world's media on a daily basis. Most of the royal family look like the back end of a bus! Not Diana. She always looked like an angel. Every aspect of her day would be covered by photographers trying to get long-range shots, car shots, images of her rollerblading in Kensington Gardens – the global demand and appetite for her were insatiable.

I got great shots on one memorable occasion when she

held a birthday party for one of the princes in the fields at the back of the palace. *The Mail* got a tip-off from a punter and I raced over and snapped them all having fun with Fergie and her daughters. They were playing on a little bus and there were clowns amusing the kids. In those days a set of shots like that pretty much guaranteed most of pages 1 to 25 at *The Mail*. Diana was in a stunning red cropped jacket and looked all class, as she always did. Fergie looked as frumpy as usual. She was the complete opposite of Diana. There would always be a disaster with her getting out of cars, and some of the things she wore I'd be tempted to hang on the Christmas tree. Sometimes it was hard to keep the lens straight because you'd be pissing yourself laughing. Fashion victim or what?

Diana certainly had her favourite spots, be it Daphne's or San Lorenzo or Scalini. She was very predictable and quite easy to do. Every day she would be in Beauchamp Place at least once, and in the early days of PapPix, John Gordon and Raphael would base themselves there. We had a lot of success with their work.

There was a real relationship between Diana and the paps. She loved the attention because she wasn't getting a lot at home. As far as I could make out, she was very isolated from the rest of the royal family. I think it was very sad. She had a mixed relationship with the media. She was probably the greatest manipulator of the press I have seen. If Charles had an official function she would often appear somewhere else looking amazing just to upstage him and make sure that it was she who made the papers the following day. Many times she would tease us and appear just for a second out of a building, meaning that we had to keep our cameras held up and ready, constantly trained on the target. At the end of the day my arms would be aching. This was a master of spin at work.

I had to desert my old pal from *The Addy*, Graham Vincent, and his wife minutes after meeting up with them for the first time in years when they came to visit me in London. The call had come through directly to me from a source at the palace and I had to head to Chelsea immediately. I arrived at the address I had been given to find Ken Lennox of *The Mirror* waiting. The address was that of a spiritualist medium whom Andrew Morton's controversial book had revealed that Diana was consulting. Diana apparently wanted to prove that the stories were true and add credibility to the explosive book as a whole. From the road we could see her pulling the curtain aside and peering through the window to see whether enough photographers had assembled before she emerged. The pictures we took that day made the front pages of the world's press, as she had known they would. Her image was everything to her.

Most of my work with Diana was London-based, though I did do some shots of her abroad, at Richard Branson's hotel La Residencia in Majorca. I was perched up on a mountain that was rapidly being washed away by the constant rain, hanging out with a Spanish freelancer that *The Mail* had cut a deal with in order to retain exclusivity. Every morning Diana would appear and do about a hundred laps of the pool. She was supremely fit and had a great body.

Diana loved playing the part of princess, as any woman would. She certainly didn't like to lose control of a situation and wanted things done her way. She would often brief reporters or photographers, either reading them the riot act or making sure they approached stories from her desired angle. On one occasion when I was covering an event in Wales for *The Mail*, Diana approached me, smiled sweetly and said, 'Make sure you get it in focus, Mr Lyons.' I was simply blown away that she knew my name! Plus, she had the sexiest posh accent you'd ever hear – used to turn me on something fierce.

Diana's relationship with the press was ongoing, but she had certain favourites. She worked closely with Jason Fraser, who was the number one at the time, and he would get fantastic tip-offs. Partnerships in this business are very handy, not just for getting great images, but also to allow for some degree of damage limitation. Jason's relationship went only so far. One evening in 1987 he caught the princess in a clinch with a guardsman named Major David Waterhouse. He managed to get a frame off before being jumped by Diana's bodyguards. Diana herself pleaded with him to hand the film over, which he did. The camera and film were returned the following day, minus the incriminating images, of course. I'm not sure that I would have handed the film over, but I'm sure her Special Branch team could be fairly persuasive. It wasn't long after that that Jason seemed to be in the right place all the time for Diana. Good for him – it's all about building relationships and he was very good at that. His background was journalistic rather than photographic and he had excellent information. In this business, taking the final picture is the easy part.

Jason and I turned up once to cover a party hosted by disgraced newspaper baron Conrad Black. There was a glittering celebrity turnout and we got some fantastic shots of the attendees, Diana in particular. We cut a deal and flogged the shots exclusively to the *Sunday Mirror* for £18 000. I think I out-shot Jason quite comprehensively that night; out of the spread of fifteen photos, only one was his.

Whenever I was covering Diana it was a waiting game. If I missed a shot, the picture desk went mad. She was pure box office – the hottest property in the world. When she arrived at an event, she arrived like no other superstar. The panic and butterflies among the public and the media were intense. She was dressed to kill and licensed to thrill. There was almost no time to nail all the different frames we needed: tight heads, full lengths and the rest. There was a blitz of white light that made looking through the lens almost pointless at times, and it was mayhem, with people kicking their colleagues out of the way. *The Mail* – and indeed BIG – would always allocate at least three photographers for Diana occasions. It was like rugby on a ladder. I think that's why I like polo so much: it reminds me of being on the road.

The full-time newspaper royal staff photographers like Arthur Edwards and Kent Gavin became very well known in their own right. Arthur in particular still enjoys a wonderful rapport with the royals, despite working for *The Sun*, which might not have made them the most obvious allies. At *The Mail*, the journalist who was closest to Diana was Richard Kay. They would have regular conversations, after which he would wander over to the picture desk and one of us would be dispatched to the scene of the story. He was the envy of Fleet Street. He would often appear in our room and whisper in Andy Kyle's ear, and suddenly it would be battle stations. Andy was hot on the royals as a picture editor but *The Mail* certainly didn't want to upset them, unlike perhaps *The Sun* and *The Mirror*. I'm convinced that Diana fancied Richard – he had an air about him. He could certainly write an interesting book on her. She would often phone him personally, but got her message across via other sources too – including the infamous butler, Paul Burrell.

I'm sure Diana knew about my growing team of guys. She knew me, of course – not least because I lived opposite the gates of her palace. You could say we were neighbours, though she had an awfully long driveway and I never popped around to borrow a cup of sugar. One truly bizarre day I came out of my flat at around 7 a.m. to be confronted by the Princess leaping out of her car to have her say. 'Why are you taking terrible pictures of me?' she demanded. I was flabbergasted, not least because I was on my way to doorstep her at the Harbour Club and now found myself being doorstepped. Talk about turning the tables. She then asked, 'Why are you chasing me, and not my husband and that woman?' At that time, though, there were no convincing rumours of anything going on with Charles and Camilla. Had I pieced it together I would have made a fortune, but it didn't make sense because the air of craziness about Diana didn't always make her utterances credible. I told her I thought the pictures had been really nice, but she told me to forget that and start tailing Charles. The chances of me keeping up with Charles's Aston Martin in my rusty Renault 5 were pretty slim!

I've got a lot of time for Charles; I think he's dealt with a lot over time and done it very well. He is known as a tremendous nutter who talks to plants, but I like that about him. He's passionate about organic food, the outdoors, architecture and, of course, polo. I think he has a grace and intelligence about him that will make him an exceptional king. Since Diana's passing I think Charles has to a degree taken on the humanitarian mantle. In his position it would be very easy to become arrogant, but I don't think he has. The royal family has never enjoyed the best PR and I believe that the nation's perception was that he was aloof with Diana and that she alone was the 'modern' royal. We commoners will never fully understand the way the royals operate. Throughout history they have been able to do exactly what they want, but in the modern world the media has been able to call them to task and this has forced a change in the way they operate.

**'Why are you chasing me, and not my husband and that woman?'**

Diana would not have been the easiest woman to live with. I think Charles just wanted to get on with the job. I suspect that some of the tension occurred because one of them loved the spotlight while the other loathed it. There's no doubt in my mind that Charles couldn't be bothered with a twit – and to some degree, that's what Diana was. She was very intuitive and sensitive, but she was also bonkers. The drama and the vanity were never-ending; she was very beautiful, but very manipulative.

Diana had a very easy manner and could deal with anyone with consummate ease. She was a strong woman, and knew the power her position gave her. She would have made a perfect president. Her power gave her the ability to change the world for the better, and I believe that as the world's biggest celebrity she had a real impact and did an extraordinary amount for the planet. Diana carried herself with real dignity and compassion, and thought deeply about what she was doing. Through her charity work she raised a huge amount of money to alleviate suffering around the world. I'll never forget the exclusive pictures BIG USA got of her and Mother Teresa in the Bronx. The two women seemed almost as one.

Diana's former bodyguard Ken Wharf says she was happiest when she was with her children and was a very loving and caring mother. He believes that her relationship with her children was the one thing in those troubled times between the separation and divorce that gave her hope and comfort. I think Diana's amazing public image hid a lot of the cracks that were appearing in the marriage, and so people were genuinely surprised when she and Charles split up. I won Press Photographer of the Year in 1992 for a shot of Prince Charles at the polo on the day of the announcement, seeming to be looking up to the heavens for help – he was gonna need it!

Diana made a huge impact on the royal family, not only because of the divorce. Ken Wharf has also pointed out that she was the mother of two boys, William and Harry, and raised them in a way that was as normal as you're going to get in royal circles. She knew how to communicate with everyone, and her thoughtfulness and honesty endeared herself to the world.

Diana was one of the first modern celebrities. For the first time in history we had a pop-star princess. She was everything – a supermodel, a movie star, a glamour girl, a personality. She wanted to become a phenomenon and she did it all right, including dying young. Of course she became a true icon. She and Marilyn Monroe have similarities in their stories and this was highlighted by Elton John's playing of 'Candle in the Wind' at the funeral. She and Elton had fallen out in recent times; I would have loved to have seen those two luvvies arguing hammer and tongs. He knew the power of Diana and that she touched hearts.

Rumours always swirled around Diana. In royal circles it was said that her first bodyguard had got a little too close to his charge and had been ridden off a Scottish cliff on his motorcycle, leaving a wife and children. Of course it was ascribed to accident – but it was a pretty strange one. Accidents like these certainly must have given Diana a 'stay away' factor for prospective boyfriends.

While she loved being treated as a princess, it's my guess that she really wanted to be treated as a movie star. Many of her friends were A-list celebrities and she loved being part of that club. She knew she was a commodity and she knew she had power. Apparently at one point she threatened to head to America and set up some kind of alternative royal family in exile; she would have fitted perfectly into the Kennedy clan and strangely had similar luck. There is no way she would have been allowed to do that, of course. Always exhibiting a real flair for PR, Diana had a truly entrepreneurial nature, though her insecurity was rampant. I think she did worry about something 'happening' to her, and that paranoia was one of the reasons she worked so hard at keeping her profile high. It meant there was always someone watching her and watching out for her. I personally believe that the only reason her erstwhile lover James Hewitt is still in the land of the living is that he has done much the same thing.

The night Diana died was one of the most traumatic of my life, both personally and professionally. The event unleashed a torrent of emotion in me and led into a scary time.

BIG Pictures had a long-standing relationship with an agency in Paris – several agencies, in fact. The guy who found himself at the centre of the Diana story was Laurent Sola, who ran LS Diffusion Press Agency. I was sitting at home on the night it all happened. It was five minutes past midnight on Sunday 31 August and Mel, Amber and I were at home at 5 Kensington Court watching the De Niro film *Heat* with varying degrees of interest. The phone rang, and Sola's unmistakeable voice came on the line. He told me that Diana had been in a major car accident. I think I was the first person outside Paris to know what had happened. He told me he had men at the scene and the pictures would be with me soon.

The agency had earlier that day received what turned out to be the only decent pictures of Diana and Dodi Al Fayed leaving the Ritz during the afternoon. The hotel's CCTV captured their images after their night out as they climbed into the car. A chandelier that hangs in my living room now is the one that was in the room the couple stayed in at the hotel – at least, that's what the auctioneer told me.

As the couple left the Ritz late that night, the assembled press scrambled off after the Mercedes. Sola's photographer lost the car when its driver, Henri Paul, jumped a red light immediately after leaving the Ritz. This error was to lead to what could have been the biggest scoop ever for BIG Pictures. While most of the other paparazzi kept trying to find the car, Sola's man decided to head for home and happened upon the wreck of the car as it lay in the Alma tunnel. He ran down and began helping administer first aid to Diana as they waited for emergency services to arrive.

Back in London, I quickly told Mel what was unfolding and then rang Len Gould at *Sunday People*. I asked him if he had heard anything about Diana being injured. He told me that nothing was running on Reuters so I knew my tip was going to be worth real money. I quickly rang around three of the editors I was closest to, offering them the tip of the year for a healthy fee of £10000 each. They reacted to the news with incredulity, but of course started chasing it up. Initially everyone was drawing a blank. Feeling slightly worried about looking silly, though I totally trusted Sola, I raced into the office. It would be five days before I slept again.

The pictures from the accident started dropping onto BIG's computer system and I realised it was serious. Sola had warned me that the images of Dodi in particular were horrible; he had been cut open at the scene and given heart massage in an attempt to revive him. To his credit, Sola had refused even to send some of the images on the grounds that nobody ever needed to see them. Certainly they were not printable. My whole body went into some kind of shock. It was a total sensory overload. I imagine it's the kind of sensation an innocent man experiences in the dock when he hears the word 'Guilty'. I whispered a prayer. I didn't know what to do. I was dealing with the single biggest news story of my lifetime and was overwhelmed

> **'Sola had warned me that the images of Dodi in particular were horrible'**

with the moment. Many people would have crumbled and I nearly did.

About an hour later all of the papers were on the case. Initial reports said that Diana was concussed and had a broken arm and the images I had seemed to confirm that. At 2 a.m. that was the story running on the wires and TV. I had a bank of nine televisions tuned to various news channels, which were blaring out updates as the story unfolded. It was amazing how far behind us they were with their facts. All were reporting that Diana had suffered a minor injury, which was still my understanding at that time. How wrong we all were. In hindsight, I can't believe how well I dealt with the situation. The pressure was really on – an understatement, to say the least. I had to decide whether to put the pictures around to everyone or do an exclusive deal.

I had rung my BIG Pictures colleague Dave Morgan on the way to the office and told him to come in fast and get the images captioned up. I told him to make up contact sheets, but to ensure that everything was provided to the papers in very low-resolution format to render them unusable without agreement from us. The contact sheets were sent out digitally to the Sunday newspapers. To this day I'm not sure what made me insist on low res. It wasn't my normal way of operating, but the decision turned out to be crucial. I believe it was an act of God.

I spoke to Phil Hall, editor of the *News of the World*, and told him what I had. He said he wanted to do a deal; apparently Rupert Murdoch was on a jet but the pair were in contact. It was not a three-way conversation, but we were in communication.

Hall offered me a quarter of a million pounds for usage of the images in *The Sun* and *News of the World*. I said there was no way I was agreeing to that; it was one-use only. I had a similar offer on the table from an American publication. We did the deal, and the high-res shot was sent to News International – the only one that left the BIG office.

And then I got a call from Phil telling me that Diana was dead and they were pulling out of the deal. *News of the World* claims that the image never got as far as the printing process.

Who knows what really happened? In any event, no money changed hands and as soon as I heard that Diana had died I immediately withdrew all of the images from the market. I was receiving big-money offers from all over the world, but no deals were done. In the early hours of Sunday morning, I told Sola that the images had to be withdrawn on moral grounds. My deal with him gave me rights for the UK, the US and Australia. He asked me if I was sure and I replied that I was, absolutely. Not selling the pictures was a huge decision. Yes, I was hungry and wanted to make a lot of money and this was the biggest news story in my life, but my upbringing meant I had no choice. I just had to answer a simple ethical question: could I make money from someone else's tragedy? It was a big call, but once the tragic news came, my mind was set. The pictures would have been the most valuable images in the world and probably still are. I almost felt like a president with his finger hovering over the nuclear button. I would love to know what other people would have done.

Neither of us knew that Sola's offices were about to be comprehensively turned over by French special-branch officers and he was to be arrested. The swift police operation meant that the only images of the incident in private hands were in my offices in London. Lionel Cherruault, a London-based photographer, had his house turned over in the belief that he had received images from another agency, SIPA, which also had its Paris offices raided. The only items that were removed from Lionel's property were computer discs and electronic equipment; the 'thieves' ignored the cash, credit cards and jewellery that were also in his study. In the words of one of the police called to the scene, it was clearly the work of 'Special Branch, MI5, MI6 – call it what you like. This was no ordinary burglary.'

Despite the fact that the images were no longer for sale and had indeed never been fully sold, the following day some of the papers and magazines, in both the UK and the US, started to demonise me

**'Some started to demonise me as the man trying to profit from the tragedy'**

as the man trying to profit from the tragedy. *News of the World* didn't pursue this line, but many of my detractors were the people who had been bloodthirstily trying to persuade me to sell them the images the previous day.

By Sunday night, no one was talking about anything else and I had been cast as the villain of the piece on the BBC's *Nine O'Clock News*. I was really feeling the heat, a sensation that I endured over the next few days. The BBC simply didn't get the story right; it was bad journalism. Of course people believed what they heard and read, and the fact that people formed the wrong impression of me hurt. One of the guys from rival agency Rex papped me outside my office and his picture stared out at the world from the TV screen. The BBC baldly stated that I was trying to sell the pictures when really I was only trying to do the right thing. Of course, the media didn't want a hero; they wanted the devil. But if I was selling the pictures, why had no one seen them?

My general manager, Greg Allen, was out of the office on holiday and we couldn't get hold of him. When he finally rolled in, he didn't even know the Princess was dead. There were death threats being made against my staff and me and it was all very frightening. I felt I had done everything right, but was living through a medieval siege without the benefit of a protective moat. Greg fielded a lot of the hate calls and was visibly shaken and ghostly white. The general office number had never been publicly listed, but we had just started a service called BIG Pictures News Line and that number had been put into the directories. It became the BIG Pictures Death Threat Line. I didn't even go home and instead checked into a hotel. I'm glad I didn't have my current haircut at that time in my life; I would have stuck out like tits on a bull.

During those days I had many conversations with people in the media, and some of them really helped me. Piers Morgan, who was the editor of *The Mirror* in those days, was a real rock. He was the only editor who phoned to offer support. (Ironically, he was forced out of his job in 2005 after printing some contentious pictures purportedly taken in Iraq.) Piers rang me very early on the Sunday morning and told me there was no way I could sell the images. I was able to tell him that they were off the market already; he promised to call me again when he reached his office. That call to a degree confirmed my course of action and endorsed what I had done. He was very direct and acted almost like a big brother. He gave me some good advice and I'll always be grateful to him for that.

This period in BIG's trajectory was very important to the future success of the company. There was a lot of respect in the industry for what we were doing; if we had sold the images we would have been blacklisted by many media outlets. (Probably only until we got the next big set of exclusives, though – that's how the business works.) This episode could have been the end of the agency if I had acted like an insensitive, greedy fool. BIG Pictures had everything to lose.

The outpouring of aggression shocked me. I dealt with the irony of getting doorstepped by the other picture agencies every time I left the office. An American film crew literally kicked the door down to get an interview with me. It was the only one I did and it turned out badly thanks to the edit, as ever in such situations. Kensington Gardens was overflowing with flowers and we were trying to run a press agency. The atmosphere was crazy, all caused by the pictures that were in my safe and not going anywhere.

Scotland Yard had been on the phone and a large deputation arrived to interview me. I don't know why so many of them were needed; they only just fitted into my office. I've never seen so many police, and wondered who was covering whose tracks. In hindsight I should have had a lawyer present, but I was naive. I made statements and handed over everything they asked for, minus a bit of insurance. Another group of police came down with a computer expert, who spent hours sifting through our hard drives and other equipment until they were completely satisfied. The whole thing was bizarre.

On a night in September I took everyone at BIG out for a meal at a local Indian restaurant called the Taj Mahal to thank them for helping us get through another difficult day. It was around 10.30 when we left the BIG building and it had gone midnight by the time I returned with a few of the staff. Immediately I realised something was wrong. The power had gone out in our building, though all of our neighbours' lights and the streetlamps were working just fine. In fact, Greg spoke to the national grid office the following day and they told him it wasn't possible to cut power to one building. Obviously someone operating at a higher level had managed it. Gazing up from street level, I saw what I thought was a flashlight cutting the darkness. The office alarm wasn't armed, probably because of the lack of power. My heart was in my mouth as we walked in and my panic reached fever pitch when I heard a steady ticking noise. In the split second before we turned tail and ran, I became certain there was a person at the back of the office. Figuring that the ticking was a bomb, we found some cover on the other side of the street and rang the police. That ticking noise worked very well as a method of buying extra time for whoever it was who had infiltrated my office.

The flying squad arrived very quickly, in five cars, and trooped in en masse. They didn't find anyone, but did identify the light source I had seen: one of the computer screens was on. That in itself was odd, as there was no power in the office. Whoever was in there wouldn't have found what they were looking for as everything had already been handed over to the police and all of the images were now in safe places.

I am certain that during this terrifying period the office phone lines were tapped. Over the following days we heard all sorts of noises on the line while making calls. The whole experience was like being haunted. It wasn't nice to be a major player in all of this, and I was. In fact, I had the fucking ball and I was running. I had jumped from one side of the camera to the other, and I didn't like it.

**'I had jumped from one side of the camera to the other, and I didn't like it'**

I know the game. My personal mauling at the hands of some areas of the media came as a disappointment, though of course I was aware that as a news story me 'selling the pictures' had much more sizzle than what had really happened – the fact that I had quietly and completely removed them from the market. I don't feel let down, because I expose myself to that kind of treatment, and to criticism in general, simply by being the way I am and doing what I do. It comes with the territory. I know I am fair game.

Not long after the accident, I went up to Kensington Palace to shoot the princes inspecting the floral tributes and discovered that even my own peers had turned against me. One of the snappers, Jane Fincher, came up and told me I was sick and had a real nerve. That was pretty rich, given that she had been shooting the royals for years. She and the others should have known better, or tried to get the facts. Nine times out of ten I like being the centre of attention, but the days after Diana's death were very difficult. I felt like I was the littlest man in the world. I wanted to hide away on my sofa, and yet I had done nothing wrong. No one understood what I was going through. The funeral on 6 September was one of the saddest days of my life.

A few days after the funeral, I received a call from John McNamara, a former Scotland Yard man who was now head of Mohammed Al Fayed's security – guys who I would have thought were among the best in the country, if not the world. He asked if he could come over to the office and meet me, as Al Fayed had a few questions. Also, Al Fayed wanted to see some of the last photos my BIG operative Ken Gough and our excellent French agency Max PPP had taken of Diana and Dodi together on their yachting holiday aboard the *Jonikal* moored

William, a 'regular Joe', does the shopping in St Andrews during his university days.

William and Kate enjoy a lovers' break in Ibiza. →

Martin Leaver/Jani Jance/Rob Morrison/Big Pictures

The two princes are very different characters. William is the more subdued of the two, while Harry fully deserves his nickname 'Harry the Hellraiser'.

← A smashed Prince Harry throws a couple of punches at photographers outside London's Pangaea club.

➤➤ The brothers on stage at the Concert for Diana at Wembley Stadium, held to commemorate the 10th anniversary of their mother's death.

◀◀ An early shot of Kylie Minogue and Michael Hutchence taken in a Sydney club.

'That dress' made Liz Hurley famous.

Catherine Zeta-Jones' fashion disaster.

Danny DeVito hams it up for me in the Mayfair Hotel.

Big Australia

Big Pictures

Darryn Lyons

John Gordon Darryn Lyons/Big Pictures

▲ Michael and Paula Yates, seen here with daughter Tiger Lily, were a constant source of great pics.

Sting was renowned for his sexual exploits. These pictures (taken at the Eden Roc hotel on the French Riviera) certainly proved that he was flexible, and were huge sellers.

Flynet/Big Pictures

Vince and Jen – we never knew whether it was fully on or not, but the camera never lies.

Penny-alty! Blonde's ticklish tackle puts rocker Rod on the spot.

PICTURE EXCLUSIVE

# THE Sun

## Its heart's Beatling!

Paul listens to Heather's tum

Leon McGowran/Will Rose/Big Pictures

Sir Paul McCartney and Heather Mills in happier times.

Flynet/Big Pictures

◄◄ Surf's up for Cameron Diaz.

Posh tackles Becks from behind on an early date. →

Adrian Turner/Big Pictures

♠ A showbiz marriage made in heaven – a Spice Girl and a supremely talented footballer. The media-obsessed Beckhams generally play the game better than anyone.

Most Wanted/Big Pictures

The infamous Beckham / Loos shot – a massive earner for us. ↘

♠ The Beckhams leave The Ivy restaurant on David's birthday in May 2007. (It was rumoured he was angry that most of the guests were Victoria's friends, not his.)

Queen International/Big Pictures

Tom Hanks and his wife Rita Wilson playing in the surf near their Malibu home.

Big Pictures

'The Body' looking stunning as ever.

The beach is a constant source of huge dollars in the paparazzi industry — fat, skinny, topless, bottomless, cellulite, toned . . . it's all good. When summer comes we feel like we've hit the jackpot on a Vegas slot machine — even the former PM couldn't resist the pull of the waves.

← Jay Kay has a booze-fuelled go at a paparazzo. He's renowned for both partying and punching.

David Beckham → mistakenly kicked a passer-by off his motorbike, thinking he was a pap! On the left, Jude Law looks ready for a punch-up!

Ewan McGregor – strangely camera-shy for a movie star – makes a run for it. On the right, Sienna Miller has a go at one of my guys (maybe she had no make-up on?).

The relationship between photographers and the stars has its ups and downs. Whether they have had a few drinks, or just don't want their picture taken, some stars are quick to go on the attack.

John Gordon/Big Pictures

KGS/Big Pictures

Paul Chesterton/Warren Richardson/Big Pictures

SHIP TEASE

Jordan goes overboard with sexy Page 3 pal

Darryn Lyons

Martin Leaver/Big Pictures

Jordan and her husband Peter André have always trusted BIG.

Rehabilitating Sophie Anderton. Before these set-up shots, I don't think she'd done a day of exercise in her life!

Steve Wake/Big Pictures

off St Tropez. All of the great pictures from that holiday are in BIG's archive. The Diana gravy train had been in full swing and we had got twenty or thirty pictures into the paper every day, all at minimum reproduction. Every day was a jackpot day and the cash till had been ringing merrily. The whole holiday was a photocall for Diana and even for her boys – I remember Harry pretending to be a paparazzo himself! They were good times for all concerned and Al Fayed wanted to be reminded of their happiness. Ironically, even after the crash those pictures continued to be huge sellers. It was like hitting the jackpot in the casino every day. And ten years on, those photographs of Diana are still in demand.

McNamara and I met up in a bar called 19:20 on Great Sutton Street, just around the corner from my office on Clerkenwell Road. He had a briefcase full of neat envelopes that I assumed were stuffed with banknotes. The phrase 'cash for questions' kept popping into my mind, but when he asked me if I would be willing to give him a brief statement about my memories of the events around the fatal crash, I saw no reason not to cooperate. He told me Al Fayed was planning to take his investigations a lot further, as he was certain that Diana and Dodi had been murdered. He pressed me on many of the strange events that followed the crash itself, but I kept my testimony as factual as I could and gave him essentially the same information I had given the police. McNamara thanked me for my help and passed me an envelope to recompense me for my 'time and expenses'. I declined to accept it, saying that I preferred to volunteer the information. I gave him a selection of 12 x 8 prints from the holiday to pass on to his boss. Al Fayed had wanted to pay for the album, but I would not accept payment for that either.

A couple of days later I received another call from McNamara, asking for a second meeting. He told me that Al Fayed treasured the images I had given him and wanted to talk again about the final days of his son's life, and also about any ways in which he could help me. They offered to pick me up, but I got my chauffeur to drive me over to Harrods, where the tycoon has an office on the top floor. As I entered, Al Fayed rose and greeted me warmly. As he shook my right hand he placed a gold bar in my left. My eyes bulged slightly, until I realised it was made from solid chocolate! He thanked me for the images and we sat down to chat. I found him very engaging. He asked me straight, 'Do you think those bastards killed my son? Because I think those bastards killed my son.'

I took 'those bastards' to be the royal family and the mandarins of MI6. There's no question that Al Fayed hates the royal family, and Prince Philip in particular. Not wishing to compromise myself, I was non-committal and stuck to the details that I was certain about. I was happy to try and help him, as I understood his thoughts and the way he felt. I don't have a bad word to say about Al Fayed. I was with him for forty-five minutes and most of the conversation seemed to be him convincing himself that something had been done to the couple. He is a very powerful man, and though I found it hard to get a word in at times, he seemed to take everything that I did manage to say as proof to back up his theories. He began telling me about his new company, which operated a series of satellites imaging the earth, and suggested we could work together.

As our meeting drew to a close he insisted he wanted to stay in touch with me, and ordered one of his flunkies to get me a new mobile phone that he could reach me on. (I returned the phone inside a month as it had never really been used other than to receive a couple of calls to clarify some details, and I felt a little uncomfortable having it.) Once more turning down payment for my time, I was presented with a whole heap of Harrods goodies – including the gold bar – and went on my way, not much the wiser, but certainly with the feeling that I had met a very decent man who had taken this very hard. He certainly wants the truth and has a large team working on it. What father wouldn't want to find the truth in such a situation?

The key picture I received from my photographers at the scene of the crash in Paris is hugely powerful. The princess looks serene in it. There are echoes of the famous death shot of Che Guevara – though crucially, in this picture the Princess is still alive. She has her back up against what is left of the front passenger seat, a smile on her face and a small cut on her forehead. She looks like an angel. The picture has something that inspires thoughts of sainthood. To my mind, it shows Diana going up to heaven. I can imagine religious fanatics getting worked up about it and I know it would have a real resonance for the public, partly due to Diana's timeless power.

The Diana pictures remain a great dinner-party topic and there are lots of fakes out there, but I can tell you they are nothing like the original key picture – 'The Angel', as I call it. Though I feel that it shows an incredible feeling of happiness and love, through my actions the world didn't see it. I don't think Diana died an unhappy person, and certainly my recollection of the pictures bears that out. Perhaps if there were some historical context for publication it would be a good thing, but I don't know that anyone has anything to gain other than money. Perhaps they could be used in a road-safety campaign – anyone seeing those images would certainly remember to wear a seatbelt. The impact of the crash was greater than anything I've seen in years of news reporting, and the only survivor of the crash was wearing a belt.

> 'If I could turn back the clock and not have her die, I would give away all my money in a heartbeat'

Of course, if Diana had just been injured those images would have made me a fortune. That said, if I could turn back the clock and not have her die, I would give away all my money in a heartbeat.

In early 1998, when Tina Brown was in the *New Yorker* editor's chair, I was approached on behalf of the magazine asking if I would be interested in selling the images to tie in with the first anniversary of Diana's death. The offer was in the vicinity of $3–4 million and I turned it down flat. It didn't come from the editor herself and I felt there was a good possibility that someone wanted to gauge whether I had anything to sell and also my willingness to do so or otherwise.

In July 2006 an Italian news magazine called *Chi* published an image from the crash featuring Diana receiving oxygen in the car. The picture was excerpted from a book by Jean-Michel Caradec'h, *Lady Diana: The Criminal Investigation*. The original images that had been held by BIG on the night had, of course, been confiscated by the police, both in France and in our London offices. The story I have been told is that someone involved with the case made copies of the images and it was these photocopies that appeared. To be clear, those images were stolen. The copyright holders, the two French freelancers, were certainly not paid for their work and the last I heard they were considering legal action. However, they may never earn a penny, as under French law the inside of a car is a private place and hence off limits to photographers. Categorically, neither I nor anyone connected with me or BIG was involved in any way.

For ten years, editors have wrestled with whether or not to dredge up one of those images, and in the end someone just couldn't resist. It's strange in a way how quickly the image has been forgotten. Of course, the precedent has now been set and the value of further pictures has fallen correspondingly, so in some way it has released a layer of tension in me. I think someone would have paid £5–10 million for the first rights to those images and the sale of the second rights around the world would have raised at least a further £50 million. *Chi* magazine has, in my opinion, blown all that away – and that is a good thing. Running the image must have been a big decision and I guess the editor felt he needed to make a name for himself; thank God I don't need to.

# Diana's Crash
# – the Truth

**THE DAYS AROUND THE DEATH** of Diana were a kind of emotional watershed for me. Although many sought information from me, I felt that I had much to learn about the circumstances of her death. Finally, in February 2006, I decided to travel to Paris to meet the eyewitnesses to the aftermath.

The Alma tunnel has become a tourist attraction. Above the tunnel a flame burns in tribute to her and the walls are covered with messages of condolence from fans. It reminds me of the walls around the Beatles' Abbey Road studio. Many of the scribblings refer to the tragic loss of 'England's rose', though others point the finger of blame.

Staring at the tributes and messages for the first time on

that dull and overcast day, I felt a real emotional connection. I still feel a closeness to the woman and to the events. Being at the site of the crash seemed to complete the images that were already in my memory. Everything seemed to be moving around me at double speed. Several people asked me to take their picture in front of the tunnel. Their big grins seemed so inappropriate, but I took the images anyway.

I spent an intense and slightly surreal hour letting the memories of that dramatic night wash over me. The events are still shrouded in mystery, but two of my affiliated freelancers, David Kerr and Fabrice Chassery, were actually there.

David and Fabrice had just started working with Sola's agency. Though both were experienced photographers, this was only Fabrice's second job for Sola and David had been in the job for less than a month. The two had been working as a team throughout that fateful day. They had taken shots of the couple arriving by private jet and were still shooting at night, covering the Ritz.

Both of them remember that nothing was normal about that night. The chauffeur Henri Paul acted differently from previous nights: he was friendly with everyone and talked to the photographers, whereas he was usually a cold fish. He emerged from the front entrance of the hotel and saw all the paps gathered there. The two bodyguards were very close to him. Paul told the press pack that the couple would be leaving through the front door in five minutes. The assembled snappers didn't smell any alcohol on his breath and he seemed steady on his feet, but they weren't very close to him and would never have suspected he was drunk, given his position within the security network.

Fabrice had a feeling that the couple would in fact leave the Ritz by the back door in the hope that no one would get a decent shot. The access road to the rear of the hotel is very narrow and there were road works going on at the time and barriers everywhere. Fabrice got there and parked, and saw through a window as he approached that the couple were waiting to leave in the hallway. He called David and told him to head around to the back in his car. The time was around a quarter past midnight French time (11.15 London time). There were several people hanging around, apparently photographers, that Fabrice didn't recognise, which was very strange. Later the police asked him and David to identify these characters, but of course they could not.

Fabrice hit a couple of shots, but due to the limitations of the area, they weren't good. The pictures everyone has seen of the couple leaving the hotel were in fact taken by Fabrice and David earlier in the day. Those pictures had already been sold exclusively and the competition had become aware that the couple were at the Ritz.

Most of the photographers thought Diana and Dodi would head back to Al Fayed's place in Paris, but Fabrice and David had a hunch that they might be heading to another property in the

Bois de Boulogne, coincidentally the place where Edward and Mrs Simpson had conducted their affair. As the 'royal' car left the hotel, David and Fabrice ran for their own vehicles. Neither was on a scooter, as reported later in hysterical press reports. David was in a good position, with just one car between him and the couple. The paparazzi who had been gathered at the front of the hotel had leapt onto their scooters and were trying to catch the Mercedes, and Fabrice was also giving chase.

In front of David, the Princess's car slowed at a red light, allowing him to optimistically bang off a couple of frames. The Mercedes then jumped a red light at the corner of Rue de Rivoli and Rue de Cambon and began to accelerate wildly away. The speed the car was doing through the crowded Place de la Concorde was unbelievable, and very dangerous. David began to slow down because he didn't want to have an accident. As a result of his reduced speed he lost them almost immediately and didn't know whether they had taken the Champs-Elysées or the tunnel. The scooter paps, who were better able to weave through the traffic, roared on ahead of David.

Having lost the Mercedes, David decided to wait for Fabrice. When he caught up they decided there was nothing more to be gained from joining a wild goose chase through the streets of Paris. The pair had already hit loads of exclusive images during the day and we at BIG had sold most of them for big money. Believing that the couple were heading to a location at which there was no chance of getting a shot, and realising that attempting a car shot of the couple was going to add nothing to their day, they decided to quit. They made an agreement to meet the following day and then they split up; Fabrice headed off down the Champs-Elysées to get some food, while David took the tunnel route to head home to Trocadéro.

Two or three minutes later, David heard a car alarm sounding and saw the Mercedes rammed up against the wall of the tunnel. The impact had clearly been enormous: the whole undercarriage of the top-of-the-range armoured car had been smashed off. The accident took place just over a kilometre from the hotel. David was, he estimated, just two minutes behind the accident itself and other than the occupants themselves, nobody had witnessed the actual crash and impact.

**'None of the paps present was actually taking images; they were all trying to help'**

Realising it would be dangerous to stop nearby, David parked safely outside the tunnel and ran down to the scene of the accident. As he arrived, there were already four photographers with scooters at the scene. David freely admits that he was in shock; he called Fabrice to give him the news. Fabrice didn't believe him initially and by the time he arrived, having also parked away from the scene, there were seven photographers there.

None of the paps present was actually taking images; they were all trying to help. One of them tried to call an ambulance but was in such a state that he kept hitting the wrong number. Later, the paps would be unfairly reproached for the delay in calling for help, but that was the reason.

All the photographers at the scene were stunned into silence. These guys thought they had seen it all, but they were wrong. It was clear that they shouldn't try to move the victims of the crash before professional help arrived. Romuel from Gamma was a qualified first aider and he opened the door of the Mercedes to see if he could help. He took the Princess's pulse and determined that she was still alive. It was obvious that Dodi was dead. The accident had been so violent that his jeans had been ripped off; one of the paps covered the body with a car mat to preserve his dignity. Dodi was clearly a lost cause, but Diana was a different case. The only blood they could see on her was from a little cut on her eye and some coming from her ear. Luckily, a doctor happened to be passing and he too got involved in the initial first-aid efforts of the photographers.

Responding to the frantic calls, police and emergency services were on the scene in the tunnel very quickly. Medical officers tried to resuscitate Dodi with electric paddles and open heart massage, but to no avail. David was in shock as the horrific scenes unfolded in front of him. As Fabrice had been forewarned by David, he was in a better state mentally and went into the tunnel-vision news mode that I experienced in Bosnia and other tight spots during my news career. He had brought all of his camera gear with him from the car and as this was a huge news event, he hit a few frames. He was doing his job. David, who had a Sure Shot camera attached to his belt, also took a couple of shots. Nobody had tried to get any pictures before professional help arrived; their focus had been on trying to assist.

Rapidly the police and ambulance presence grew very large and David told Fabrice it was time to go; there was nothing more they could do. Some of the local residents who had gathered to see what was going on started to shout at the snappers to cease, so the duo left, along with another freelance. They were the only three not to be picked up. The other photographers stayed where they were and were all arrested. David rang Laurent and told him what had happened, and Laurent told him and Fabrice to get to the office to process the film. Laurent then placed the call to me.

Even upon arrival at Laurent's office, David was still very shaken. He and Fabrice started to discuss with Laurent what should be done with the images. David had realised quickly that the situation could be very difficult and dangerous for them. Laurent overrode their concerns and the images were scanned and supplied to me in the BIG offices in London. Laurent kept the negatives and the pictures were not sent anywhere else.

When the French police raided Laurent's office, they took all the images they could find as well as the negatives. I don't believe that he kept any copies. The police were perhaps initially alerted to the fact that Laurent had the images because one of his salesmen offered the picture to a paper called *Le Nouveau Détective*. That bid turned out to be a covert police sting and the salesman was arrested.

Later, Laurent was interviewed on French television and said that Diana had been beautiful even at the end. By this point, David and Fabrice knew the police were looking for them and were concerned that they were about to become the victims of a witch hunt. The pair decided between themselves to contact a lawyer and on the Thursday they presented themselves at a police station in Paris.

There has been a lot of conjecture about what happened that night. I am still extremely suspicious about some of the things that occurred. Many aspects of the affair just don't add up, and I am by no means a conspiracy theorist – in fact, my usual way of thinking is black and white. I think there are huge gaps in what we know and some of those gaps will never be filled. Of course, conspiracy theories grow to fill gaps in information.

The paparazzi – without a shred of hard evidence to back up the allegations and plenty to refute them – were made the scapegoats for what happened. All very convenient. Should the paps have been following the Princess? It's hard to answer that, but one fact remains: she wanted her picture taken that night. My guys were tipped off; they knew which exit the couple were going to be using and at what time. It is very easy to sneak someone out of a hotel like the Ritz if you want to. Diana and Dodi both had the best security available. OK, so the bodyguards have said there was no conspiracy – but since one of them was in the car, I don't know how he would know one way or the other if there had been a plot.

Whatever the truth, David and Fabrice maintain that a well-known UK pap told his partners in France not to turn up and follow Diana that night. Certainly it is odd that they alone were not represented at the Ritz or afterwards. These guys are highly regarded pros, and it was strange that they weren't around. Just another mystery.

There's no doubt that Diana would have stood a much better chance of survival if she had been taken to the hospital ten minutes away instead of being driven around for fifteen minutes. Additionally, it is well documented that a British woman who lived in Paris reported driving through the tunnel the night before the crash and noticing that all of the security cameras had been turned away from their usual orbits to point at the wall. The *Daily Mail* published a letter to this effect in February 2000.

The photographers at the scene were all known to Fabrice and David. The rumours about French photographer James Andanson being present are simply not true: he wasn't there. It had been said that Andanson was driving a white Fiat Uno that collided with the Mercedes, causing the accident. David and Fabrice refute that. Since Andanson wasn't there, the other more ghoulish rumour, which centred on him stealing the engagement ring from Diana's finger, can also be discounted. Conspiracy theorists have adopted him as a potential killer who may have fired a laser weapon to blind Henri Paul and cause the accident. Andanson himself will never be able to state his side of the case: in 2000 he was found mysteriously burned to death in a car deep in the forest near Nantes in France.

I have no doubt that at some point someone was seriously discussing having me killed. Whether that was someone in the establishment or one of the nutters out in the streets who had elected me Public Enemy #1 I don't know, but it would have been unfair, as I had played it so straight. The event had offered me an unparalleled chance to make an awful lot of money very quickly, but the financial aspect was never paramount in my mind.

**'I have no doubt that at some point someone was seriously discussing having me killed'**

I'm a salesman and I love to close a deal, but I'm glad I decided not to shift those pictures. Something tells me there's a good chance that there might have been another interesting 'accident' for the conspiracy theorists to chew over on the Internet. This book would have been a few chapters shorter, too. Type 'Darryn Lyons' and 'Princess Diana' into Google to see how embroiled I became anyway.

Eventually, rightly, no case was brought against Fabrice and David, though they are still involved in a nominal legal battle with Mohammed Al Fayed. It is my opinion that they were just doing their job and then when the horror began to unfold they helped as much as they could. Neither profited in any way from the events. In fact, David and Fabrice fell out with Laurent over non-payment of royalties that were due to them for the use of the pre-crash Diana pictures. Laurent paid them for the hours they worked, but not for the sales their work generated. Other than one chance meeting in Perpignan I have not seen Laurent in the last ten years, and his agency has folded. David and Fabrice now run their own agency in Paris, KCS Presse.

Sitting in that hotel room with them discussing how the scenario unfolded truly brought back the memories from that difficult time and confirmed my feeling that many people made up their minds too fast about what happened. The paparazzi were the perfect 'get out' and the average person in the street believes that version of the story. I am happy to tell it from another perspective. David and Fabrice have been silenced due to the legal set-up and the cases that are still pending. All of their problems could be solved by the payment of one symbolic euro to Al Fayed, but in order to make the nightmare go away they must accept culpability, which neither, naturally, is willing to do.

Is it right or wrong to chase people in order to get a picture? My answer is simple: the only person who did the wrong thing was Henri Paul, by drink-driving, jumping red lights and speeding. The crash became the biggest news story since the assassination of President John F. Kennedy and any newsman worth his salt – myself included – would have covered the events.

Any editor would have wanted his man or woman on the scene to get the pictures and would have been hugely disappointed had they failed. That's not to say that the pictures would have been used, but the photographers were there, and once they had done what they could to help out, they were there to do a job. A professional photographer switches off and does the job.

My discussions with David and Fabrice brought me a feeling of closure and also total exoneration. I know I did the right thing that night by not selling the pictures. I could have made a fortune and by doing the right thing I ensured that I didn't. It's easy for people to forget that I was just an agent. I didn't even take the pictures!

After Diana died, the paparazzi world went into meltdown. I had the sense to force BIG to diversify immediately into animal shots, cute shots, weird and wonderful stuff, extreme sports, anything we could pull in to keep the till ringing. Other operators panicked and wondered what the hell they were going to do now. The gravy train had just been derailed in truly spectacular fashion. However, despite the initial shock and temporary drop in the market, nothing fundamental really changed in the light of what happened to Diana.

Though the processes we use today are much the same as those employed in 1997, I think that to a degree the whole Diana incident made the paparazzi grow up. A lot of the cowboys exited the industry pretty quickly, while the professionals took stock of what the business was really about. I hope people realise, though, that chasing for pictures has always happened, and that for the quarry, the option to take is not to break the law and start driving at crazy speeds in order to lose people. Paris has always been famous for its teams of scooter-riding paps. Scooters are, in fact, a way of life in all of France. It was like that in 1997 and it is like that now. BIG recently got some great shots of Angelina Jolie and Brad Pitt that were taken by one of our guys operating from within a pack of scooters following the stars' car through Paris.

There's no real code of conduct, particularly for freelancers, but BIG does have its own stringent code – and my safe is filled with images that infringe privacy and whose publication is not in the public interest. Often these are decisions I will take with a Fleet Street editor, and sometimes they are tough calls. I always tell my guys not to even bother shooting into someone's private property, but as we receive images from all kinds of sources, sometimes amazing pictures do pop up. The public are becoming the new paparazzi with the evolution of camera phones and the like, and there really is nowhere to hide. The business is changing and that's why I launched my new initiative, MrPaparazzi.com. In the old days, the Duke of Edinburgh could get away with whatever took his fancy. Wouldn't happen now. Only recently the BIG Pictures safe received a new addition supplied by a member of the public: a mainstream TV presenter brandishing a shotgun in his garden. Is that a private moment? In the end it didn't run, though one of the Sunday papers was close to printing it.

Until very recently the royal gig was much less interesting. I don't think many of the papers currently bother with a royal team and no one is making millions as a royal pap with current images, that's for sure. That situation is undoubtedly about to change, though, with the two princes becoming seriously hot property. But getting images of them will be far harder than it ever was with Diana. Both William and Harry seem to toe their father's line and relationships with the media are not being built in the same way as they were with their mother.

Diana will always conjure up great memories for me of a wonderful but flawed individual who brought a lot to the world and in many ways got very little back – not even a fucking statue in London. I'd love to see a statue placed somewhere, even if it's just of her rollerblading. I personally think Kensington is the place it should be and obviously it should be the biggest statue in the park. I do like the Princess of Wales Walk through the park, but where's the focus? They've got a Peter Pan statue there, but where's the Princess? There's only that pathetic water feature that keeps breaking down.

Diana is irreplaceable. She had a heart that touched the world and I think it will be many years before someone with that much to give comes along. She will be remembered through our pictures. She was the greatest thing on earth to photograph and any decent picture of her was guaranteed to make publication somewhere in the world.

I recently spoke to John Edwards, the picture editor at *The Sun*, and he said, wistfully, 'I still miss her.'

So do I, mate.

# Catwalks and Dance Floors

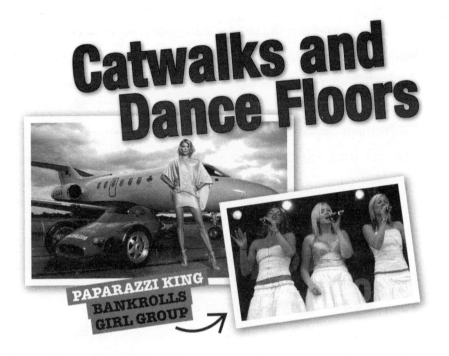

PAPARAZZI KING BANKROLLS GIRL GROUP

**BY HARNESSING PASSION,** drive, instinct and experience, I have made most of my business decisions work. When I moved into the nightclub business in Geelong I felt that I was buying into an enterprise that I not only truly understood but could ensure made a profit and a real difference to the town.

George Ramia, my lifelong buddy and the guy who made me into DJ Scoop, alerted me to the fact that there was an old wool store for sale on the foreshore in Geelong. When I was a kid the place to be was the top of the town, but I knew that the heart of Geelong was moving towards the water so it seemed like a good bet. I asked if he would be interested in starting up a business there with me. The money would come from me and George would run the business. He had been locked into his family business since he was fourteen and wanted to do something on his own. He had made the family business a huge success and had run the first proper discos in the area.

We had discussed working together for a couple of years and the time felt right. We would have some fun and do something for Geelong. I reflected for a while and then told him to attend the auction on my behalf and bid for the wool store, up to about half a million dollars. The auction was under way when George rang me at about midnight UK time in a bit of a panic to tell me he couldn't purchase the building. When I asked him why, it became apparent that George's father was also in the running and he felt very uncomfortable fighting with him. I overrode him and told him to pass me to Tim Darcy, who was an acquaintance and former Geelong footballer. I told Tim that whatever the final price was, I would top it. George's father, Ray, thought he had the property, but I whipped it out from under him. I was determined to get the building, no matter what it cost.

I flew out to look at the property and get started. I knew we needed to do something special and told George that doing it up on the cheap was not the way forward. I wanted this to be one of the best nightclubs in the world, and that meant not scrimping or saving on anything. I have partied at the best clubs in the world: from London to LA, from Rome to St Tropez, and I wanted something on the same scale. Opening the nightclub meant risking bringing down my whole empire.

Two nightclubs had already failed at the site. The first was called Platinum and despite a fair bit of investment its consortium had gone under. Various rumours circulated as to why it had failed. Some claimed it was an Aboriginal burial site. When I took the place over it wasn't much different from a bare wool store and I was going to have to spend a couple of million doing it up. Whatever your budget on a job like that, it will always be busted. I spent an enormous amount of money on it. If I had taken a financial hit on the UK business at the same time, I would have been in trouble. But the project was about realising a dream, being the best of the best and leaving a legacy for my home town.

George and I commissioned designers to come up with a look for the club, and hated them all. In the end, the name 'Home House' came to me on a flight to Australia from LA and I sketched out the whole concept and decor on a paper napkin. Working to my brief of 'new with the old', the designers then got it right and even managed to buy in much of the set from the film *Moulin Rouge*. The scheme was really coming together.

The opening night shaped up to be a huge night in Geelong's history. Australians like a party and anything can happen. (I was once told a hilarious story about Elton John's 40th birthday party, which was held aboard a huge yacht in Sydney harbour. One of the guests was reportedly Australian music doyen Ian 'Molly' Meldrum. Apparently it was the party of all parties and the guest list was stellar. Running late, Molly decided to cadge a lift from a police pontoon that happened to be berthed next to where he had parked. As they neared the party ship, Molly nudged the driver and said, 'Let's give them a wind-up – switch on the lights and the siren.' The story goes that unknown to Molly, a massive amount of cocaine and various other substances went over the side of the ship when they saw the police boat approaching. Molly clambered up the ladder, proclaiming 'Surprise!', to be met by stony-faced silence. I bet the sharks had a good night – maybe that's why they are called great whites.)

**No corners had been cut – the staff were even wearing $600 Swarovski crystal-studded T-shirts!**

By opening night, anticipation was at fever pitch. The paint was still wet when we opened the doors. No corners had been cut – the staff were even wearing $600 Swarovski crystal-studded T-shirts! The menus had real gold leaf on them (sadly, they ended up ruined after three weeks). It was beautifully done. We ended up with three and a half thousand guests that night. It was so rammed you could hardly see what the place looked like. The bar went through fifty-six barrels of beer! Though drinks were free until 1 a.m. when we let the public in, we still took more money that night than most clubs took in a week.

My intention had been that Robbie Williams would open the club on our VIP night. A good buddy of mine, Michael Brown, had strong links with Robbie and said he could sort it. I met Michael at the Sandy Lane hotel in Barbados when he asked me if I wanted to play a round of golf. He was in Barbados holidaying and was booked in to get married on the beach. Michael told me that he did some business in Australia. When I said I was after a big name to open my club, he asked who would be my ideal. I told him that Robbie would be a dream booking. I had followed Robbie all over the world in his Take That days, when I was with *The Mail*, and papped him many times since then. These days, of course, he is a megastar. I love his music. He does have an issue with the paparazzi, but I think that's partly because he doesn't want to be famous any more. There was a period when he would don a Robbie Williams mask whenever the paps were around, which I found very funny.

A couple of weeks after being on the golf course in Barbados, I was sitting in Crown Casino in Melbourne staring at a rider agreement with the 'RW' logo at the top. Silk Cut, Snapple, all kinds of weird things were requested. That fax is framed and on the wall in the club. On the appointed day my driver was waiting at the airport to get Robbie, the hotel was booked, and I had spent quite a lot on presents for him and Rachel (Hunter, who he was seeing at the time). Sadly, when the plane landed they were not aboard. To this day I don't think Michael knows what happened – I certainly don't. But he almost pulled it off. Luckily we hadn't released the news that Robbie Williams was coming to Home House, just that there was going to be a big surprise. As it happened, I was the one who got the surprise. Though all of our outgoings were refunded, it was a shame. I had really wanted to do it for my home town. Robbie probably just thought, 'I can't be fucked getting on a plane to Geelong.' A lot of people think I bluffed about his planned appearance, but it was all on the level.

The nightclub business really needed to work. I had drained a lot of money out of my other ventures in order to give Home House a real chance. Luckily the risk paid off. Since those early days the club has continued to be a success, though after the first three crazy weeks we went through a lean patch, which I think was because Geelong wasn't used to such an opulent, over-the-top place. Geelong is often known as 'Sleepy Hollow', and when the Darryn Lyons Circus set up in town it raised a lot of eyebrows. If the club had been in London or New York, it would have been packed every night.

George left the business after three years to concentrate on his family and pursue other business interests. In fact, as he had contributed so much to the success of the place I bought him out. I was a little disappointed to lose him, of course, and I know he still misses the club – he's often to be found at the bar!

Home House has stood the test of time because it truly feels like home; it's the biggest and best place in town. It's beautiful. I've had great times there. My work is all around the walls and the VIP room is packed with my photos and memorabilia. Every bloke wants to own a nightclub, I guess.

It's a magnet for babes. I have on drunken occasions kicked the DJ out and had a go, usually for a little too long. When I'm pissed I love getting on the mic and entertaining the punters – it's all good fun.

I would certainly love to be able to open a place like Home House in London, though I had a dabble in the club scene there when I went in with the bank and the administrators to try and save the Attica venue. My great mate David Mills was involved in attempting to resuscitate the business and he asked if I could help. I was friends with – and had a lot of respect for – the man I thought was the previous owner, Marios, but it turned out that the business was owned by the bank. He used to hold dinner parties where he'd invite his favourite people and was surrounded by hordes of assistants having a good time.

Unfortunately, after getting involved with Attica I had disagreements with the new management. Promises were broken and in the end I resigned as director, having worked really hard and brought the celebrities back into the venue. One of the accountants who was involved thought he knew how to run a club. Fatal – he should have stuck to his numbers. I'm not bitter, but it's a shame, because I think the place has suffered since then. BIG helped Attica get excellent publicity, but management didn't know how the game worked. They were scared to take pictures of celebrities in the club despite my protestations that this was what these people wanted! I was promised a free hand, but ended up with my hands tied. Attica could have been great again but I couldn't be bothered with a battle. By the end of my tenure I was actually made to feel unwelcome there and that hurt me. I had fantastic times at the place, but I don't go any more and neither do any of my clients. David remains a good mate, though.

Having access to a private jet for a year was a fantastic feeling and it came about in part through my association with David and Attica. Money brings you choice and this was a choice I was lucky to be able to make at the time. I joined the board of a company called Club 328 as an adviser; David was working with the company to turn it around financially. It was run by a great Aussie guy by the name of Warren Seymour, and specialised in providing services for the super rich. Members paid €328 000 to join, which then gave them a set number of points that could be exchanged for fast cars, a private jet, incredible houses in the middle of the Rockies, you name it.

I brought in Jodie Kidd to be the public face of the company and organised a media photo shoot featuring her wearing a gorgeous winged dress liberally festooned with Swarovski crystals. The shoot did well and made a lot of the papers. We also put together a launch event in Monaco's harbour that was attended by the great and the good, including many of my clients. The company then offered me a pretty amazing deal on a certain number of hours on the private jet, which I seized upon. The discount meant that I still paid out fifty grand, but it was well worth it. I loved it – the jet meant that

I could travel from London to my place in St Tropez in a quarter of the usual travel time. My car could pull up at the plane, let me out and off I went. You can do anything you want aboard your own private jet, and believe me, I did! Having the jet really made me feel that I had made it. The runways used by private jets are truly a prime meeting point for the world's movers and shakers; many a time I wished I had my camera round my neck.

Like the boat, the jet was supposed to pay for itself by being used to take celebrities out for exclusive shoots. In reality it probably didn't work as well as it should have, because I became too selfish with it. Perhaps it would have worked if more of our clients could have leapfrogged me in the queue. I didn't take on the jet again, which was a wrench but a commercial decision I had to make. I loved the years I had it. I made a lot of people happy with it – the boys used it, and I was able to fly my sister's family down to the yacht, which made me proud.

David Mills was also involved, to a degree, with my entry to the rag trade. The decision to have a crack at the fashion business came about as a result of my association with the fiancé of model Lucy Becker. Lucy and I had been working together very successfully for a while. My interest in fashion had always been strong. Various initiatives had almost come about and some ideas were better than others – though I do wish I had stuck to my guns to launch TNUC (The New U Couture). I thought the name was hilarious, but I got outvoted.

Lucy's fiancé (now husband) Julian Tendler had just sold his fashion business, Lollipop, and was looking for a new venture. He had been impressed with the barrage of press coverage I had been able to put behind my friend Robert De Keyser's label, Wheels & Dollbaby in the UK, and suggested that we team up. I would bring the publicity and the celebrity endorsement aspects; Julian would take care of the logistics of supply and manufacture. We put a team of designers together and started working on a range. Through my connection with David Mills and his administrators, we found a company in Turkey called MSG who could knock out the pieces for us. We were off.

We went for a 'rock chick' look and settled on the names Celebrity Couture and Twisted Ribbon. While I was away in Australia, Julian as majority partner declared to me that we were ready to start manufacture. Deferring to his greater knowledge of the rag trade, I agreed. We got the range into most of the High Street stores and did OK. Out of our line of twenty items, six or seven sold like hot cakes. Had our range been smaller we would have been away.

I was disappointed that we only broke even; I think sales could have exploded. The reason they didn't was probably that Julian let someone else take over the sales function. My experience in business always demands a hands-on approach. Going halfway rarely works and that is what we did. I should have been pushier. The rest of the collection sold out eventually, albeit at heavy discounts. My nieces and female friends certainly appreciated all the free remaindered stock we were able to push in their direction. Even today when I walk down the street I often see a girl in a Twisted Ribbon top and it gives me a wonderful feeling.

The whole process was a huge learning curve for me. The margins weren't great, and given that we were operating on a shoestring relative to the big boys we did really well. I got my fingers burned a little in that one, but you win some, you lose some.

Businesses interweave and I have always been amazed at how people's paths can cross and re-cross as we journey through this life. As one door closes another one opens, and though the fashion venture wasn't fated to set the world on fire, it did indirectly lead me into the world of music.

My journey into the music business started with Tanya Robinson, a woman who had been a buddy of mine for a long while, but certainly isn't now. I asked her to model for me at the launch of the Celebrity Couture range and we soon found ourselves talking about a new and entirely different project.

Our paths had first crossed when Tanya became one of the first clients of BIG Management, a venture that ended in disaster. BIG Management came about after I was approached by Camilla Storey, who was representing Tanya and her partner,

The golden couple. Forever? ↑
The million-dollar exclusive. ↓

Moving on,
Jen and Vince.

EXCLUSIVE PHOTOS!

US WEEKLY

JEN REACTS TO THE NEWS
RING DETAILS

BRAD & ANGELINA
SECRET LOVE TRIP
12 PAGES OF NEW PICS THAT PROVE THE ROMANCE IS REAL

Ben Spends $500,000!

The world is obsessed with celebrities and especially their love lives. Publications will pay millions to secure the scoops. 'Brangelina' was the big one and our pap Raymond Field got it. Who needs a lottery ticket?

Tom and Nicole in golden times.

The incredible world of Tom Cruise, with its bizarre twists and turns, has always been a draw for photographers. In his heady early days he could not stand the paparazzi – now he courts us.

Max PPP/Big Pictures

← Tom and Nicole and their adopted son, Connor.

Big USA

Nicole and a mystery man on Bondi Beach.

Big Australia

⬆ Yet another photocall from the couple who are fond of saying how much they're in love.

Steve Wake/Big Pictures

Big Pictures

KYS Press/Big Pictures

← Pete and Kate – I love 'em!

The former British PM's son wins over another voter.

Nothing sells like pictures of an A-list romance. Some of these relationships, of course, can be ones of convenience – all in the name of publicity.

Fame/Big Pictures

**NEWS** OF THE **WORLD**
HAVE WE GOT MORE SCREWS FOR YOU!

Which one of these stars has NOT slept with Deayton's hooker?

**SHE'S THE ONE**

World picts

Rumoured to be nothing more than a clever set-up, these pictures nevertheless made a fortune.

Robbie and Rachel: The love they tried to hide

**NEWS** OF THE **WORLD**
WE'RE STILL ONLY 65p

EXCLUSIVE
WILLS
The most amazing pictures ever

**WORLD EXCLUSIVE**

# KYLIE'S WRECKED MY LIFE

By lover James Gooding

The sex, the rows, the drugs, the...

One of my favourite 'Neighbours' in London, Kylie is the consummate professional who always plays the game with real class. She sang 'I Should Be So Lucky', but poor Kylie has not been all that lucky in love.

*Kylie takes a stroll with Olivier Martinez's dog, Sheba.*

*Argent au Poids*
*Silver by weight*

EXCLUSIVE: PILLION PICTURES SHOW SHE'S SO IN LOVE

# It's Ol's Angel Kylie

SEXY

HUNKY

By DAVID JEFFS

RACY

Celebrity shockers are always huge sellers.
Everyone forgets that celebrities are real
people too – we're here to remind them!
This is Mr Paparazzi's Yuk Page.

**Kurt & Goldie:
THE NAKED TRUTH**

CENSORED!

Keeping it all in is a big part of a female celebrity's life, and some are better at it than others.

John Gordon/Big Pictures

Goldie Hawn after a very heavy night.

Elle Macpherson has trouble keeping her assets in as boyfriend Tim Jeffries looks on with glee.

The paparazzi will be with the stars for the good times and the bad. It's not our fault that the bad times are the funniest!

Darryn Lyons

Marco Deidda/Big Pictures

Jack Nicholson is one of my all-time faves. Here he plants a kiss on a homeless man outside Tramps Nightclub.

This shot was taken backstatge at the Whitehall Theatre after the show Voyeurz, which featured a stage full of naked actors

Big Pictures

Michael Douglas denied a face-lift, but the camera tells a different story.

Big Pictures

THE NATIONAL

# Enquirer

·BIGGER·BOLDER·BET

## PLASTIC SURGERY
## DISASTER

EXCLUSIVE PHOTOS MORE INSIDE!

MICHA DOUGL FACELI Shocki secre revea

Tama Hassan. They liked the BIG brand and thought we could work together. They talked a good game, and the fact that I had always wanted to add a management arm to the company drew me in. There was something in the back of my mind saying no, but I went ahead anyway.

The results of the tie-in are probably a prime example of the need to perform a process of due diligence before proceeding on a venture. The whole affair was a mistake – albeit not an expensive one, but a mistake for the brand, and that pissed me off. Once the deal had been done, and I'd set firm targets and financial restraints, Camilla and her clients suddenly became a lot more demanding. There was a degree of mistrust between us and it began to fester. My experience of partnerships is simple: they are hard unless there is a leader. Even in a 50/50 deal someone needs to be the dominant character and run the engine. Also, a partnership must be completely transparent or it will fail. That said, if an entrepreneur doesn't have trust in other people, he will never find out if the potential in his ventures could have been realised. Whatever the business, there comes a time when a businessperson is forced to rely on other people, and with that there is always an element of risk. My failed partnerships have come about because people haven't been able to deal with my forthright manner and extensive vision for the future of the firm.

In the end a deal was done and they bought me out. My only regret is that they kept the name BIG Management – but I have BIG Group Management now, so it's not a huge problem. A name is a name, but I do worry sometimes that BIG Management is associated with me. At the time of the dissolution I didn't have a huge amount of choice. There was a very difficult atmosphere and a total divergence in how the separate parties thought business should be conducted. Luckily I got out quickly and cleanly – sometimes making the decision to get out can be even more difficult than deciding to invest or expand. Whatever else happened with BIG Management, it did put me in touch with Tanya Robinson and that led on to all sorts of ventures – most of them disastrous!

Tanya and I met up again when I took over Attica and booked her to launch Celebrity Couture and Twisted Ribbon. A couple of days after the launch she asked to meet as she wanted to discuss another project. She told me she had hooked up with two other girls, Shereen and Charlotte, to form a girl band. They'd already made a record deal, but it had fallen through and now they wanted to have another crack. My heart sank. I knew I needed involvement in the music industry like a hole in the head. Doubting that Tanya could even sing, I agreed to meet up with the girls for dinner.

They sang for me and I was astonished at how good they were. Their talent, allied to the fact that I really wanted to help Tanya out, led me to sign them to a management deal with my newly incepted Little Women Management. The band is just another one of Mr Paparazzi's mad gambles – I'm a very normal crazy guy!

My great friends in the music business are legendary

record producer Bryan Morrison and his son, Jamie. (Bryan is the owner of the Royal Berkshire Polo Club, where I play.) I mentioned the girls to Jamie the next time I saw him, and secured an appointment for them to audition for Bryan. Though he'd never worked with a girl band, he had been involved with everyone from Pink Floyd to George Michael and Wham!, which I figured was close enough. He liked what he saw and within days had signed them to his label, Believe Music – it was probably the fastest deal ever done.

Bryan knew how difficult it would be to break the band, but my promotional skills and his unrivalled experience made us a good team. The girls were a terrific package and my BIG Pictures team produced some fantastic publicity shots. I didn't scrimp and save with the girls, as I do with many of my businesses. I concentrated on making everything absolutely the best it could be. Sometimes I allow myself to eat into the profit margins a little in order to make myself proud and to surpass people's expectations. Image is everything.

Bryan brought an excellent songwriter, Ryan Laubscher, into the fold and he came up with some material that was immediate and had a real pop edge, but also with an intelligence that I thought would give it longevity. Once we got the girls into the studio, the results were pretty amazing. Shereen has a wonderful voice and Tanya was taking vocal lessons and improving every day. However, I knew Charlotte was going

**'Once we got the girls into the studio, the results were pretty amazing'**

to be trouble. Right from the off, she didn't seem to recognise the opportunity she was being presented with or understand the amount of work that needed to be done.

The girls cut a track under the name Kalinka for Chelsea Football Club, and the feedback was great. In the end we didn't release the track commercially, but the buzz was growing. Meanwhile, cracks were starting to appear in the band and it was time to act. Charlotte's lack of tact and direction were becoming a problem. Rumours about her were circulating and I didn't have time to deal with three squabbling wives – I was living the life of a Mormon! Acting decisively, I gave her notice and brought in the fantastic vocalist featured on Ryan's demos. Losing Charlotte was difficult for me and the other girls, but we all knew this was their chance and nobody was going to stop us having a crack at it. Paula was an outstanding talent and the missing piece. She was desperate to get involved. Her chance had nearly come a year before when she had reached the final of *Pop Idol* before the judges found out she was under their minimum age. The timing was good as we had yet to cut any tracks for the album. Paula's voice gave us something truly special.

The band was now named Twisted Sisterz, but we soon received notice that the veteran rock band Twisted Sister wouldn't allow us to use that name. Bryan told me it didn't matter what the band was called, but that we did need a moniker, and quickly. After some terrible suggestions we settled on Mrs Robinson and were away. The contract we signed gave the girls a real incentive to graft and was very fair – almost unique in the business, I would imagine – as all monies were to be split equally four ways. I could be very hard on the girls and sometimes they were frightened of me, but they needed discipline. I didn't see them as employees, though I was their boss.

Bryan and I put together a treatment for a video and had it produced. I enjoyed working with him; we had a real understanding. I think he found my ideas refreshing. I might have been new to the record business, but I knew how to make a group of girls look good. I was pushing hard on publicity and the girls were very well known nationally before they had even recorded a track.

Standing in the studio listening to the band laying down tracks felt wonderful. I was very decisive and knew what I wanted. We were all very proud of the results. When I opened the first box of CDs and saw my concept brought to life I felt a real swell of pride.

I think the world of music suits me because I understand business and I understand people. I have been described as a magnetic character and I love getting in the midst of the action, coming up with ideas and really making a difference. It wasn't an easy process. We had huge arguments and differences of opinion at times. I was a father, brother, husband, grandfather and sister to all of the girls at some point along the road. Everyone connected with them worked their arses off for the band and friendships were cemented; in particular, I formed a strong bond with Shereen's boyfriend, John Ball, now one of my closest friends in Britain. Life is about ticking boxes; the music business was just another box.

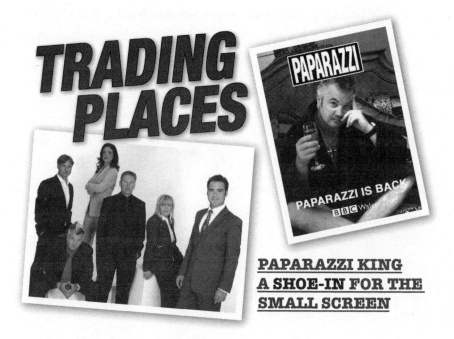

# TRADING PLACES

**PAPARAZZI**

**PAPARAZZI IS BACK**
BBC Wales

**PAPARAZZI KING
A SHOE-IN FOR THE
SMALL SCREEN**

**I AM NO SHRINKING VIOLET** when it comes to commerce, and that's why people in television have latched on to me – to give their shows some serious colour. I am lucky that I don't get nervous or scared. Pre-recorded is a piece of piss, but coming up with the goods on live television is harder, and like everyone I need a glass of water followed by a couple of deep breaths before I get started. Still, I have a real confidence in my knowledge of the subjects I am interviewed about, and my persona as a naughty boy involved in naughty businesses seems very popular with the public.

The first series of the BBC show *Paparazzi* came about after I was approached by Mags Gavan from BBC Wales.

She was trying to pull together a series about the industry as a whole. I told her straight that if any other agencies were involved I wouldn't be. Luckily they decided that I was the most compelling character they had discovered and the series would focus solely on BIG's operation. When the show aired, Andy Coulson of *News of the World* told me he was very relieved it had been me and not any of our rivals. I took Andy's comment as a compliment and knew I had a responsibility.

I trusted Mags, even though I realised I would have only a small amount of control over what went out. I didn't want to damage my business, but knew that when push came to shove, if something was unfolding that I didn't want to have filmed, then despite the lack of editorial control I could just throw the camera out of the window. BIG has operational secrets that it wouldn't be wise to broadcast around the world on BBC1! In all seriousness, that situation didn't arise. Ventures like this only truly work if a great relationship is established early on, and we certainly had that. I liked the producers, Jerry Gibson and Christine Macaulay; the director, Brian, and the main cameraman, Marcus, were great people; and of course I had a lot of time for Mags. I knew we had struck gold with this and that it would be fantastic TV. It was sold to fifty-nine countries.

The process was very intense, but it was good to open up the business to the public gaze. The BBC was amazed at the access we gave them and the fact that I never really kicked up a fuss. However, I knew I couldn't afford to be precious when someone was intruding on my life. There was an obvious parallel with my business and I was well aware of it. I thought to myself, 'Just deal with it.' No celebrity can come back to me now and say I don't know what it's like to be followed 24/7.

I enjoyed the process and am very proud of the results. It was a wonderful experience that allowed me to become a spokesman for the business. I took to it like a duck to water, as I do most things – I'm the archetypal jack of all trades, master of none. Parts of the series did us damage, but others made us an even bigger brand. Of course I cringed at times when I watched – the shots of me in Speedos, in particular!

**'No celebrity can come back to me now and say I don't know what it's like to be followed 24/7'**

Six and a half million people tuned in to the BBC. It was one of the highest-rating programs of the year – we were only a million viewers behind the launch of *Desperate Housewives* and they had a multimillion-pound budget for advertising alone. We just had me, Amber and my driver, Robin! Some of the reviews were very kind. Victor Lewis-Smith, whom I respect enormously because few escape his wrath, said that if there were any man he would go to war with it would be me. I was proud of that.

Because of the success of the series, the BBC decided to make a sequel. I did it because of the relationship that had been established and because the BBC was willing to be flexible. For the second series things were different as business was deadly slow and I had come back from six weeks in Australia to a bit of a nightmare. There had been a couple of changes in the crew; one of the girls had been trying to stitch me up and another was trying to shag me, so they both had to go! Filming started in March and went right through until the end of the year. During this time I restructured the business, got rid of some piss-takers and turned the whole thing around – all with a camera in my face.

None of the film crews ever turned up on time, of course, and they drove me nuts by missing some outstanding footage, but that's television. I was constantly kicking their arses and probably acted like an executive producer. I made it clear if I was unhappy with anything. One girl had to go because she kept missing key scenes, not least me scoring a goal at polo. I expect professionalism from my own guys and I expect it from anyone I work with. There's no doubt they found it hard to keep up with me, even though they were able to switch teams during the day.

I didn't try to hide the changes I was making to the business. This was a fly-on-the-wall documentary and I had to operate as usual. The public know when they are being conned. Right after the restructuring we hit big with the Angelina and Brad story and the year kicked off. In the middle of the filming process Joe Sene, who had been a wonderful CEO for me, left to picture-edit the *National Enquirer*. This left us with a gap, which Alan Williams filled admirably. He was a great appointment. He had been in my orbit for a long time and in fact asked me for a job while we were sitting in my good friend Leo's cafe Rimini in Geelong (which still serves the best scrambled eggs in the world). During the filming the 7/7 bombings in London happened; the crew got some powerful footage of that. Steve, the guy who edited the shows for Wiseguy Productions, did a great job.

When I was asked to be on *Dragons' Den* in Australia, I hadn't seen the UK version of the show. My Australian manager and old friend Mario took the call from the production company representative, who said, 'We want the crazy guy with the hair. We've really gotta have him.'

I wasn't inclined to do the show. Business was tough at the time and I knew the filming would eat into my schedule. I asked them what they were paying, and they told me 'Nothing' and said it would take three weeks and I would have to spend my own money. This was starting to look worse by the second! Mario and I discussed it; he was very keen for me to do it to raise the profile of the Australian businesses. He pleaded and in the end I agreed and flew to Sydney. I did it because I wanted to spend some time at home and it was a prime opportunity to plug my home town of Geelong on Channel 7. Contributors to these kinds of shows tend to be from the major cities, so it was a great chance.

The idea of the show was for people with business ideas to pitch to a panel of experts – the 'Dragons' – in the hope of getting the experts to invest in their idea and make their dream come true. Apart from myself, the Dragons were Peter Higgins, founder of home-loan business Mortgage Choice, who also has substantial interests in technology and data companies; Sarina Russo, whose self-titled group includes education and training institutes and employment agencies; advertising genius Siimon Reynolds; and Suzi Dafnis, publisher of the bestseller *Rich Dad, Poor Dad*, personal development educator and leading light of the Australian Businesswomen's Network.

The first stint of filming took five days, the second three and the final stage four. In between each phase I returned to London to keep my eye on BIG. They were tiring times; each day of filming went for at least thirteen hours. It was a slog, but a memorable experience. The team were paranoid about me swearing as they didn't want to have to 'bleep' the program. Of course, moderating my language wasn't a problem and things went very smoothly.

I had never met any of the other Dragons before, though I was given a brief resume of each. They were all very different from me and I have to say I think the casting was brilliant. There's no doubt I was the least qualified to be there. I was a bit of a fish out of water, but I dealt with it and was pleased with the results, and I think I made four new friends.

The Dragons were competitive. It was a battle of egos for some of the other guys and to a degree I enjoyed sitting back and watching the drama unfold. There was competition to be the first to invest. The women gave me the shits at times, but we all got on well. Naturally the show was a great source of new contacts and I met some good people.

We weren't shown beforehand what the pitches were going to be. The first one we saw was complete crap and it went on for three hours. I was planning to walk off to make a statement. Obviously the production company was keen to make good TV as well as flesh out the business aspect, but this was shaping up to be excruciating. All of the other Dragons were new to TV and anxious to get involved and talk and talk. I was unique in that I didn't really care how I came across. I knew people would either love me or hate me. My previous TV experience meant that I knew the editing process favours the short, pithy remark, and so I kept my comments brief. The first BBC show had shot 900 hours of footage of me running around the world that was cut down to three programs, after all.

**'I didn't really care how I came across. I knew people would either love me or hate me'**

I was just myself on the show. If someone needed attacking I would do it, and if I thought they were wasting my time I would tell them. I didn't mind telling someone that they had pitched badly and had a crap product. I loved having a go at people. I tried to be funny and to understand the people pitching as well as I could. The guy who pitched an invention called the 'Anywhere Tent' was a kid I wanted to help. He had spent time in the bush perfecting his design and his dedication was amazing. Four of us invested with him, though in the end the business didn't go ahead.

The funniest one, which was never actually shown, was a guy who had invented what he said was the first robotic vacuum cleaner. The product had apparently cost millions to develop and it later transpired that a competing product was already available. I smelt a rat immediately, though the others were initially interested. I feigned sleep during much of the pitch. Once the filming of the segment had finished, I went over to the robot and had a look inside it. To my astonishment I saw that it was basically made up of three rubber bands and a set of wheels sticky-taped together. I found out later that when the crew had gone to film the prototype it had actually exploded just after the cameras were switched off. I pissed myself laughing.

Peter Higgins has become a great mate of mine. He's a mad polo player and with his brother has built a fantastic business. Peter's kids love me and I love being the cool character. Peter has a natural intelligence. He's a supremely brilliant man but, like me, he didn't go through the university system. He is an accountant, an analyst, and on the show I couldn't compete with him on that level – at one point they gave us all calculators and I really wasn't sure what the hell to do with it!

Sarina Russo was a great performer. She couldn't stop mentioning all her powerful mates in Queensland so she would get kudos when she went back to Brisbane – I bet! Despite that, she blew me away and I love her. She's a skilled networker and has been very successful. I think she has a fantastic team around her and that has been integral to her rise. Suzi Dafnis is very bright and a really hard worker. She and Sarina were really competitive. Each would ask me about the other and I loved stirring them up. It really kicked off between them on one segment and Sarina and Peter had a serious spat too.

Siimon Reynolds is an advertising guru and I got on well with him. He is very softly spoken, charismatic and intellectual and would come out with the best and most apposite quotes from prominent businessmen. I phoned Mars after the first show and said, 'Mars, get me some fucking quotes – I'm going down here!'

My performances probably weren't helped by the fact that I was out on the razzle. Despite the fact that I was supposed to be on a health kick, I was in party mode and Mars and I went out clubbing on one of the nights before filming. He left me to it after a while, being the diligent Aussie business manager he is. I ended up staggering back to my hotel room with two women at God knows what time in the morning. At seven o'clock I was woken by Mars telling me that I had to be in make-up in half an hour. I was still slaughtered on the air and how I got through the day I have no idea – though the final cut looked fine.

Most of the businesses I was interested in were those that had scantily clad women coming on to the set during the pitch. Lusty Threads swimwear scored highly there. When their model walked on in a bikini, I shouted, 'I'm in!' – I didn't care what the business was. I invested in an eco-friendly cardboard coffin business probably because I was feeling so seedy, and a Sydney-based hair-care business initially got the nod too. I was interested in a high-fashion shoe company called Heirs & Grace, but it fell down on due diligence; sadly the woman had spent the money before she received it. I really liked her. She was a real goer and that's the way it works sometimes – you back the person as much as the business. I made an emotional investment in Paw Paws 'pet hotels' for Amber, but again that business wasn't financially viable and the actual investment didn't progress.

At the end of the show a wrap party was organised in a bar overlooking Sydney Harbour and each panel member was presented with a *Dragons' Den* trophy as a memento. I really enjoyed working with them; they were a truly professional bunch and we had great laughs together too. When my name was called out to go and get my trophy there was a huge roar and that made me feel really good. Andrew O'Keefe, the presenter, was a highlight for me and Keiron 'Spud' Murphy, the director, was also a funny fucker. Michael Horrocks, the executive producer, was a terrific guy to be around and was very interested in all of us.

Entertainment aside, I knew that in the end most of the businesses we had seen on the show would fall down for one simple reason: no serious businessperson is going to make a final decision on investing in a business in forty-five minutes. I believe in taking risks, but I don't throw money

away. Good TV, yes; good investment, no – not without
due diligence. Of the six or seven pitches I was interested in
during the show, one is now going well, another looks like
it's on its last legs and the remaining five didn't go ahead as
the businesses didn't stand up to a proper inspection. Due
diligence revealed that one of them had debts of 150 grand.
I was initially interested in investing the same amount, but
to do that would have been paying off someone's debts and
leaving no capital to invest in the business. It would have
been just throwing the money away.

*Dragons' Den* certainly made me an instant celebrity in
Australia and hopefully raised the profile of Geelong. As a result
of my appearance I've had lots of inquiries from companies
about bringing me in as an adviser or joining the board.

There is never a dull moment running BIG – someone,
somewhere, is always doing something very bizarre! Being
a press photographer gives me an understanding of the way
the celebrity industry works, but generally I'm not interested
in being anything other than myself. I don't care what people
think of me. I just don't give a shit. I'm not insecure – if I
was I wouldn't have hair like this! Anyone who believes their
own hype is given a one-way ticket to somewhere I don't
want to visit.

At the moment I see both sides of the fence in the fame
game. I'm sure that some of my friends on the picture desks

at the papers have a good laugh about it. Though I don't see myself as famous, I love the attention at times. Of course, I'm easily identifiable. There aren't too many peacocks like me around, so I make a simple target.

Fame in itself doesn't attract me, but if it happens as a by-product of successfully doing the things I enjoy then I will embrace it. Standing on the stage at Wembley Stadium in front of tens of thousands of people as the front man of a rock band is something I would love to do for one night, but it's not the way I want to live my life. I would rather be known as a great character, or be remembered as the originator of a great quotation, than just be famous. I love doing television because it can be such a buzz, but I realise of course that it pushes me into the limelight. The kind of fame that comes my way will, I hope, be down to some talent I have; that is the kind of fame that I admire in others.

Fleet Street editors have in the past called to warn me that people are circulating rumours or stories about me. I appreciate that, but I genuinely believe that there is no such thing as bad publicity. If I were caught doing copious amounts of cocaine and shagging twelve hookers, many of my mates would think I was a legend! Still, they'd better make sure the story's true before they print it or they'll find out how sharp my lawyers' teeth are! Sometimes I've baulked at the public exposure and I've gone back to my advisers and asked why I've been misquoted or lied about. There's a delicious irony about the Paparazzi King worrying about his public profile, of course. Maybe someone will turn me over one day – and good luck to them – but I won't be bleating.

In 2006, I was invited by *Sun* editor Rebekah Wade to a News International drinks event at the Royal Academy of Arts, attended by Rupert Murdoch. I couldn't miss the opportunity to shake his hand. Murdoch is one of my real heroes, a brilliant man. He's a freak and he controls the world. The power he has is awesome, and he could probably start World War III if he wanted to. I think he is far more important than the President of the United States. (And let's face it, he's a bloody joke. I say bring back Blowjob Bill.) I am just happy that Murdoch seems to run his empire in a responsible manner. The last time I had met him was in that lift at the News International building in Wapping, and now, nineteen years on, I had the chance to meet him as the biggest single contributor of images (in financial terms) to his company, and as a guest of their elite.

**'Murdoch is one of my real heroes, a brilliant man. He's a freak and he controls the world'**

All the British political grandees were at the event to meet Murdoch, the most powerful man in the world, and I enjoyed conversing with them. They were, in the main, very nice people. I found myself chatting to Gordon Brown, who was then the British Chancellor of the Exchequer and is now the prime minister, for twenty minutes about Australia's performance in the football World Cup. Brown is a really likeable bloke, which surprised me. If he didn't tax me so much, I might even be able to vote for him! I know Murdoch admires Brown's work ethic. When the new Tory leader, David Cameron, left the function, Brown called out a friendly goodbye. Cameron was completely thrown by this and just walked off without responding. To me that showed immaturity, but also ambition.

While I was able to introduce myself to Murdoch, sadly there was no time for a proper conversation. As I left the function, I thought to myself that there was probably a billion pounds worth of automobile parked along the road outside. I thoroughly enjoyed the evening and it felt amazing to be invited to rub shoulders with such illustrious company.

Due to the high-profile nature of my business dealings, I feel that I have crossed over – not only from the world of business to that of celebrity, but also from one side of the camera to the other. Many people fail to realise that these days I tend not to take many pictures; more and more, I find that people are taking pictures of me. In Barbados airport recently I found myself crowded by autograph hunters, who completely ignored the very famous model I was with. I won't even mention her name because she was so pissed off. I actually overheard her say to her partner, 'Who the fuck is he, anyway?' – which I loved.

These days I am probably more famous than some of my clients. The *Paparazzi* show has been sold in fifty-nine countries worldwide. In New Zealand recently, the Australian series of *Dragons' Den* was broadcasting on one channel while *Paparazzi* was on another. Given that they only have four channels there, that was a situation approaching domination! Wherever I stop around the world, someone recognises me – obviously it's pretty hard to miss the hair. Though I get more attention than I ever expected, I enjoy it. My exposure is only going to increase with MrPaparazzi.com – the cartoon version of me will be splashed all over TV, London buses, the Tube and magazines. I like the cartoon, not least because I took about five stone off myself.

At the end of the day, I have an ego – and a Leo ego at that. Even if the attention isn't positive I don't mind – I love a debate. Since the *Paparazzi* show, people have gained an insight into what we do and they understand the capricious, difficult nature of many of the stars. I have had a lot of fan mail, hate mail, you name it – even death threats, one of which was made out of letters cut out of a newspaper. It was nice of them to take the time, and I reckon you've really made it when someone sends you something like that! I even have a couple of stalkers – regular contributors to what I call the Strange Mail Society.

On a cold Thursday night late last year, I was sitting drinking in the bar at Claridge's Hotel with my friend Bryan Morrison. It had been a long day at work, but my celebrity radar was still working and when I noticed a little face peep around the corner of the bar, I knew immediately that it was Victoria Beckham giving me her trademark pout.

'Hello,' she said, giggling. Despite all the water under the bridge, this was the first time we had met socially. As it became obvious that she was there to talk, my respect for her went up a huge amount, though I have always rated her as a media player. It would have been far easier for her to ignore me or give me a glare, but instead she came over to say hello. This is a woman who knows how things work.

'David and I were in the shower this morning talking about you,' she told me. As I tried to digest this news and deal with the mental image it conjured up, I responded that I was delighted to meet her. Truly, I told her, she was astonishing, a real icon, and she played the game amazingly well. I'm never star-struck, but I was struck by her warmth. She continued, telling me, 'I think you're a wonderful businessman. You do what you do, of course, and it's never going to make us happy all the time, but we do have a lot of admiration for you. Also, I so look forward to you doing the paper review on Sky News.'

Victoria confounded my expectations. I've always admired her amazing style, but I was surprised that up close she was so polite, affectionate and courteous. It was a strange moment, as if we'd known each other for years – which of course we had, through a lens. You could say that our relationship had come into sharp focus. Maybe the next headline will be: 'Posh Spice and Paparazzo in Spicy Sex Romp'. If that happened, it would be one story that I would never sell. Giddy up!

# The Knack

**BIG'S BUSINESS OFFERING IS SIMPLE.** Of course we offer our clients pictures, but more than that we offer them the chance to increase their circulation by printing those pictures. I run the agency like a newspaper. My background is journalism and I've never forgotten that. I know what makes a great picture because I've taken scores of them. Hard work doesn't faze me and I expect the same from my team. I never let the office tell people I'm on holiday – I'm always available. My guys work fucking hard. Yes, they run around the world shagging flight attendants and staying in exotic locations, but they work hard.

The business has changed a huge amount in the years since

I started, and the simple reason for that is that there are more media and more cameras. The protection or non-protection of celebrities never used to be an issue; now it is an industry. The world's awareness of celebrity has grown to resemble a religion and with the advent of camera-phones and the like everyone can get involved. There are no hiding places left.

Technology has altered the root and branches of the supply side of the business. When I started as a photographer, I'd be looking at half an hour to develop the film after I'd hit the shot. Once I had my negative, it would take five minutes to make an edit (basically cropping the image as I saw fit) and then I would put the image into a scanner. The process of scanning would take at least ten minutes and once this was done I would plug the computer into an analogue phone line – assuming there was one available – and send the image to the paper, which would take at least forty-five minutes. The whole process would take at least two hours. These days I can move an image from a digital camera to my laptop and it can be in my office and then all around the world within minutes. The new technology still blows my mind – and it is constantly evolving.

Despite these changes, the basic ethos of the agency has remained fairly constant. We receive images as raw material from our employees and partners around the world and edit them to sift the wheat from the chaff. Because of the digital revolution, people are able to submit much higher volumes of images and it is a Herculean act to manage them all. Of the inflow that we receive, a maximum of 10 per cent is chosen for processing and offered for sale. Every day, Big Pictures sends 3500 to 4500 images around the world.

Believe me, editing a set of images is one of the hardest jobs in the world. The responsibility is to know what is going to sell. To a degree it is a skill that can be learned, but I also believe that some people have an innate ability for it. I regard myself as being one of the best in the world and that is what the business was founded upon. It is easy to miss the key aspect that may sell a picture for big bucks. For instance, we had a set of Kate Moss come in that looked pretty bog standard. I blew one of the shots up and spotted a needle in her ear with a tiny bit of tape over it. Was it there for drugs, smoking or diet reasons? I didn't know – but I do know that the picture made about twenty grand around the world as opposed to maybe a couple of hundred if we hadn't been able to highlight such a good story. That is the talent and it takes a real eye for a story. Is there a ring on the finger? A new tattoo? Anything out of the ordinary?

**'Is there a ring on the finger? A new tattoo? Anything out of the ordinary?'**

Once the pictures have been selected, most are cropped and captioned with our copyright details and digitally watermarked to prevent any unauthorised usage. Generally we own the licence to the copyright in perpetuity, through our deals with the photographers we employ. There is software available to us now that can tell exactly where an image has come from, and even if someone tries to create a shot by tacking two images together we can identify the 'DNA' of a BIG Pictures image.

All the studio shots we release are PhotoShopped, but none of the pap stuff is. While the pap shots are not touched up, they will be cropped or perhaps the brightness or the colour ratios will be adjusted – but nothing more than that. Once we have arrived at the finished product, it is passed to the sales team for sale and syndication to our clients. Our team has a morning conference based on sales strategies. Discussion revolves around the list of exclusive sets and images that we are prioritising that day, which will be written up on the whiteboard for all to see. Generally the first people we target for 'first rights' (the right to use a picture exclusively over a set period, usually a day) are the newspapers and then the magazines. The magazines will also often come to us once they have seen an image in a newspaper and will bid for second rights. An increasing part of the business is electronic rights – usage on mobile phones, hand-held devices and, of course, the Internet and television.

As well as the morning sales meeting, we also hold an evening conference to discuss who's hot and who's not, which helps us narrow our targeting and sales. That evening session would be heartbreaking for some celebs to witness. I'm sure that some of them would moan, 'Oh fuck, I'm not on the BIG board this week!' Every week we decide that some people are 'over'. By factoring that into our overall approach, to a degree we also set the agenda and force our predictions to come true by cutting certain characters out of our offering and supply.

If the papers and magazines are not receiving images of a certain celeb then obviously they won't be printed and the oxygen of publicity is cut off. So keep the Christmas hampers coming, guys!

A non-exclusive image will be pumped out to every contact from whom we think we have a chance of a sale. We call this 'all-round' distribution. Minimum reproduction rates will be added if we believe we have better material than our competitors. Obviously in the larger markets, particularly the UK, we deal directly with the magazines and papers and make sure that none of our contacts miss out on having the option to buy. Exclusives are dealt with separately. Sometimes, if we have a really big set, we will negotiate a share of exclusivity so that two (or more) publications run simultaneously with the same set.

If our first target for the sale of a set of images, or indeed a single image, declines for whatever reason then we move on to our second-tier target. We will not accept crap money at BIG and will never cheapen ourselves. We are a prestigious agency, and I know that our rivals don't get the money we do. People buy from me because they know the images are good quality and legit, and also, to a degree, to ensure that they get a look-in when the next major story comes in – we get the most exclusives. That's simple business, looking after your best suppliers. Building that reputation took a long time, and I protect it fiercely. My clients know that if I make a call, it is worth picking up, and that they are going to get something that's pure gold. They also know they're going to have to pay for it.

When an exclusive comes into the office on a normal day, Mel will take charge. These days I am only hands-on for the really big deals. Mel is exceptional at what she does, probably the best salesperson I have worked with. She and the team of eight sales staff (in the UK) will discuss the most likely buyer for the image and will start the process of making the client aware of what we have, moving to negotiations when interest is expressed.

Mel and I have very different approaches. There's something about her that makes you buy. The fact that she's a stunning woman doesn't hurt, but she also remembers birthdays, has throat lozenges delivered if a picture editor is feeling bad – just attention to detail. Mel has an air of purity and honesty about her; I certainly have *one* of those – but I'll leave it to you to guess which! If anyone at BIG is indispensable, it's Mel. She's the international sales director and you couldn't find a better one in the world. I have perhaps a more logical and convincing persona – the direct approach is the one I favour, and I will only deal with the top person. I'm a great sales thinker and know who is going to be interested in certain shots. Jane Fonda in a wheelchair: where's that going to go? One place: the *Daily Mail*. There are some celebs who will sell to everywhere – Kate Moss, for example – but someone like Kate Winslet is one for the *Daily Mail*, and the *Telegraph* loves people like Liz Hurley. The targeting is driven by experience and a knowledge of who is hot at the various titles and exploiting that knowledge. My team needs a nose for who wants what, and when they want it. Most editors trust my judgement. I don't ring them up claiming to have something great unless I truly do. In fact, these days it is more common for them to ring me begging for something!

As well as our own images, we sell other agencies' images in the UK. When we work with an agency from a different territory there is usually a dual sharing of images; we sell their pictures in our territory and they sell ours in theirs. Often we have more than one partner agent in each territory, as we have a reputation for being the best at selling people's work. I am always looking to bring in good agencies and also individual operators. We have representatives in more than forty countries, and differing levels of commercial involvement with each. The most important territories for us are the UK, US, Spain, France, Germany, Italy and Australia. Many of the nations that we do not deal with regularly have their own home-grown celebrities who would not interest the global market. Germany is a huge celebrity market, but we very rarely get images from there – there aren't many beaches for celebs to frolic on in Germany!

I still love the feeling of bringing in a great picture – and selling it, of course. The amazing picture of England footballer Wayne Rooney doing a scissor kick in training at the 2006 World Cup and proving to the nation that he was fit again after breaking a bone in his foot was a good example. Some of the football authorities didn't like the fact that we got that shot, but the British public loved it. The job has got harder, but I still get the buzz. If I didn't have that feeling of exhilaration, I would move on. I routinely experience some of the most important managers and corporations in the world trying to slime up to me or buy me off, but I don't care what they say – I do it my way. If I think a picture should be released, I release it.

I love selling and am good at it. I can get heated and frustrated at times and have been known to scream at editors. Generally it is a tough fight to get the best price, though if we have a truly outstanding set then the process is easier – the sale of the Beckham pictures to *News of the World* came at the end of one of the easiest negotiations I have been involved in; I named my price and got it – simple.

'Once you start to worry about the competition, you take your eye off your own game and that can be fatal'

That one picture gets used over and over again at a high minimum reproduction price, so it keeps earning for us and the photographer. Usually we get the pricing right, but we have had occasions when we know in our heart of hearts that we have undersold a set (though that happens perhaps 1 per cent of the time). My team is good and knows the game inside out – in sales, if you don't know the market you are fucked. It is hard to stay number one over time, but we have done it. Once you start to worry about the competition, you take your eye off your own game and that can be fatal. If you gave my enemies a sword, they would stick it in and twist it with relish – and, yes, if the situation was reversed I would do the same thing. That's just business.

People always ask me what a picture can be worth. The

answer is simple: it is worth exactly what someone in a given place at a given time is prepared to pay for it. I have a feeling for the figure that someone has settled on almost before they do. That value can and does change – for example, images of British actor Patsy Kensit and her new man were worth four and a half grand on the first day of sale and nothing the following day. There is no such thing as an average picture in terms of value because everything depends on who the picture is of and what the context is. If there's a story, the value can skyrocket.

When someone gives me an image, be they a staffer, a freelancer or a member of the MrPaparazzi.com website, they buy into my experience and reputation and I ensure that they get good service and of course a good result. There is no doubt I have sold the world's most expensive pictures. Not long ago a member of the public hit a wonderful shot of Gwyneth Paltrow surfing and was offered £300 by a paper. She came to me and I got her nine grand. I know the picture editor concerned got a serious bollocking for letting that one get away. If he had offered the girl a decent price he could have bought it exclusively; in the end he had to share.

The point is that a layperson will not generally know if they have an image that is worth a million quid or twenty. That can be allied to the fact that anyone going directly to a paper to sell an image will get turned over anyway. If a newspaper says it's worth twenty, I'll get you a hundred. MrPaparazzi. com recently sold for £40000 a picture that one of the papers had offered two grand for. That is why people need an agent and the knowledge I built the business on: knowing the value of an image and negotiating to get that price. I know for a fact that even our big competitors have no idea what their images are worth. I could walk in and guarantee that I would make them at least three times as much as they are making now if they turned that arm of the business over to me.

Knowing what a picture is worth is essential, and I have a happy knack of being on the mark. That is one of the reasons I set up MrPaparazzi.com. Any member of the public offering a great picture to a national newspaper will get the same response: 'We'll give you 250 quid for it.' Newspapers know they can get images from 'citizen journalists' on the cheap. And television companies expect them for free! I am putting myself in the frame as the public's agent to redress the balance.

Obviously not all images are equal. The minimum that we would sell a picture for is around £40 for something probably taken from our library. As for the upper limit, well, I am still trying to set that record – and I try every day to beat my own world record. Our picture library is one of the best in the world and an ongoing source of revenue. It probably generates around 40 per cent of our turnover.

I will never be a sheep. Sheep are not effective leaders, after all; all they do is follow each other around all fucking day. On very rare occasions we have had a set rejected by everyone because of price, but I very rarely lower prices below

Graham Trott

## We're Engaged

Melanie Pettitt to Darryn Lyons
20th July 1991

◄◄ Mel has always been a great friend and confidante – and always will be.

The boys, then and now. Whether I'm driving a battered XA Falcon or a Lamborghini Diablo VT, I have as much fun as ever with my lifelong buddies.

▲ Vanny (Shayne Van Dreumel), me, Cam (Cameron Byars) and Mars (Mario Gregorio).

▲ Me, Lewy (David Lewis), Mars and Vanny.

❦ BIG Pictures now and then. It's been quite a journey from our first small base in St John Street to our five-storey colossus overlooking St Paul's Cathedral.

← The prince and the paparazzi. I am at the Royal Berkshire Polo Club with my Geelong FC jersey watching Prince Harry play polo.

Polo is a huge part of my life.

← Tough job! Another hard day's work on board my yacht Australia IV in St Tropez.

Nice spot for a hangover. It's hair of the dog at 50,000 feet on my private jet.

◄◄ This was taken on my yacht after I'd had several tinnies to celebrate the day's 'catch'.

Organising and directing shoots with the world's top models is all part of the fabulous fame game. Jodie Kidd is a polo pal and a joy to work with.

➤ Since filming *The Dragon's Den* in Australia, we've been inundated with business proposals from all over the country. I went for this proposal because it would inject a lot of money into my home town if it came off.

Don't let the hair fool you – a serious businessman lurks beneath.

Being an entrepreneur is the core of my life. I may mix with the stars, but my true passion is seeing something built from nothing and making it last.

The love of my life: Amber.

Unusual for me to be shy, but when you're going out with Jordan there's no alternative.

Paul Chesterton/Big Pictures

Lindsay Lohan's bag was stolen, but I tracked it down.

Babies are big business, as this page of big-selling pics shows.

The first pictures of Liz Hurley where her pregnancy bump was showing clearly. This one was taken in Beverly Hills.

The first picture of Jordan's baby – another BIG Pictures scoop (this one by Steve Ward).

Posh Spice shows off a new addition.

Madonna proves that she really is the Grandma of Pop.

Britney's baby escapades always hit the headlines.

I'm being ribbed about my size, says Liz

SUNDAY **PEOPLE**

WORLD EXCLUSIVE **Jordan & baby ..first photo**

Madonna always turns it on, unlike her shy husband, Guy.

← The camera does lie. Mel B wasn't topless here, but looks can be deceiving.

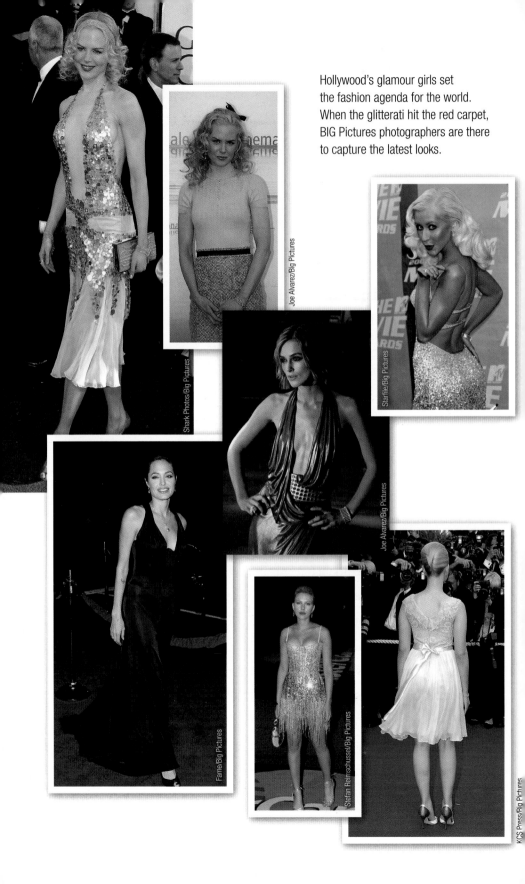

Hollywood's glamour girls set the fashion agenda for the world. When the glitterati hit the red carpet, BIG Pictures photographers are there to capture the latest looks.

Joe Alvarez/Big Pictures

Shark Photos/Big Pictures

Starfile/Big Pictures

Joe Alvarez/Big Pictures

Fame/Big Pictures

Stefan Reimschussel/Big Pictures

KGS Press/Big Pictures

the level that I feel is right. When you've got Gucci products, you don't offer Marks & Spencer prices. I know that any photographer reading this won't like that tactic, but I stand by it. My stance protects future prices and makes a lot more money for photographers.

At BIG these days I deal with running the show rather than working in it. In this job, a typical working day is one that never ends. I'm usually awake by around 5 or 6 a.m., and most of the time I don't get to bed till 2 or 3 a.m. As soon as I get up, I head straight out for my daily walk through Kensington Gardens. It really wakes the brain and gets me ready for the day. I'm generally picked up by my driver around 8.30. Once I reach my London office, I'm pretty much straight into meetings – very often I'll have breakfast, lunch and dinner meetings. My PA then schedules meetings around those meetings.

**'I like the idea of making money even when I sleep. Not that I get to sleep much'**

It's a pretty power-packed day. My input is simple: ideas and actually running the business. I always wanted a 24-hour business, and now I've got it. I like the idea of making money even when I sleep. Not that I get to sleep much – I'm out networking most nights, dealing with celebrities, their agents, the papers, PRs and my other businesses. My phone never stops ringing. I hear it in my dreams. I have to deal with everything the day throws at me. Much of it comes directly to me, but I'm a delegator and make very quick decisions.

I love ideas and that's what I deal in. I jump from thought to thought very quickly; my brain works in an erratic but detailed way. Every so often I clear my schedule and make some time for myself. I love to watch *Seinfeld* and *M\*A\*S\*H* and my latest passion is polo. It is like Australian Rules football on horseback, and I fucking love it. Most of the time, however, I'm on full alert. If you make a mistake in business it can bury you. I've come very fucking close a couple of times. I hide a lot of stress, but I get off on it too. If I end up going back to Geelong with the $500 I arrived in London with, well, it's simple – I've had a bloody good time! Always remember: the brave do not live forever, but the cautious do not live at all.

As my experience of the corporate system has increased, my management style has evolved and softened. I used to be the biggest shouter, stamper and screamer. I used to throw chairs. I was a rock-star boss, without any question. I even sacked Mel on one occasion; that's how bad I was. These days I am much shrewder, much more of a thinker.

I am a real listener, which is learned behaviour, and these days I can admit when I am wrong. Just recently at our office conference we were looking at a set of pictures of Elle Macpherson getting into a car, which Alan was confident he could sell. I laughed in his face and promised him a case of wine if he did. The call came through at lunchtime – Alan had sold the lot to *The Mirror* – and I asked my secretary to sort him out. Ten minutes later Mel buzzed through and told me she had sold the set to *Heat* magazine, too. Luckily I hadn't made a deal with her! I had been going to say that I would hang naked from Tower Bridge if they sold the images, so I guess I got off lightly, and so did the British public.

I try to instil my work ethic in my team and motivate them. Mel and Alan in particular have taken to it like ducks to water. They get it. Focus and dedication are the keys. I will tell any businessperson in the world that if they return home after a long flight or business trip, no matter what hour of the day or night, and don't immediately head to the office then they are a wimp. I don't come home; I go straight to the office.

I am building the business into a 360-degree digital media company to include television production, the Internet and mobile phones. I want to see BIG Pictures become the best company in the world. I am very lucky to be in a business where something different can happen every day. It's strange, however, that often the first subject discussed in the office conference will be who's getting sex. It seems that usually no one is – though I guess most of them are married! Sometimes I find myself out of touch with the company environment. Sitting at the top of the BIG Pictures tree looking down, I find that I don't know the name of some of those who work for me, and that is terrible.

The biggest danger for me is becoming bored. I will get

up and start screaming around the office just to get some excitement going. I make the place into a bit of a movie set. My directors get driven mad by me appearing in their offices during quiet times. I need things moving and a hundred things going through my head to have had a proper day.

MrPaparazzi.com is a huge priority for me. The site will democratise my business by allowing the public to upload their own pictures and take advantage of my skills as an agent and a salesman to make them top dollar and avoid getting ripped off. The potential is there for MrPaparazzi.com to be a much better business than BIG Pictures. It is the future and I am putting a lot of thought and money into it, though the business is already self-funding – as

**'I have around 800 photographers running around the world for me – but I would rather have a billion'**

was BIG when I started it. We have had millions of hits and sold plenty of fantastic pics; we made one contributor more than $100 000 by brokering the sale of one image. The site won Yahoo International Entertainment Website of the Year in 2007 and has now become the number-one entertainment site in the UK. Over a million people are getting their celebrity fix every hour of every day, and the numbers are increasing daily – it's celebrity junkie heaven!

We live in a very media-savvy world and people know the value of celebrity images. Any member of the public can become a photographer for me. As it stands I have around

800 photographers running around the world for me – but I would rather have a billion, which is a distinct possibility! Already, people are interested in working with us or acquiring the site and I need to make the right decisions. I've had plenty of million-dollar offers for the site, but I'm holding out for the right partner who can make it fulfil its potential.

My credo at the moment is simple: back to basics. Sometimes you have to take your business back to the basics. It is useful to think about how things started and where the initial success came from. Simplicity is often underrated. All of my energy is focused around BIG and drawing in from some of my corollary activities. I have achieved a lot of my ambitions through commercial ventures, and I love taking those punts, but now I want to lead BIG into the future.

# LIVING THE DREAM

## LOCAL BOY MAKES GOOD

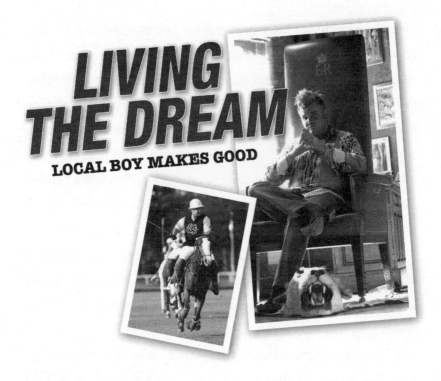

**THE ENTREPRENEUR** is a rare beast and an animal that people seem to be afraid of. I'll never again make the mistake of telling a bank manager that I am an entrepreneur – he couldn't get me out of his office fast enough. I remember sitting with a banker who had been introduced to me by David Mills, with whom I had worked at the Attica club. I ran the guy through my business portfolio and he turned white. Afterwards, Mills told me that perhaps I had overplayed my hand and that I had probably scared him off with the extent of my dealings (and my hair!). More entrepreneurs fail than succeed and I have done a bit of both along the way. My ethos is that if one plan fails, I quickly implement another.

The public love entrepreneurs – anyone who is willing to have a go. I don't believe that you get anywhere in life without taking big risks. I have doubled up mortgaging assets with banks across the country to get the money I needed for a project. I need rapid results; things have to happen now, preferably yesterday! These days it is probably harder to get away with this approach – if it all goes wrong then big trouble is on the cards – but there isn't a successful entrepreneur in the world who hasn't made major mistakes along the way. Most have had more failures than successes. This certainly doesn't make them bad businesspeople. I believe that failure will always teach you more than success, on both a personal and a professional level.

To be a success, an entrepreneur must focus on being the best and going with their gut instincts. If I have to work around the clock to make something happen, then I'll do it. People don't want to work the hours I work, and nobody works as hard as I do. They simply can't do it – but work is the reason we went from 'little' pictures to fucking BIG Pictures. I keep a notepad by the side of my bed to jot down the ideas that come to me every night. An entrepreneur has to act quickly. I don't stop to think about things – when I have an idea it has to be acted on immediately. As a businessperson very often you have to wing it because you're not sure what the fuck you're doing. That's not a formula for success, of course. Everyone has their own approach and mine has worked for me. Sometimes I can go off on several different tangents at once and at times I lose interest in aspects of my business. I've always got an eye on the next newfangled idea. I see myself as a builder. I have the ability to think out of the box. I love edginess. Everyone has creativity within them, but not everyone is able to express or use it.

The opposition or competition shouldn't be something you think about too often. I think that being blinkered is a good thing in business. Be like a racehorse: focus on your target and just go for it. I have always said that if I could be an animal I would be a racehorse: you'd spend the first half of your life with someone on top of you and the second half out to stud! The competition can't keep up with me and that's why we prevail. I don't care what the opposition is doing and I won't have my competitors' tactics discussed in the office.

My approach to business is that it isn't rocket science. To be successful you need to be honest and loyal and avoid being greedy. It is essential to come up with a big idea and see it through, work hard and take a big risk. Treating a venture as a journey is hugely important. The process can be very stressful; being an entrepreneur is 'worry, worry, worry'. I used to get off on stress; it was my drug. I loved working out how to get out of ludicrously hard situations just so I could test myself.

My flair and outrageous nature have helped me in business. The heights I have scaled and the depths I have plumbed cannot be reached without upsetting a few people along the way. People are very clear in their minds about how I do business. I'm not a double-dealer. I am warm and sensitive on the inside, but most people don't get to see that; they just see the ego. My relaxed approach in meetings helps me to break the ice. I'm a straight-to-the-point guy. There's no bullshit with me – I'm always 'Get it? Got it. Good.' I can't deal with people that will not get to the point; I tend to stop people mid-flow just to get them to cut to the chase.

Just remember that while a touch of arrogance can be the other side to greatness, it must be used in the right way – with charisma. I have my knockers and I always will. Some call me arrogant, but others call me honest and say that I voice what others are thinking. I believe in confidence and find it an attractive quality in others. I can be bold and disruptive, but people always remember who I am. Perhaps my dress sense helps there, too! I've always been a colourful person.

**'I can be bold and disruptive, but people always remember who I am'**

I know that I fascinate people because they can't work out how I've become so successful wearing what I wear and being how I am. I love to intrigue people. Even if I was flat broke in the gutter I would still be invited by the rich and famous to the same parties I go to now because I'm a character. (If I was in the gutter I'd probably have saved my Cavalli snakeskin jacket and trousers so people could laugh at the rich tramp.) My life will be a roller-coaster whether I like it or not. I didn't plan it – I'm just like that. I'm a grafter, and best of all I'm an Aussie – there's more behind the hair. Never underestimate me.

My mate Bryan Morrison and I often meet in a little bar in the Milestone Hotel. The building used to be an asylum – maybe that's what attracts us. He told me once that I was in the top tiny percentage of the world's population because I allowed my idiosyncrasy to express itself and enjoyed being truly different. What he said took me aback, but it's true that there are differences between me and most other people. I think we all have talents and mine lies in being instinctive yet also able to forecast and be forward-thinking. I can see the beginning of a business and the end of a business. Seeing the end is incredibly important, and predicting events is certainly more important and lucrative than reacting to them.

I think business today lacks great characters. You look at a guy like the late Kerry Packer, who I sadly never got to meet. He was a bit of a nutter and could be like thunder in the office, always with fifteen fags hanging out of his mouth. Packer did a massive amount for cricket and was also a huge polo fan. I guess we had a couple of things in common.

I heard a wonderful story about Kerry spending a day playing polo down at Cowdrey Park in Sussex with his team. It was late on a Sunday when the tournament finished, and he decided to take the boys out because they had won. They went into the local village and stopped at the nearest restaurant. The owner told Packer that it was too late to serve them and they should be on their way. They headed down the road and found another place where they were welcomed despite the hour. The owner cooked up a meal for them and when the bill came they left a cheque and walked out. Packer then walked back up the road to the other place and shouted through the door, 'You really missed out, mate – the bloke down the road just made a hundred grand!'

I love people who make their own success. It's about doing it on your own, not inheriting wealth. They say that every third generation loses it, and that's why Murdoch isn't guaranteeing to any of his kids that they will inherit his fortune, though they won't be eating from the gutter. Such an incestuous set-up can spell the death of the mightiest corporation. People in that situation can't compete on their own terms with the success that has gone before them and their experience of wealth means that they often have a skewed appreciation of the real world. As Oscar Wilde said, 'Some people know the price of everything but the value of nothing'. It's no accident that *BRW*'s rich list in Australia doesn't feature people who have inherited their wealth, only those who have created it. That's why I like Paris Hilton. She could just sit at home all day and do nothing, but she has developed her own corporation. Naturally she had a good start, but she's built it. No one gets anywhere in life sitting on their arse at home. Look at the world and see what is happening. People, listen to me – get off your arse and just have a fucking go! I hate to think what would have happened if I'd been born into money: I would have been a crazy man. Worse than I am, anyway.

I am a great ideas person; that's what I do. I mix with some of the best, and though I sometimes envy their sheer brainpower, I know I'm more of a creative, 'make it happen' person. I don't have a huge amount of patience and everyone will tell you that is important in business. I'm very good with children and animals, though. I do get judged negatively – whether it's the hair, I don't know, but I don't really care.

I am ruthless in business, but loyal to my friends. I have chosen my friends really well, and I can't put into words how much I love them. I've had great times with them and I like to think that I've been part of their great times too. I think for someone in my position it's unusual to be able to keep friends for as long as I have. I'm a very lucky man.

**'There are so many fuckers out there who want to cut your balls off'**

As well as my friends, I choose my employees carefully. Employing the best people is essential. People laud entrepreneurs like Branson, and he's an amazing guy, but he keeps it simple. If he's going to start a new company he poaches the best people available to advise him. The most important aspects I look for are loyalty and integrity. I think if you find these factors then you are more than halfway there. There are so many fuckers out there who want to cut your balls off. Backstabbing is a fact of life and I have certainly had my share of injuries. I need hard workers and I hate people who clock-watch. Even people who go out for lunch bother me! My dad was that way, too. I know what he went through to put food on the table every night. I will always back a hard worker who comes into my office, but be disloyal and you're finished.

The way I see it, I take the risk so I can comport myself as I see fit. I expect my employees to care about the company and see it as their company as well. I enjoy 'making' people and pushing them to achieve their potential. Of course I get it wrong sometimes and have promoted the wrong people. I think young people now expect everything straightaway; they don't understand that it's a journey and rewards have to be worked for and earned.

The danger in doing what I do is getting trapped. I walk with a noose around my neck every day. The noose is responsibility. The boss is the most talked-about person in any business. You're talked about at people's dinner tables. I pay 200 rents or mortgages, pay for 600 meals a day, and multiply that for all my employees' families. You're the best bloke in the world, or the biggest prick. That's the responsibility. But I accept that I have to pay these people's bills and I take it very seriously and I stress about it. I get fed up with people thinking, 'He's got this, he's got that', but not understanding all the risks I take, what I put on the line. Those figures in the media come from assessing what I could make if everything was sold tomorrow. When the *Business Review Weekly* 'rich list' came out in Australia saying I was worth $58 million, people started speaking to me differently. But I haven't changed – though I did ask Mars where the hell the millions were. It was funny walking into the Bank of Melbourne in Geelong holding a copy of

*The Addy* proclaiming my wealth and having a laugh with the cashier, who could see what was actually in my account! I don't care about money, but I do care about having enough to pay the bills. I like to think that I've had more successes than failures, but I don't think of myself as successful. There isn't enough time – there's too much to be done.

Looking after my employees is a frightening responsibility, but one that I take extremely seriously. That's why I find it so hard to fire people unless I do it in a rage or temper, when I never actually mean it. In fact, I don't think I have ever sacked anyone. I find it incredibly hard, which is a terrible thing to admit. I always get someone else to do it because I get quite emotional. That's a bad trait to have as a businessperson because it can lead to holding on to people or assets for sentimental reasons. My nature means that sometimes people can have me over, but I am a great believer in karma and I like to think of the ones who have done me wrong dreaming about a wild, coloured-haired bloke pointing the finger and saying, 'I told you so!'

Being rich doesn't make people happy, and success shouldn't be gauged by how much money is in the bank. Money is a by-product of success. People should go and do what they want and the success will come. They should stop thinking about how much money they are going to make, and enjoy the journey.

I haven't been successful because I wanted money. I don't

see myself as a brilliant businessman; what I am is a grafter and a builder. When people talk about P/E ratios and all the rest of it I glaze over. My great mate Peter Higgins, from *Dragons' Den*, is amazing at all that, but it's not my style – show me a profit-and-loss statement and I'll say, 'The business is fucked' or 'Giddy up – let's buy a Bentley'. I'm no analyst!

I see success differently from many of my peers. Bringing up a happy family, staying married for forty years, busking on the Tube and bringing a smile to people's faces – that's success. I'm not intimidated by anyone and I don't wish for anything – other than to walk through my front door to a lovely wife and two beautiful kids, which is something I haven't achieved yet. There is no one formula for success. Once people have tasted big success, striving to better themselves is rarely about the money any more. They then crave power, or desire to leave some kind of legacy. I certainly fall into the latter bracket and don't dwell on the success I have achieved; I am always looking for the next challenge. I have the will to be the best, but I never will be. Your life runs out!

> 'Bringing up a happy family, staying married for forty years, busking on the Tube and bringing a smile to people's faces – that's success'

You never know when something is going to happen that is beyond your control, but if you plan for contingency things will fall into place. I'm a very ambitious person and always desperate to achieve the unachievable. That means that I will never reach the top. I'm never going to be the richest or the poorest, but I'm having a crack. Going down to my corner shop and spending a pound on a lottery ticket and winning a million pounds wouldn't make me happy – but trying to achieve my own success with that same pound would.

Money buys choice, not happiness. I play with big, big money but I'm not afraid of it and so I don't lose any sleep over it. My background wasn't materialistic and I think that has helped. I can certainly be materialistic now, and I can afford to be. I don't mind admitting that I love the bling and the Lamborghinis and the Ferraris. Why not? It was my dream at twelve and it will be my dream at 112. I don't give a toss whether people think it's ostentatious or not – at the end of the day a Lamborghini is just a lump of metal with four tyres. Some people may think that I don't deserve to own such a car if I can say that, but it's the truth. I have part of my dad's attitude in me; he drove his Hillman Hunter for hundreds of thousands of miles until it fell apart.

Some very rich people don't spend money, but that's not my style. I like a good time and good crack. Do I need a boat? No. Do I need a Ferrari? No. Did I need a jet? Again, no, but they're great things to have. I started BIG Limos to be able to afford a chauffeur, and the yachts I have bought into pay for themselves through third-party charters. As long as a purchase of that ilk can break even, it is worth doing.

I don't ever want to be like the old couple from Geelong I

heard about who were so tight with their cash that they even reused their cling film in order to save money. They were found dead underneath their washing line, both having had a stroke. I wouldn't want to end up like them or with a reputation for being tight.

Stressing about the almighty dollar has shortened my life and will shorten the lives of many readers of this book. I've seen it ruin lives. If all you want is money, then you may fulfil your ambitions, but you'll never be happy. You should never go into anything if you don't love it. You've got to passionately want to do it. The money is a by-product if you're successful. Money is paper, and it burns. Remember! It burns.

A guy like me is always going to be worth a lot, or nothing. I don't have anything tucked away for a rainy day because I like to gamble with everything I've got. One important maxim that has always guided me is that when I have to make a real gamble, I make it on myself and not on someone else. No one can be trusted to commit themselves totally to achieving something with someone else's money. Deep down, I always know whether or not I can pull something off, and I rarely let people know exactly what is going on in my mind.

If you don't think in cycles as a businessperson, you've lost it. That's why it's a shame that I don't have an heir – though I have set up a trust to benefit photography and the arts. I'm not going to leave millions to people in order to let them have an easy life; I certainly haven't had one. Children don't know how to handle responsibility. Wisdom comes with age and experience and that's the purpose of life – you have to climb the hill to get the view. I will make sure my family is looked after, but I don't feel a responsibility to make them wealthy as I think it would make them worse people. The only thing money can give you is choice, and it's important to exercise that choice wisely.

Many roads have led me to my current position, some planned and some random, some lucky and some disastrous. I have always been a confident little sod and have never been afraid to knock on doors to achieve my dreams. Sometimes you have to knock a hundred times, sometimes they just open.

My life has been blessed by adventure and opportunity and, as Mr Paparazzi, it has been lived through a lens. My father used to lead the Lyons family in a grace before dinner. At the time I found it funny, but now it seems about right. 'For what we are about to receive, may the Lord make us truly thankful. For Christ's sake, amen.' It's been a long road from my early days in Geelong, but my journey has taken me to the heights of London society to the madness of the Bosnian conflict to the realities of building a business. It's been a blast.

I enjoyed the early days, but I wouldn't trade places now. If I didn't have the stress, I wouldn't have the freedom. I love new things and my position now allows me to really take myself on a journey. The journey is what money can't buy and it's what you make it: the hunt, the chase, being alive. Someone said to me recently, 'Why don't you just take a couple of mill and put it to one side?' It would make sense, of course, but for me, that's just not cricket. It's all or nothing.

My comfort zone is work. It's a compulsion that I can't control, an innate behaviour. I've never known how to deal with not being busy. It's important to keep the brain ticking, and I don't think I'll ever change. I have never been a great sleeper. My mind buzzes and races with ideas. Every night, to try and get to sleep, I play in my mind an image of me walking out to bat for Australia at the MCG and hitting the first over all around the ground. Thirty-six off that one over is a regular achievement. I wish!

I am a creator, and I hate being bored. I love building and liken myself to a kid with a set of wooden building blocks and a box of matches. There's no doubt I have been guilty of running around doing too many things, but I'm a crazy man. Sustaining the requisite energy levels is a challenge, though. The only thing I miss from my early career is my fitness; I had such high energy levels in those years. I should make the effort to rebuild that fitness.

My work ethic is a family trait. When I was a kid my father used to turn his nose up at the surfers and tell me they were a bad example. Now it's part of the way I am, and I think it's good. Ironically, Dad is now the loudest voice telling me to slow down and take more time off. He doesn't understand why it's always 'Push, push, push' with me.

I'm very scared of relaxing and would never go away on a

break if there were work to be done or the business needed my input. I am always contactable. Turning the mobile off is not an option. There is only one thing that could ever make me slow down – and that's a wife and family. I do want to carry on the family name, as my brother's children are both girls and my sister changed her name upon getting married. That's still important to me: the pride of Lyons! I am making a bit more time for myself at the moment because I have come to the conclusion that life is short. I am playing polo and heading down to St Tropez more often than before. I'm tired and I need to clear my head and look to the future. I have excellent people around me and my involvement isn't as critical as before. My input in the day-to-day operation hasn't been huge for some time, though I am always on hand to provide pep talks and handle the big deals. I see my role now as developmental. I can't help but watch the sales targets like a hawk, though, and if we are down on my expectations it drives me crazy.

I need to ensure that the company evolves. If we don't, our path will follow that of the tabloid newspapers – namely, down. BIG must change and plug into the technology tidal wave. The digital revolution is something I used to think was unlikely to affect me, but now I realise it has changed everything on a global scale and will continue to do so. The future of BIG is the Internet and Internet TV. Not only do I want to be part of the process commercially, I also want to free up time to make a creative impact on the television industry with my own productions. Every new communications development offers me another stage on which to test my skills. Any businessperson who doesn't see what is happening on the digital front is an idiot. It gives me such a kick to look into the future and think, 'This is fucking right.' The new challenges are huge, but also potentially rewarding on every level.

Mel and I still have a very strong relationship, despite the end of our marriage. Neither she nor I believe this is born out of commercial necessity – though neither of us wanted to leave BIG Pictures when the divorce loomed. There was never a point when either of us wanted to cut our losses and walk away. We both worked very hard to set BIG up and we are both good at what we do. The company would have been far weaker without us. Some people can't get their head around our current situation, but it works for us. I don't regret getting divorced because it made Mel and me into great friends – which is probably what we should have been to start with. We have never lost our trust in one another and we're really like brother and sister now. Mel says that she believes the change in our domestic set-up freed me up to be more dynamic, travel more and really be myself. She's probably right. She still visits my family in Australia and my nieces and nephews still call her Aunty Mel, which is nice, though it makes her sad in a way. We saw a lot of the world together and still travel together.

Going it alone gets harder and harder. I risk everything every day for the business, and it can take its toll. That's the reality. If business was easy, everyone would be doing it. Mum often offers to come over to London and visit if she senses

I'm down. I always tell her not to bother and that by the time she gets there I'll be better. She thinks that every time I visit Geelong it gets harder for me to leave and return to London because I am starting to enjoy the pace of life they have in my home town. She's right, but the magic of London is hard to turn my back on.

There are certain aspects of my life that frighten me. Sometimes I am scared to think about the success – it's almost an embarrassment. I am just a boy who grew up, travelled around the world, took some pictures, shagged some beautiful women, got shot at and got kidnapped – but I'm a Geelong boy and I'm not going to change. I'm not scared of losing everything. As long as I've got my friends and family, I don't give a toss. On the way up I had a fantastic time and if it all goes wrong then that's part of life. I live my life to the fullest.

I have acquired wisdom and perspective, but still work harder in an hour than most people could imagine. I regret nothing that has happened to me along the journey; the knocks are what I have learned from. Whatever happens along the road happens for a reason. I don't believe that anyone is truly in control and I like the bits that are uncontrollable! I will never be content and I don't believe that anyone with an entrepreneurial attitude ever is. My ambition has always been to 'achieve the unachievable'. It keeps me going. I love what I do, but I've got a lot more to achieve. When I met Richard Desmond (the *OK!* magazine magnate) the other week, he asked me how I was. 'Trying to make a buck,' I replied. 'Me, too,' he said. It made me laugh, but there's a truth there.

Whatever people think of paparazzi, at the end of the day we produce images that don't lie. They're a record of our times, and I'm constantly amazed by the number of people who phone me or my company and ask for prints of pictures we've taken of them. We capture moments, treasured by some, hated by others, but that's life. Love it or hate it, it's my business and it's BIG business!

At this point in my life I am looking forward and feeling excited. There are plenty of things on the horizon, but I will wait and see how the chips fall. I have been offered great deals before and rejected them in order to maintain my independence or my standards. I think that I could fit into a corporation, but I like my freedom.

Life is like a series of amazing pictures and we live by progressing through a magnificent gallery. I love surrounding myself with great images of our time. Despite the slant of my companies, probably none of the images I consider to be my best work are those of celebrities. Rather, they are of animals, children or war. Some of the images recorded by my company have been truly iconic. Photography is a celebration of life, and the one regret I probably have is that I haven't taken enough pictures of myself. My career has been largely concerned with recording the passage of others through this life and I have neglected to record my own. Perhaps that's what this book is about – an attempt to redress the balance.

# ACKNOWLEDGEMENTS

Heartfelt thanks to Mum and Dad – there's nothing much more to say except I love you. And thanks to my brother, Greg, and sister, Vikki, who I regularly kicked under the dinner table – sorry!

Whatever the truth, David and Fabrice maintain that a well-known UK pap told his partners in France not to turn up and follow Diana that night. Certainly it is odd that they alone were not represented at the Ritz or afterwards. These guys are highly regarded pros, and it was strange that they weren't around. Just another mystery.' To Mel, the girl I married, divorced and who is now my best friend – thank you for being my eyes and ears all my business life. You've given me a very special gift.

Thanks to Mars and the boys. Mars has been my twelve-year-old best buddy for my whole life. He's taken care of businesses in the southern hemisphere, which isn't the easiest thing to do with a boss who is also a best mate.

To my faithful and most loyal friend in the world ever – my golden cocker spaniel Amber, who has seen things in life that a dog shouldn't see; and to my heroes Dennis Lillee and Rupert Murdoch, and friend Simon Cowell, for the inspiration to succeed in everything that I do.

Many thanks also to Chris Hewlett for his help in writing

the book, and to my clothes designer, Sebastian di Natale, whose jacket I'm wearing on the cover of this book.

Finally, thanks to the most important people of all in my business – my loyal and hardworking photographers and staff. Without you this book wouldn't have happened.

And to all the bastards who have turned me over, I have one final word: KARMA.

# INDEX